ELIZABETHAN PRIVATEERING

ELIZABETHAN PRIVATEERING

ENGLISH PRIVATEERING DURING
THE SPANISH WAR
1585-1603

BY

KENNETH R. ANDREWS

*Lecturer in Economic History in the
University of Hull*

CAMBRIDGE
AT THE UNIVERSITY PRESS
1964

PUBLISHED BY
THE SYNDICS OF THE CAMBRIDGE UNIVERSITY PRESS

Bentley House, 200 Euston Road, London, N.W.1
American Branch: 32 East 57th Street, New York 22, N.Y.
West African Office: P.O. Box 33, Ibadan, Nigeria

CAMBRIDGE UNIVERSITY PRESS
1964

Printed in Great Britain
by Robert MacLehose & Company Limited
at the University Press, Glasgow

PREFACE

This book is divided into three parts. The first is introductory, dealing with the general context of privateering, its administration and the necessary materials. The second describes various types of venture and attempts an economic analysis of them. To this part are attached, as prelude and tail-piece, two contemporary narratives, placed thus as reminders of the crude realities of our subject-matter. The third part concerns the role of privateering in English overseas expansion. Readers are advised to begin with chapter 1, even if they know the period well, and to leave Part III to the last, but otherwise the order of the chapters is not vitally important, and the reader who wishes to get to grips quickly with events and people would do well to turn directly from chapter 1 to chapter 4.

This study makes no claim to be comprehensive or definitive. Elizabethan privateering is a subject that has been neglected by serious students of history, even though some of the more famous voyages have been examined in detail. Whatever the reasons may be for this neglect—and it would be interesting to examine them historically—the consequence has been to make my task largely exploratory. In some areas there were already substantial clearings (the semi-official joint-stock expeditions have been investigated by W. R. Scott, and there is much detail on the fate of neutral shipping and goods in E. P. Cheyney's *History of England from the Defeat of the Armada to the Death of Queen Elizabeth*); such topics I have skimmed lightly here in order to concentrate on what is new. Even still, much work remains to be done before the structure and role of this phenomenon can be firmly defined. Local studies of privateering—at Weymouth, Plymouth and Bristol, for example —are needed; a survey of Elizabethan shipbuilding and shipping would be most valuable; a full study of the administration of privateering could go much further than I have gone; above all, Charles Howard, Baron of Effingham and Earl of Nottingham, one of the key figures of his time, deserves a major biography. I can only hope that the present work may stimulate interest in such themes.

I am grateful to Mr R. T. Spence for permission to use his

unpublished thesis on the Earl of Cumberland, and to Mrs J. L. Thomas (née Wiggs) to use hers on the trade of Southampton. Miss Irene Wright has been as generous as ever in placing her unpublished transcriptions and translations of Spanish MSS at my disposal—without them chapter 8 would have been much the poorer. I also wish to thank the Hakluyt Society for permission to reproduce the map of the West Indies from volume CXI of their Second Series; and the Huntington Library for permission to reproduce the Grafton pamphlet (H.M. 82178). Above all I owe a great debt to Professor David Quinn, whose example as a scholar has been an inspiration to me for many years and whose practical help and advice have made this book possible.

K.R.A.

September, 1962

CONTENTS

MAP

SOURCES AND ABBREVIATIONS

The following is a list of the contemporary manuscripts, primary printed sources and secondary authorities that have been of major importance for this study. References to other MSS, books and articles are to be found in my footnotes. This list also explains such abbreviations as I have used.

A. *Contemporary Manuscripts*

In the Archivo General de Indias, Seville

A. de I., Santo Domingo, *Legajos* 15, 51, 73, 74, 81, 127, 128, 129, 184, 186, 187
   Santa Fe, *Legajos* 38, 190
   Guatemala, *Legajos* 10, 39, 44
   Panamá, *Legajos* 44, 45
   Indiferente General, *Legajos* 742, 1866
   Contratación, *Legajos* 5109, 5110

At Appleby Castle

'A Brief Relation of the severall voyages undertaken and performed by the right honorable George Earle of Cumberland'

In the British Museum

Additional MSS 11405, 12505, 12506, 12507, 36316, 36317
Harleian MS 598
Lansdowne MSS 67, 69, 70, 73, 75, 78, 115, 129, 130, 133, 134, 135, 140, 142, 143, 144, 145, 148, 157, 158
Sloane MSS 2292, 3289

At Magdalene College, Cambridge

Pepys MS 2870 (Miscellanea, vol. 2)

In the National Library of Wales

Journal: Sir Thomas Myddelton, 'A jurnal of all owtlandishe accomptes begyninge this 14th May 1583'

In the Public Record Office

H.C.A. 1 : High Court of Admiralty, Oyer et Terminer, 39, 40, 42, 43, 46

H.C.A. 13 : High Court of Admiralty, Examinations, 17–37, 96, 101–104, 148

H.C.A. 14 : High Court of Admiralty, Exemplifications, 9, 10, 23–35

H.C.A. 23 : High Court of Admiralty, Interrogatories, 4

H.C.A. 24 : High Court of Admiralty, Libels, 42, 44, 53–71

H.C.A. 25 : High Court of Admiralty, Letters of Marque, Bonds, etc., 1, 2, 3

H.C.A. 30: High Court of Admiralty, Miscellanea, 840, 842

Court of Requests, Proceedings, 30, 35, 43, 46, 97, 109, 240, 247

S.P. Dom. Eliz. : State Papers, Domestic, Elizabeth, *passim*

At Somerset House

P.C.C. : Prerogative Court of Canterbury, various wills

B. *Primary Printed Sources*

Anderson, R. C. (ed.). *Letters of the Fifteenth and Sixteenth Centuries* (Southampton Record Society, 1921)

——. *The Book of Examinations, 1601–2* (Southampton Record Society, 1926)

Anonymous. *A True Discourse of the late voyage made by the Right Worshipfull Sir Thomas Sherley the yonger, Knight . . . Written by a Gentleman that was in the Voyage* (1602).

——. *The Honorable Actions of that most famous and valiant Englishman, Edward Glemham, esquire . . .* (1591)

A.P.C.: Dasent, J. R. (ed.). *Acts of the Privy Council* (New Series, vols. 7–32, 1893–1907)

Arber, E. (ed.). *An English Garner* (10 vols., 1903)

Bamford, F. (ed.). *A Royalist's Notebook. The Commonplace Book of Sir John Oglander Kt. of Nunwell* (1936)

Beaven, A. B. (ed.). *Bristol Lists, Municipal and Miscellaneous* (1899)

Boteler's Dialogues: Perrin, W. G. (ed.). *Boteler's Dialogues* (Navy Records Society, LXV), 1929

Cal. Salis. MSS: Historical Manuscripts Commission, Calendar of the Manuscripts of the Marquess of Salisbury (Parts I–XV), 1888–1930

Cal. S.P. Dom. Eliz.: Calendar of State Papers, Domestic Series, Elizabeth, *1581–90* (1865), *1591–94* (1867), *1595–97* (1869), *1598–1601* (1869), *1601–3* (1870)

Cal. S.P. Spanish, Eliz.: Calendar of State Papers relating to English Affairs preserved in the Archives of Simancas, 1568–79 (1894), 1580–86 (1896), 1587–1603 (1899)

Cal. S.P. Venetian: Calendar of State Papers, Venetian, 1581–91 (1894), 1592–1603 (1897), 1603–7 (1900), 1617–19 (1909)

Chanter, J. R. and Wainwright, T. (ed.). *Reprint of the Barnstaple Records* (1900)

Cooley, W. D. (ed.). *Sir Francis Drake his Voyage, 1595, by Thomas Maynarde, together with the Spanish Account of Drake's attack on Puerto Rico* (Hakluyt Society, First Series, IV), 1849

Corbett, *Spanish War:* Corbett, J. S. (ed.). *Papers relating to the Navy during the Spanish War, 1585–87* (Navy Records Society, XI), 1898

E.P.V.: Andrews, K. R. (ed.). *English Privateering Voyages to the West Indies, 1588–1595* (Hakluyt Society, Second Series, CXI), 1959

Fisher, F. J. (ed.). 'The State of England (1600). By Sir Thomas Wilson', *Camden Miscellany*, XVI (1936)

Foster, *Lancaster's Voyages:* Foster, Sir William (ed.). *The Voyages of Sir James Lancaster to Brazil and the East Indies, 1591–1603* (Hakluyt Society, Second Series, LXXXV), 1940

Further English Voyages: Wright, I. A. (ed.). *Further English Voyages to Spanish America, 1583–94* (Hakluyt Society, Second Series, XCIX), 1951

Gribble, J. B. *Memorials of Barnstaple* (1830)

Hagthorpe, J. *England's Exchequer, or a Discourse of the Sea and Navigation* (1625)

Hamilton, G. H. (ed.). *Books of Examinations and Depositions 1570–94* (Southampton Record Society), 1914

Harlow, *Raleigh's Guiana*: Harlow, V. T. (ed.). *The Discoverie of the large and bewtiful Empire of Guiana, by Sir Walter Ralegh* (1928)

Kingsford, C. L. (ed.). 'The Taking of the Madre de Dios', *Naval Miscellany*, vol. 2 (Navy Records Society), 1912

Laughton, *Defeat*: Laughton, J. K. (ed.). *State Papers relating to the Defeat of the Spanish Armada* (Navy Records Society, I and II), 1894

Marsden, *Law and Custom*: Marsden, R. G. (ed.). *Documents relating to the Law and Custom of the Sea* (Navy Records Society, XLIX and L), 1915–16

Marsden, R. G. (ed.). *Select Pleas in the Court of Admiralty* (Selden Society, VI and XI), 1894, 1897

McClure, N. E. (ed.). *The Letters of John Chamberlain* (American Philosophical Society, Memoirs, XII), 2 vols., 1939

Monson's Tracts: Oppenheim, M. (ed.). *The Naval Tracts of Sir William Monson* (Navy Records Society, XXII, XXIII, XLIII, XLV, XLVII), 1902–14

Mote, Humphrey. *The Primrose of London, with her valiant adventure on the Spanish coast* (1585)

Moule, H. J. (ed.). *Descriptive Catalogue of the Charters, Minute Books and other Documents in the Borough of Weymouth and Melcomb Regis, 1252–1800* (1883)

Principal Navigations: Hakluyt, Richard (ed.). *The Principall navigations, voiages and discoveries of the English nation* (Hakluyt Society, Extra Series, I–XII), 1903–5

Purchas: Purchas, Samuel (ed.). *Hakluytus Posthumus or Purchas his pilgrimes* (Hakluyt Society, Extra Series, XIV–XXXIII), 1905–7

Quinn, D. B. (ed.). *The Voyages and Colonizing Enterprises of Sir Humphrey Gilbert* (Hakluyt Society, Second Series, LXXXIII and LXXXIV), 1940

Raleigh's Works: Oldys, W. and Birch, T. (ed.). *The Works of Sir Walter Raleigh* (8 vols., 1829)

Roanoke Voyages: Quinn, D. B. (ed.). *The Roanoke Voyages, 1584–1590* (Hakluyt Society, Second Series, CIV, CV), 1955

Roberts, Henry. *Our Ladys Retorne* (1592)

R., H. (Henry Roberts ?). *News from the Levant Seas* (1594)

Rutherford, J. (ed.). *The Miscellaneous Papers of Captain Thomas Stockwell, 1590–1611* (Southampton Record Society), 1932

Stevens, *Dawn*: Stevens, H. (ed.). *The Dawn of British Trade to the East Indies, 1599–1603* (Court Records of the East India Company), 1886

Taylor, E. G. R. (ed.). *The Original Writings and Correspondence of the Two Richard Hakluyts* (Hakluyt Society, Second Series, LXXVI and LXXVII), 1935

——. *The Troublesome Voyage of Captain Edward Fenton, 1582–3* (Hakluyt Society, Second Series, CXIII), 1959

Warner, G. F. (ed.). *The Voyage of Robert Dudley into the West Indies, 1594–5* (Hakluyt Society, Second Series, III), 1899

Williamson, J. A. (ed.). *The 'Observations' of Sir Richard Hawkins* (1933)

Worth, R. N. *A Calendar of Plymouth Municipal Records* (1893)

Wright, I. A. (ed.). *Historia Documentada de San Cristóbal de la Habana en el Siglo XVI* (2 vols., 1927)

——. 'The Spanish Version of Sir Anthony Shirley's Raid on Jamaica, 1597', *Hispanic American Historical Review*, V (1922), 227–48

C. *Secondary Authorities*

Andrews, K. R., 'Christopher Newport of Limehouse, Mariner', *William and Mary Quarterly*, 3rd Ser., XI (1954), 3–27

——. 'The Economic Aspects of Elizabethan Privateering' (unpublished thesis in University of London Library), 1951

Beaven, A. B., *The Aldermen of the City of London, temp. Henry III to 1908* (2 vols., 1908–13)

Brown, *Genesis*: Brown, A., *The Genesis of the United States* (2 vols., 1890)

Chaunu, H. et P., *Séville et l'Atlantique, 1504–1650* (11 vols., 1956–9)

Cokayne, *Lord Mayors and Sheriffs*: Cokayne, G. E., *Some Account of the Lord Mayors and Sheriffs of the City of London* (1897)

Cheyney, E. P., *A History of England from the Defeat of the Armada to the Death of Queen Elizabeth* (2 vols., 1914)

Corbett, J. S., *Drake and the Tudor Navy* (2 vols., 1893)

——. *The Successors of Drake* (1900)

D.N.B.: *The Dictionary of National Biography* (63 vols., 1885–1900)

Dodd, A. H., 'Mr Myddelton the Merchant of Tower Street', in *Elizabethan Government and Society, Essays Presented to Sir John Neale* (ed. Bindoff, Hurstfield and Williams), 1961

Edwards, E., *The Life of Sir Walter Raleigh and his Letters* (2 vols., 1868)

E.H.R.: *English Historical Review*

Foster, W., *England's Quest of Eastern Trade* (1933)

H.A.H.R.: *Hispanic American Historical Review*

Haring, C. H., *Trade and Navigation between Spain and the Indies* (Harvard Economic Studies, XIX), 1918

Oppenheim, *Administration*: Oppenheim, M., *A History of the Administration of the Royal Navy and of Merchant Shipping in relation to the Navy, 1509–1660* (1896)

Powell, J. W. D., *Bristol Privateers and Ships of War* (1930)

Shillington, V. M. and Chapman, A. B. W., *The Commercial Relations of England and Portugal* (s.a.)

Sluiter, E., 'Dutch-Spanish Rivalry in the Caribbean Area, 1594–1609', *H.A.H.R.*, XXVIII (1948), 165–96

——. 'Dutch Maritime Power and the Colonial Status Quo 1585–1641', *Pacific Historical Review*, XI (1942), 29–41

Smyth, W. H., *The Sailor's Word-Book, an Alphabetical Digest of Nautical Terms* (1867)

Spence, R. T., 'The Cliffords, Earls of Cumberland, 1579–1646' (unpublished thesis, University of London Library), 1959

Stone, L., 'Elizabethan Overseas Trade', *Economic History Review*, 2nd Ser., II (1949), 31–58

——. 'The Fruits of Office: The Case of Robert Cecil, First Earl of Salisbury, 1596–1612', in *Essays in the Economic and Social History of Tudor and Stuart England* (ed. Fisher), 1961

Taylor, E. G. R., *Late Tudor and Early Stuart Geography, 1583–1650* (1934)

Wernham, R. B., 'Elizabethan War Aims and Strategy', in *Elizabethan Government and Society, Essays Presented to Sir John Neale* (ed. Bindoff, Hurstfield and Williams), 1961

Wiggs, J. L., 'The Seaborne Trade of Southampton in the Second Half of the Sixteenth Century' (unpublished thesis, Southampton University), 1955

Willan, *Studies*: Willan, T. S. *Studies in Elizabethan Foreign Trade* (1959)

Williamson, G. C., *George, Third Earl of Cumberland* (1920)

Williamson, J. A., *Hawkins of Plymouth* (1949)

Wright, I. A., 'Rescates, with Special Reference to Cuba', *H.A.H.R.*, III (1920), 333–61

Part I

CONTEXT AND ORGANISATION

Chapter 1

PRIVATEERING AND THE SEA WAR

In May 1585 a number of English ships in Spanish harbours were arrested, the crews imprisoned and the cargoes confiscated. One, the *Primrose* of London, managed to escape, bringing home with her the *corregidor* who had been charged with the task of making the arrest. There was an immediate outcry in England, and in particular the merchants who had suffered loss clamoured for redress. On 7 July the government instructed the Lord Admiral to examine the claims of the merchants and issue letters of reprisal to those who proved their losses to his satisfaction. Such letters would license the holders to set forth armed vessels for the capture of Spanish goods at sea. The English government was not hereby committing itself to an act of war—these were private wrongs. Thus at first the formal procedure for obtaining letters of reprisal was taken seriously by both merchants and lawyers. A pleading would be filed in the High Court of Admiralty, supported by witnesses, and later a decree would be promulgated stating the amount of the losses sustained and declaring the right of the plaintiff to recover his losses by force. Letters of reprisal, valid for six months, would then be issued. But this event came at a time of crisis in Anglo-Spanish relations, a crisis which did not, as Elizabeth herself hoped, quickly pass. Before long it became obvious to all that the two countries were in fact, if not in law, at war, and that Spanish ships and goods were fair game for any who wanted to take a hand in the business of plunder. As Sir George Carey, one of the advocates of strong measures, put it as early as 25 June: 'her Majesty shall not need to espy the faults of those that will venture their own to do her service'. In this category of persons he included 'one Flud, a valiant and skilful pirate, weary as he protesteth of his former trade', whom he now proposed to victual forth to reconnoitre the Spanish coast.[1] It would in any case have been impossible to prevent legitimate grantees from forming partnerships with merchants and gentlemen who had not

[1] S.P. Dom. Eliz., clxxix, f. 84.

3

themselves suffered loss; but further the whole procedure of prov-
ing losses lent itself to abuse. Who could say, other than the
merchants and factors interested, how much had been lost? Who
would bother to gainsay them?—such actions were not contested.
Soon, and inevitably, proof of losses became little more than a
legal fiction, and reprisal ventures were promoted by men who
had never dreamed of trading in Spain. Before long the promoter
of a venture had merely to perform a routine which amounted to
buying a licence from the Lord Admiral through his court. Many
did not even bother with this formality, but obtained a private note
from the Lord Admiral direct, or even sailed without licence
altogether, strong in the conviction that any objectors could be
bought off in the unlikely event of a day of reckoning. Those with
influence at Court might by-pass the admiralty by obtaining a
commission in the form of letters patent.

Thus in the summer of 1585 the first of a host of voluntaries took
to the sea—some genuine ships of reprisal, some private men-of-
war equipped by gentlemen, some mere pirates 'weary of their
former trade'. In September Sir Francis Drake sailed for the
West Indies and before long the reports of his triumphs roused
enthusiasm to fever pitch. Drake's voyage, wrote John Hooker,
'inflamed the whole country with a desire to adventure unto the
seas, in hope of the like good success, [so] that a great number
prepared ships, mariners and soldiers and travelled every place
where any profit might be had'.[1] During the next eighteen years
hundreds of private expeditions were organised for plunder;
merchantmen on trading voyages were also expected to take prizes
when opportunity offered; promoters of colonisation, exploration
or new trade routes usually authorised their commanders to do
likewise. Certain ports, such as Weymouth and Southampton,
gave themselves over largely to the business of fitting out ships of
reprisal and disposing of prize-goods. Long after the war John
Hagthorpe asserted that the Spanish had 'good cause to remember
how they were baited in the queen's time, there being never less
than 200 sail of voluntaries and others upon their coasts'.[2] He was
probably exaggerating, but it is unlikely that the number in any
year of the war fell below a hundred. Well over two hundred
private vessels made reprisal voyages in the three years 1589-91

[1] W. J. Harte, *Gleanings from the Commonplace Book of John Hooker*, p. 39.
[2] John Hagthorpe, *England's Exchequer, or a Discourse of the Sea and Navigation*
(1625), p. 25.

and towards the end of the war the number was probably as great as it had ever been. In 1599 Thomas Nashe observed that 'voyages of purchase or reprisals . . . are now grown a common traffic'.[1]

This, briefly and roughly, is the phenomenon we call privateering—retrospectively, because this term did not come into use until the seventeenth century and was therefore unknown to Elizabethans. It is to be distinguished from plain piracy on the one hand and from the semi-official enterprises of the sea war on the other, though in neither case is the line easy to draw. The proper distinction between privateering and piracy is a legal one: the privateer had a commission from a recognised authority to take action against a designated enemy; the pirate had no commission and attacked anyone. But what constituted a commission? Were commissions issued by the Portuguese pretender, Dom Antonio, valid? Were English subjects lawfully entitled to accept the commission of a foreign prince? There were no certain answers to these and many similar questions. International law was in its infancy and governments freely manipulated what law there was to suit the political needs of the moment. Thus once hostilities with Spain had begun legal niceties gave place to practical considerations. A captain without letters of reprisal would not be treated as a pirate so long as he confined his attentions to Spanish commerce, though a properly commissioned man might be indicted for piracy if he spoiled an English or neutral vessel.

The essential difference between the privateering venture and the semi-official expedition is that whereas the former was wholly financed and directed by private individuals, the latter was a national undertaking in which the queen's interest predominated, though her financial share might not be large. Drake's West Indies raid in 1585 is a case in point. Elizabeth supplied only two of the twenty-five sail and these, with her additional cash subscription of £10,000, gave her an investment officially assessed at £20,000 in a total stock of £60,400. But Drake on this occasion was acting as the queen's admiral and had his official instructions. His fleets of 1587, 1589 and 1595 were of much the same mixed character, but, like some other semi-official expeditions, they had a strategic purpose apart from mere prize-hunting. There were of course a few ventures in which, although the queen invested, the direction of the voyage remained completely in private hands. The earl of Cumberland's 1589 voyage, for example, was essentially a

[1] Thomas Nashe, *Lenten Stuffe* (1599).

private venture, although the queen lent the earl the *Victory* for his flagship.

We are concerned, then, with private anti-Spanish enterprise at sea, legally authorised, or at least permitted, by the English government. However, the boundaries of the subject also indicate its context, and the significance of privateering will be missed unless it is considered in relation to the war as a whole. For privateering was not merely an incidental by-product of this war, as it was, for example, of the eighteenth-century wars. In the Elizabethan war with Spain it was the characteristic form of maritime warfare, the essential embodiment of the private initiative and enterprise that dominated the sea war. The explanation of this lies partly in the queen's political strategy and war policy, and partly in the maritime ambitions and activities of the English in the pre-war decades.

Elizabeth did not want war with Spain. She did all she could to avert it, and when it came she waged it reluctantly and defensively. As Sir Julian Corbett regretfully observed: 'Through it all she was craving for peace, and in her eyes the brightness of every victory was dimmed with an anxious regret that it widened the gulf between her and Spain. For that strange idea is to be seen at the bottom of all her half measures. She never shared the confidence of her officers, and never believed she could strike her enemy a fatal blow.'[1] Certainly Elizabeth saw no necessity for a fatal blow. Her concern throughout her reign was simply to preserve the safety of her kingdom and there was sense in her view that England's security did not depend on demolishing Spain's power. She may have been mistaken in this, though the fact that she and England survived without destroying the enemy would seem to indicate the opposite. What matters now, however, is not what she ought to have done, but what she did and why.

As a political realist Elizabeth could not think in terms of a life-and-death struggle for supremacy with Spain, for France and Spain, not England and Spain, were the two great powers of her time. England could not hope to vie with these giants. The most she could expect was to consolidate her strength, and in aiming at this, as Elizabeth did, she had always to keep one eye on France and the other on Spain. Hence her ambiguities, disconcerting changes of direction and evasive tactics. Hers was an intuitive

[1] *Successors of Drake*, pp. 3–4.

grasp of politics, and that tendency to prevarication which was the despair of her ministers was fundamentally rational. Under all her moods lay an almost instinctive fear of commitment, a reluctance to close any door, and among the considerations which shaped her diplomacy perhaps the most important was a deepseated distrust of France.

When she came to the throne it was France that presented the chief threat to her security. Ever since the Hundred Years War France had grown from strength to strength and just before Elizabeth's accession had completed the recovery of her northern shores by the capture of Calais. To make matters worse there ascended the throne of France a queen who was the legitimate ruler of Scotland and in Catholic eyes the rightful queen of England. The prospect of a Franco-British empire dominated by the Guise family was likely in 1560, and only the death of Francis II and the success of the Lords of the Congregation caused it to recede. Yet the Guises remained strong and for ten years Elizabeth stood mainly in fear of France. In this period her relations with Spain were by no means perfectly amicable, but her religion and other causes of friction mattered little beside the fundamental rivalry of France and Spain for the hegemony of Europe. So long as this lasted and so long as England stood in the way of French expansion, so long would Philip II tolerate the heretic queen and even take steps to preserve her political existence.

It was the Netherlands revolt that changed this situation. Elizabeth had little sympathy for Calvinists or for men in rebellion against their lawful sovereign, but she could not suffer the Low Countries to be occupied by so powerful a force as Philip's, particularly in view of his known hostility to the reformed religion. From the time of Alva's arrival there in 1567 the Low Countries became a wedge driving England and Spain apart. Elizabeth's difficulty was that she feared a French occupation of the Netherlands even more than a Spanish; she supported the rebels' claims to self-government and toleration because these implied the removal of Spanish troops, but she wanted Philip to keep his suzerainty to prevent a French conquest. She was prepared to use every weapon in her diplomatic armoury to bring Spain to terms in this matter, but she was always willing to accept a compromise so long as it provided reasonable security for England. During the first phase of tension she sought to bring pressure to bear on Philip by a series of hostile measures and eventually, in 1572, moved towards France. The tension was reduced, however, in the same year, chiefly as a result of the massacre of St Bartholomew. For a time Anglo-Spanish relations improved and it even seemed for a moment in the mid-seventies that the Netherlands problem might be liquidated. But the opportunity passed and western Europe entered a new phase of tension mounting to general war in 1585.

Spain now visibly gained ground on all fronts. In the Netherlands the duke of Parma took over command in 1578 and steadily drove back the rebels. In 1580 Philip occupied Portugal without serious opposition, thus not only adding the wealth of the East to that of America, but providing himself with the nucleus of an ocean-going force, the effectiveness of which was soon proved by the crushing defeat of the French at Terceira. In France decomposition was setting in; the Catholic League, formed in 1576, moved rapidly into alliance with Spain; from 1578 Philip and the Guises were allies; Philip's doubts about supporting Mary Stuart were soon dispelled and by 1582 he was subsidising the Catholic League and lending a readier ear to the champions of the Enterprise of England.

To Elizabeth each possible course seemed fraught with appalling dangers. In consequence she pursued them all by turns and none of them wholeheartedly. She encouraged the duke of Alençon's intervention in the Low Countries and was even inclined to marry him, but in the end drew back for fear of Spain. On the other hand there was some hope of dragging France into war with Spain if Henry III could be induced to support Alençon. In the event mutual distrust was sufficient to frustrate any common action by the two countries, though Alençon's activities, however feeble, and the prolonged Anglo-French negotiations kept Philip anxious. Thus the back door of compromise with Spain was kept open, and when Alençon ruined his prospects in the Netherlands by the French Fury, Elizabeth veered sharply towards Spain, ordering the withdrawal of English volunteers from the Provinces and the arrest of Dutch ships as security for her loans to the rebels. There were obvious risks, however, in a policy of placating Philip. Antagonism between Spain and England had grown so great now that it was difficult to envisage peaceful relations between them. The revelations of Francis Throckmorton in November 1583 served as a timely reminder of Spain's menacing aggressiveness.

Hopes of a compromise with Spain were in fact receding at

much the same rate as prospects of a French alliance and the events of 1584 seemed fatal to both. In January the Spanish ambassador, charged with complicity in the Throckmorton plot, departed vowing revenge. Parma exploited Alençon's collapse to quicken his relentless advance. In June the prince of Orange was murdered. Few expected the rebellion to survive without much more substantial foreign help. The rebels looked first to France, but in October the death of Alençon, making Henry of Navarre heir presumptive to the throne, brought that country to the verge of civil war, with a king too weak to resist the pressure of the League. Thus at the very moment of greatest danger in the Netherlands the balance of power collapsed and Elizabeth was faced with the alternative she had always tried to avoid—that of confronting Spain with force, assembling under English leadership the motley band of European Protestants.

It was with extreme reluctance that Elizabeth embarked on this policy in 1585. Moreover, confronting Spain with force did not mean, in her eyes, committing herself to war, nor abandoning other courses. Philip must be kept at bay in the Low Countries and induced to agree to a compromise. Such were the purposes of Leicester's expedition to the Netherlands and Drake's to the West Indies. These hostile measures were the physical aspects of diplomacy. Her main object was limited—a Netherlands settlement favourable to English security. If Philip would not concede this peacefully, then the presence of English forces in the Netherlands was for the time being necessary, but naturally she looked forward to a time when she could withdraw her troops, either because Philip had come to terms, or because the Dutch had become capable of keeping him busy without assistance. With the coming of the Armada Elizabeth was forced to recognise the existence of the war, but she could never regard it as more than a provisional state of affairs, necessitated by an emergency, which must pass when the European system resumed its normal shape. France, after all, had not disappeared, and from 1589 this was increasingly evident. So was the gathering strength of the Dutch. Thus whereas before the Armada Elizabeth was merely using rather forceful methods of diplomacy, after it she had time on her side.

Elizabeth's war strategy, then, was determined by the same considerations that had governed her peacetime policy. Her objects were to ward off Spain's blows and to develop sufficient pressure on the enemy to bring him to terms. To go further would be to turn the scales too far in France's favour. For the time being, since Philip was intent on aggression, effective resistance must be maintained in France and the Netherlands, especially to prevent his establishing a northern base for an attack on England. The mere fact of England's survival as an independent state was of incalculable value to her allies, and the money and troops she supplied helped to tide them over the worst dangers. As for English sea-power, its essential functions were defensive: to protect English shores, to maintain communications and supply lines between the allies, and to deny Spain the use of western European waters. Other operations of a more offensive nature were indeed undertaken, but in these the queen was not vitally interested. She could be persuaded to give grudging support to various projects, but she regarded them as secondary campaigns and treated them as such, leaving the initiative—and particularly the financial initiative—to her subjects, and measuring their success largely in financial terms.

For the queen lacked not only the will but the means to wage offensive war. Her resources were small and had to be distributed not only to the continental fronts, but also to maritime operations and, after 1595, to the enormously expensive Irish campaigns. Her total annual revenue did not exceed £300,000, and her appeals to parliament for money met with the same sort of generosity that she herself showed in her dealings with her servants and allies. In such circumstances there was little room for ambitious strategy, involving as it must the mounting of a sustained counter-offensive. Instead there was merely a sequence of improvisations, concerned for the most part with immediate dangers.

The prominence of private enterprise in the sea war was thus in a sense the converse of the queen's preoccupation with defence and the continental war. It also arose, however, from the positive interest of some of the queen's subjects in a maritime offensive against Spain. The maritime ambitions of the pre-war period were not the main cause of the war with Spain, and to some extent the growing anti-Spanish bias of English maritime enterprise before the war can be attributed to the mounting political and religious hostility between the two countries. Nevertheless the energy of English maritime expansion did in those political circumstances become a serious source of conflict with Spain and when war finally came it was canalised to a large extent into forms of sea warfare. For purposes of analysis we may distinguish two aspects of English maritime ambition which tended to lead to conflict with Spain: the one mercantile, the other predatory; the drive of the merchants to extend trade, and the drive of the gentry for plunder. The two trends, never entirely unconnected, were fused into one by the course of events, but the fusion was not completed until the outbreak of the war itself.

Most English merchants interested in overseas trade were anxious for peace, mainly because they knew that war would interrupt or endanger their trade. Those who stood to lose most were those mainly interested in trade to Spain and Portugal. Yet the Iberian trade was itself the growing-point of commercial rivalry. The trades of the Iberian peninsula were of immense importance for Europe's commercial system in the later sixteenth century. The Spanish-American trade and the Portuguese trade with Africa and the Far East were two giants, with which no other trades of the time could compare in value.[1] Moreover they differed from Europe's traditional commerce not only in scale but in kind. From the East and the West came a rich stream of goods bought cheap and selling dear—colonial or quasi-colonial goods offering a rate of profit that attracted merchants from all over Europe to Seville and Lisbon. English trade with both countries grew steadily, English cloth and other goods being exchanged for Iberian products and for the products of the two empires.

But merchants interested in Spain and Portugal naturally sought a share of the colonial trade. Already in the thirties and forties Englishmen were trading through Spain to America, and even directly from England to Brazil and Guinea. In the fifties the commercial penetration of Morocco and Guinea assumed serious proportions, and the leaders of this movement in England were the Iberian traders.[2] The Portuguese were much offended, and although in Morocco they were too weak to frustrate their rivals, in Guinea their resistance was determined and bitter. One after another William Towerson, the Fenners, John Hawkins and others came into conflict with the Portuguese, capturing their shipping or defending themselves against attacks. At length matters came to a head with the seizure of a vessel of Sir William Winter's on the Guinea coast in 1568. Portuguese ships in Falmouth were arrested by way of reprisal and in return all English goods in Portugal were sequestrated. Meanwhile a commercial dispute

[1] Pierre et Huguette Chaunu, *Séville et l'Atlantique, 1504-1650*, I, 12.
[2] Willan, *Studies*, pp. 95-6, 100-1.

with Spain had been developing along similar lines. Among the English merchants—chiefly Bristolians and Londoners—trading to Spain, a number took up residence in Seville, Grand Málaga and San Lúcar, conformed to the Catholic faith and engaged in the West Indian trade. Roger Bodenham, who conducted trade first with Morocco and then, in the sixties, with the West Indies, was typical of these Hispaniolised Englishmen, and he, like Anthony Parkhurst and Henry Hawks, passed on his knowledge of Spanish America to Englishmen at home, including the Hakluyts. Such was the commercial background to the Hawkins voyages, supported as they were by a mixture of mercantile and court interests, and ending as they did in the disaster of San Juan de Ulloa. The Hawkins family had long been trading in Spain and the Canaries, and even in Henry VIII's time had branched out into the Brazil and Guinea trades. Now in the fifteen-sixties John Hawkins resumed the family tradition. His slaving voyages to West Africa and Spanish America, however, took place at a time when the Spanish government was taking measures to strengthen and preserve its monopoly of colonial trade. However pacific Hawkins' intentions may have been and however much he may have wished to render a service to the king by his periodic visits to the Caribbean, it was made crystal clear that neither his service nor his presence was desired. The culmination of his voyages in a bloody encounter was almost inevitable.

Anglo-Spanish commercial rivalry had already been given an ugly edge by religious animosity. English seamen and factors in Spain had fallen foul of the Inquisition even in the reign of Henry VIII. The connections of the English ports with the Low Countries and La Rochelle made them breeding grounds of advanced Protestant opinion in England. The shedding of blood in 1568 thus marks the beginning of a feud for which the ground was well prepared. At the beginning of 1569, when Hawkins was demanding revenge, French Huguenots and Dutch sea-beggars were swarming against French Catholic and Spanish shipping. Trade between England and Spain was stopped and English sailors needed no encouragement to join in the plunder. The princes of Orange and Condé and Admiral Coligny distributed commissions freely; La Rochelle and the southern ports of England became recruiting and victualling centres as well as plunder marts for Protestant ships which conducted an increasingly indiscriminate war on all 'papists'. The Hawkins family were deeply involved in all this activity, as were the Winters and Fenners, and during the ensuing three years of crisis they did not miss the opportunity to extend their operations to the West Indies. Drake's successive voyages of 1570, 1571 and 1572 on behalf of the Hawkins interest are well known, but there were other Caribbean raids at this time, including one organised by a Winter and another led by a Fenner.[1] When, at the end of 1572, the queen brought her seamen to heel in home waters, voyages across the ocean continued and the feud remained alive.

The crisis of 1569–72 marks the appearance of a split in what might be called the Iberian interest. Henceforth the Hawkinses, Fenners and Winters pursued their private war with Spain and urged an aggressive, anti-Spanish policy for the nation. On the other hand the majority of the merchants wished to preserve amity with Spain and were apparently ready to accept the sacrifice of American and West African prospects for the safer dividends of trade with Spain and Portugal. This split, however, was the outcome of an ambivalence rooted in the nature of the Iberian trade. Those who now resumed that trade were soon bedevilled by the same sort of temptations that had led Hawkins, the Fenners and the Winters into trouble. English overseas trade had been focused for many years on Antwerp, and the Iberian trade itself had been, at least for Londoners, largely a triangular trade involving the Low Countries. But as political troubles grew in the Netherlands, Antwerp became less attractive as the focal point of England's overseas commerce. The direct connection between England, especially London, and the Iberian ports now assumed greater importance and the growth of Anglo-Iberian trade in this period was part of a general decentralising movement. But in this decentralisation there was a marked southward trend. The same period witnessed the development of English enterprise in the Mediterranean (to Marseilles, Venice and its dependencies and Turkey), to Morocco, the Atlantic islands and (abortively) Brazil. Cheap English cloth was now beginning the conquest of the southern markets, and the drive to find a 'vent' for the nation's main product was no doubt partly responsible for a commercial offensive which was to become irresistible after the war.[2] Nevertheless the

[1] H.C.A. 1/39, 27 Oct. 1572 ; *Cal. S.P. Spanish, Eliz.*, II, 429, 432, 434, 438, 464.
[2] F. J. Fisher, 'London's Export Trade in the Early Seventeenth Century', *Economic History Review*, 2nd Ser., III (1950), 151–61 ; C. M. Cipolla, 'The Decline

chief attraction of the southward trades for the merchants who developed them (as distinct from the government and the clothing interests) was probably the high rate of profit to be gained on the return cargoes. As the Company of Merchants Adventurers complained in 1579, English merchants could afford to sell their goods cheap in Spain because 'their gain lieth rather in the foreign commodities there bought'.[1] Seville and Lisbon were pulling England's trade southwards; and it was the merchants of the 'Spanish Company' who played the largest part in pioneering the other southward trades. The produce of southern Europe—fruits, wines, oils and salt especially—the sugar of Barbary and Brazil, the cochineal, indigo and dyewoods of America, the ivory and pepper of West Africa, the spices, calicoes, drugs and jewels of the Far East, the sweet wines and currants of the Near East, the carpets, silk and damask of the Middle East—these were the goods they coveted.

The attitude of these merchants nevertheless remained strongly pacific, and the divergence between them and the aggressive element became obvious in 1577, when the establishment of the Spanish Company coincided with Drake's departure on a voyage which was to combine exploration, trade-reconnaissance and plunder. The voyage was backed by Winter and Hawkins as well as by certain courtiers and (for her own reasons) the queen, and when Drake returned with his booty in 1580 the merchants trading to Spain and Portugal greeted his exploit with a mixture of alarm and hostility.[2] In the same year Philip assumed the throne of Portugal, driving the pretender Dom Antonio to seek assistance in France and England. This event provided the champions of anti-Spanish action with two arguments: that Philip's gains would make him all the more dangerous, and that

of Italy: the Case of a Fully Matured Economy', *Economic History Review*, 2nd Ser., v (1952), 178–87. Both writers are concerned with the rapid growth of northern cloth exports to the south in the early seventeenth century. The general movement of the English and Dutch into the Mediterranean is, however, already noticeable in the seventies and in full swing in the last decade of the century, being part of a general shift in the European commercial system, a shift which has been illuminated in F. Braudel, *La Méditerranée et le Monde Méditerranéen a l'époque de Philippe II*; F. Braudel et R. Romano, *Navires et Marchandises à l'entrée du Port de Livourne, 1547–1611*; and A. Tenenti, *Naufrages, Corsaires et Assurances maritimes à Venise, 1592–1609*.

[1] R. H. Tawney and E. Power (eds.), *Tudor Economic Documents*, II, 54.
[2] *Cal. Salis. MSS*, II, 515; *Cal. S.P. Spanish Eliz.*, III, 130.

the opportunity to forestall him in the Azores and the East Indies should not be lost. English commercial interests on the other hand hoped to exploit the situation by developing peaceful trade with the Portuguese empire, especially in Brazil and the East Indies. Thus the Spanish Company exerted its considerable influence against the scheme put forward by Leicester, Walsingham and Drake for the occupation of Terceira, the object of which was to establish a base for the interception of Philip's treasure. The scheme, as it happened, came to nothing, largely because the English, the French and Dom Antonio failed to work amicably together. On the other hand the lure of colonial trade did lead members of the Spanish Company to take part in various attempts to establish trade with Brazil, as well as in Edward Fenton's disastrous venture of 1582–3. This last was ostensibly a trading voyage to the Moluccas, but the Terceira projectors has such a large hand in the arrangements that nothing was achieved except a serious blow to the hopes of Brazil trade and some small contribution to the worsening of Anglo-Spanish relations.[1]

The Iberian traders of the pre-war decade were clearly no warmongers. Yet the commercial ambitions which inevitably arose from the Iberian trade, and which had contributed so decisively at an earlier stage to the formation of a militant maritime party, were still latent in these men of peace. War when it came not only deprived them of their normal trade, but presented them with the chance of gaining by force the imports they most desired; and the losses they suffered in Spain at the outbreak of the war provided them with all the excuse they needed. Thus it happened that in the final crisis of 1585 the Iberian interest moved over *en bloc* to the war party and became the chief force behind the privateering war. The very men whose business was with Spain seemed fated to become her worst enemies.

Trade and plunder were inseparable in the sixteenth century. The business of sea-plunder attracted all kinds of men, from criminals to noble lords, and took forms which varied from uninhibited piracy to licensed privateering. What is significant about Elizabethan sea-plunder up to 1585 is that it increasingly identified itself with Protestantism and patriotism. This is not to say that there was a general change of heart among pirates, nor that the government ceased to condemn them; ordinary indiscriminate

[1] See ch. 10 below.

piracy remained a serious social evil and the government's attempts to suppress it were unavailing. But in times of crisis pirates could be useful, provided they concentrated on the right prey. At such times, moreover, seamen and gentlemen who were not ordinary pirates took to the sea to do themselves and incidentally the queen a service. In all this activity the gentry took the lead, especially the west country families connected with the sea, for whom Protestantism, patriotism and plunder became virtually synonymous. It was the participation of the gentry that transformed the petty Channel roving of the earlier years into the oceanic ventures of the seventies and eighties, fusing into one diversified movement the ambitions of plunderers and traders.

The process started before the end of Mary's reign, when the Cornish Tremaynes and Killigrews embarked upon an unofficial war with Spain, sailing under French commissions. The next stage came with Elizabeth's intervention in France, from the end of 1562, when the English privateers, now properly licensed by the English government, freely included Spaniards among their victims, especially when Anglo-Spanish relations deteriorated and the trade with Flanders was suspended. In 1565 this spate of spoil subsided, only to revive on a larger scale in 1568, when the links with La Rochelle were re-formed and the Dutch joined in, making all the waters from the North Sea to the Bay of Biscay their hunting-ground.

In the sixties most of this marauding was small-scale, not markedly different from petty piracy either in law or in its conduct and results. The ships—usually mere barks or pinnaces of under fifty tons burden—operated chiefly from the Channel ports, especially from Devon and Cornwall, making short trips in home waters to bring in fishing boats, Flemish hoys and such small prizes. The booty was sold along the coasts to all and sundry of the local people, to regular receivers among the gentry or provincial merchants, or at recognised plunder marts like Mead Hole in the Isle of Wight, whither flocked buyers of all kinds. The captains, who often owned or partly owned their ships, usually had some connection with minor gentry, being gentlemen themselves or backed by gentlemen, and most of them would be able to produce some sort of commission from a foreign prince. John Chichester of Barnstaple is typical. He obtained a commission from Henry of Navarre to attack French Catholic shipping and in 1569 with his own 50-ton privateer took six French prizes, including one with a cargo belonging to London merchants. The English goods were restored to their owners and Chichester was bound in £300 to return home and go no more to the sea. He defied the ban, repeated his misdemeanour and probably ended his life on the gallows.[1]

Alongside this petty marauding, however, there developed a more ambitious type of venture. The *Castle of Comfort*, for example, was a powerful ship of 200 tons burden. George Fenner used her in his Guinea expedition in 1566, and in 1569 she came into the hands of Sir Henry Compton. Then with a licence from Coligny and victuals supplied by a substantial London merchant she set forth under the command of Thomas Jones, a gentleman of Lynn. Among her prizes was a French ship with a cargo worth some £800, the largest part of which went to a London merchant, who at the captain's request passed on £30 to Coligny and £10 to the Lord Admiral of England. In 1571 the *Castle* left for Morocco on what was ostensibly a trading venture; but she was now commanded by John Garrett of Plymouth, the same captain who, the following year, left a message of warning for Drake at a secret harbour in the Gulf of Darien. It is not unlikely, then, that the *Castle* was in the Caribbean in 1571 or 1572. In 1574 Richard Grenville bought her, having in mind a South Seas expedition. He had already entered the game of local sea-raiding in 1569 and was now contemplating something more ambitious. The scheme fell through, however, and Grenville and his partner Hawkins allowed the ship to a French captain called Henry Joliffe, who had strong connections with the Isle of Wight, for use as a privateer under licence from the prince of Condé. In such fashion grew the scale and geographical scope of plunder under the patronage of men of position.[2]

The political crisis of 1568–72 brought about the first important junction between the drive for trade and the drive for spoil. While the Hawkinses, Fenners and Winters turned from trade to plunder, directing their efforts to American as well as European

[1] H.C.A. 1/39, Aug. and Sept. 1569; H.C.A. 14/9, nos. 22, 137–8, 176, 199, 204, 215–16, 289–90, 318–19; H.C.A. 14/10, no. 167; Lansdowne MS 142, no. 80.

[2] H.C.A. 1/37, 1 June 1569; H.C.A. 1/39, 25 Nov. 1569; H.C.A. 13/17, 6, 18 March 1569/70; H.C.A. 13/18, 12 Sept., 13 Oct., 7, 10, 20 Nov. 1570, 18 Jan. 1570/1; H.C.A. 14/9, nos. 31, 158, 172, 238; H.C.A. 24/42, nos. 153–4, 193; H.C.A. 22/44, no. 11; A. L. Rowse, *Sir Richard Grenville*, pp. 118–21.

waters, the bolder spirits among the Channel-roving gentry launched out into oceanic voyaging. Edward Horsey, for example, had been one of the Channel rovers of Mary's reign. He was now Captain of the Isle of Wight and in that capacity permitted the island to become one of the main bases of French, Dutch and English freebooters. In 1572 he set forth Captain James Ranse, who joined Drake in the West Indies. In 1578 he supported Sir Humphrey Gilbert's venture, with which William Hawkins was also associated, a venture aiming to establish a North American base for raiding Spanish shipping. This enterprise failed chiefly because some of the captains and men preferred immediate gains to long-term prospects. Gentry and courtiers became increasingly interested in this sort of maritime enterprise during the seventies and early eighties. The great took less and less care to conceal their patronage of pirates, and themselves openly sponsored or took part in ventures of discovery, trade and colonisation from which ambition to 'annoy the king of Spain' was rarely absent. Their motives were mixed: some, like Walsingham, who sponsored Drake's South Seas venture, the Terceira project and Fenton's voyage, as well as less aggressive enterprises, were moved chiefly by hostility to Spain and Roman Catholicism; some wanted lands beyond the seas; some were genuinely concerned with exploration; and an element of mercantile endeavour made itself felt in some voyages; but the dominant note was predatory. Thus Frobisher's north-west passage ventures turned into a treasure hunt; Gilbert's colonial expedition in 1578 into a field day for pirates; and meanwhile others like Oxenham made straight for the obvious target—Spanish bullion. The lesser kind of piratical adventurer found an increasing demand for his services in anti-Spanish projects. In 1582, for example, at least eleven English vessels were sailing under Dom Antonio's flag. Two of these were commanded by notorious pirates; another belonged to the earl of Shrewsbury; Drake owned two. In 1584 Edward and William Fenner took to the sea in the company of the pirate John Challice (or Callys), plundering Portuguese shipping in the name of the pretender.[1]

In 1585, as we have seen, this bellicose alliance of revengeful traders and rapacious gentry gained the adhesion of a powerful body of merchants, and the social force which was to dominate the sea war reached its full shape.

[1] See below, pp. 91, 202–3.

It did not, however, dominate the strategic conduct of the sea war. In this, as in every phase of war and politics, the decisions lay with Elizabeth, who did not share the outlook of such 'men of war' as Drake, Hawkins and Raleigh. They had enough influence to persuade her to adopt now one, now another of their strategic notions, but they did not make policy; they were the queen's servants, not her masters. No Albuquerque, no Chatham could arise so long as she occupied the throne. Nor could her 'men of war', in their position, even organise their ideas into a coherent system. Their suggestions remained mere unrelated sketches for a general design that was only dimly conceived. There is evidence that they would have liked to transform England's sea effort into an effective bid for Atlantic power, cutting off the supply of treasure upon which Philip depended and opening up America to English trade. But for a clear statement of this purpose we look in vain. Instead we find various proposals for offensive operations at sea implying this purpose, all of them variants of three main schemes.

The most important of these envisaged the holding of Cadiz or Lisbon or some other base on the Iberian coast, from which Spanish commerce could be completely disrupted. But it was one thing to surprise and sack Cadiz, as Essex did in 1596, and another to maintain it against a Spanish army operating on its own soil. For amphibious operations of this kind England required a much more efficient army than she had, and far greater financial resources. More alluring was the project of holding a base in the Spanish Indies—Panamá, Havana, Cartagena or Puerto Rico—or alternatively establishing an English colony nearby. Cartagena was captured in 1586, Puerto Rico in 1598; both were immediately abandoned; the Roanoke colonies, too, were virtually abandoned. Such bases in the midst of the Spanish empire could only exist if Spanish naval forces ceased to exist. So long as Spain had some power at sea any such base presented a target to all the forces she could mobilise. Unfortunately Spanish naval power was never destroyed. Finally there was the plan of blockade proposed by Hawkins. A substantial squadron was to be kept at sea between Spain and the Azores with the main object of intercepting the treasure fleets. The plan was simple and it neither required the use of an army nor offered the enemy a sitting target. Above all, it was comparatively cheap. Hawkins submitted the plan in 1589, when Spain's naval power was at its weakest, and it is possible that this policy might have prevented the revival of Spain's marine and gravely injured her war effort. On the other hand it is doubtful whether even Hawkins realised the magnitude of the task. Spain was already in 1589 beginning to use the fast-sailing *gallizabras* for transporting the king's treasure, and a very thorough blockade of the Iberian coast would have been necessary to intercept them. If the English fleet had been split up for patrolling purposes it would have been unable to face a fleet of Spanish warships sent out to escort the silver galleons home. This was exactly what happened in 1591, when Lord Thomas Howard withdrew from the Azores in the face of Admiral Bazán's superior fleet.

Hawkins' scheme was practical, but its success really depended on the destruction of the Spanish naval power. So did the various projects for a West Indian base. As for the Iberian projects, they depended on the creation of an efficient army and strong financial backing. In fact all these plans required the sort of wholehearted war effort that the political circumstances rendered inconceivable. It is not surprising that such attempts as were made to carry them out were unimpressive. It is futile to argue, as historians are inclined to do, about what should have been done and who was to blame. The queen had her limited war aims, and achieved them; her 'men of war' groped towards a different conception of English maritime strategy—one which could not reach clear expression until the interests they stood for had taken command of the state. Then, from the days of Blake onwards, the navy would become their weapon, to use as they wished. Meanwhile the navy belonged to the queen.

The government neither would nor could develop a systematic offensive against Spanish sea-power, but it naturally expected voluntary forces to play their part, as they had always done, in damaging enemy commerce, and it was weak enough to employ its own ships in the same way, since the queen expected them to pay their way in prizes. For although the sixteenth century saw the emergence of the royal navy as a force distinct from the irregular sea-forces of the nation as a whole, there was as yet no clear division between the functions and personnel of the two. The management and command of the queen's ships were in fact to a large extent in the hands of the leaders of private maritime warfare. Hence the domination of offensive operations at sea by those whom we have identified as the aggressive elements of the pre-war period, now joined by the embattled merchants. Hence the prominence of the semi-official enterprise, financed and led by the merchants and sea-gentry. Hence the inevitable cloud of privateers which accompanied such expeditions, either as consorts attached and under orders for an agreed period, or simply 'in company', with no formal obligations. Hence, while strategy foundered in a confusion of aims, haphazard plunder became the rule.

Privateers far outnumbered the queen's ships throughout the war. Their depredations could not, of course, win decisive victory at sea, but there is some evidence that, although largely concerned with private gain, privateers did on occasion co-ordinate their movements, either to assist each other or to provide more formal fleets with timely information. Privateers were frequently employed as scouts on the Spanish coast or in the Azores, and when they actually sailed with an organised fleet they would have their allotted tasks. At the beginning of the war, indeed, there may well have been some loose plan to co-ordinate private effort in the main theatres of Atlantic action—the Spanish coast, the Azores, the Caribbean, Virginia and Newfoundland.[1] After 1588 there was probably less collaboration, and after 1592 very little. It would be rash, however, to attempt more than these tentative suggestions for an inquiry that might yield fruitful results, but is not our main theme here. An examination of the contribution of privateering to the war would, moreover, attempt to assess the impact of commercial losses upon the Spaniard, both in weakening his economy and in spurring him to its defence, but this again is not our purpose here, though the detail that follows will throw some light on this question. Rather we are concerned with privateering as an English phenomenon, for two decades one of the main forms of English maritime activity. Circumstances had conspired to give it a more important place in English sea life than it ever held before or afterwards, and in tracing its anatomy we may perceive from a fresh angle the main lines of maritime and commercial development.

[1] D. B. Quinn has indicated 'some over-all co-ordination between what Francis Drake planned for the Indies, Raleigh and Grenville for Virginia, and Bernard Drake for Virginia and Newfoundland' (*Roanoke Voyages*, p. 32).

Chapter 2

REGULATION

Privateering, though a form of private enterprise, was also a political phenomenon, since it was of interest to the state in several ways. In the first place, Englishmen could hardly be allowed to take action against the subjects of a foreign power without some specific authority from their own government. Secondly, disputes were bound to arise between Englishmen and neutrals, and the government was obliged to have some legal machinery for dealing with them, as well as some disciplinary powers to keep them to a minimum. Thirdly, it had a revenue interest in privateering, partly because private shipping was thus being mobilised to fight the enemy without imposing any burden on the exchequer, but more directly because customs duties were paid on prize-goods and an additional tenth on prize-goods provided the Lord Admiral with an income. Dr Julius Caesar, judge of the Admiralty Court, maintained in 1590 'that her Majesty hath gotten and saved by these reprisals since they began above two hundred thousand pounds'.[1] Privateering also, it was argued, helped to keep shipping and commerce alive in the midst of wartime difficulties; Raleigh and Caesar both thought that without it English shipping would decay 'and her Majesty lose the best part of her custom'.[2]

The government therefore had responsibility for and could well benefit from the licensing, control and taxation of privateering. In practice the system of licensing was very loose, depending, as we have seen, on a legal fiction; control over the conduct of privateers at sea was so inadequate that the government was seriously embarrassed by constant complaints from neutrals; and even the financial gains of the Crown from privateering, either directly or through the admiralty, were slight in comparison with those of its private subjects. In fact the working of the machinery for the regulation of privateering provides a striking example of late Elizabethan administration at its worst—feeble and corrupt.

[1] Lansdowne MS 157, f. 434. Caesar to Howard, 18 Dec. 1590.
[2] Lansdowne MSS 69, f. 60; 157, f. 446.

The Lord High Admiral of England from 1585 to 1619 was Charles Howard, Baron of Effingham and (from 1596) Earl of Nottingham. He was responsible, under the Crown, for all matters concerning prize, and he exercised his powers through the High Court of Admiralty, whose judges and other officers he appointed, and through the vice-admirals of the coast, likewise appointed by him. The judicial and administrative functions of this apparatus were hardly distinguishable from each other. The vice-admiralty officials, for example, saw to arrests of ships and individuals, bound individuals to appear in court, made inventories of ships and cargoes in suit, executed the sentences of the court, examined witnesses, collected the Lord Admiral's tenths and took bonds from privateers for good behaviour at sea. The court itself issued letters of reprisal, adjudicated prizes and had both civil and criminal jurisdiction in matters of prize, spoil and piracy. In the court the Lord Admiral could institute *ex officio* proceedings against privateers who had sailed without letters of reprisal, evaded payment of the tenth or in any other way infringed his rights or disregarded the rules he laid down for their behaviour. Foreign merchants, or foreign diplomats on their behalf, could bring actions in the court to reclaim captured property; English merchants, seamen or any other participants in a privateering venture could here appeal to the law to arbitrate in their frequent disputes over the division of the spoil. And in addition to its prize jurisdiction the court had wide powers in all kinds of maritime and mercantile issues. Theoretically, at least, the Lord Admiral did not lack the necessary authority. What he did lack was the standard of efficiency and honesty necessary to impose restraint upon a pursuit such as privateering. The standard was no doubt unattainable then and difficult enough at any time, but the admiralty men probably fell even further below it than their contemporaries.

In the first place, a considerable traffic in letters of reprisal seems to have developed. The Lord Admiral complained that they 'have been and daily are by some disorderly handled, bought and sold for money, and both ships, captains and masters oftentimes rased out and others inserted in place thereof, and used so as granted by my authority'.[1] On one occasion a commission was offered in exchange for shares in a venture, and on another a local admiralty official acquired a blank commission, which he then

[1] H.C.A. 14/26, no. 137.

allocated to a venture in which he had an interest.[1] The Lord Admiral himself was in the habit of by-passing his own official machinery by granting commissions without even notifying the Admiralty Court. The result of all this was that the court, which was nominally responsible for all commissions of reprisal and all 'controversies arising thereof', could not have known how many commissions were issued nor by whom they were being used. Furthermore a number of privateering enterprises were authorised, not by letters of reprisal, but by letters patent. Such commissions were only granted to people of some influence, and were preferred for reasons of prestige and for certain practical advantages attached to them. Here again the court was by-passed, and its normal procedure for regulating the behaviour of privateers at sea and ensuring the proper adjudication and disposal of prizes could not in these cases be applied. Many ships sailed without any licence at all, and the lenient attitude of the Lord Admiral in this matter did nothing to strengthen the authority of his office.

The promoter of a reprisal venture, when he acquired his letters of reprisal, had also to enter into a bond to observe certain rules in the conduct of the enterprise and the disposal of the prizes. He was forbidden to attack any but enemy commerce and was ordered to proceed directly to the coasts of Spain and Portugal or other waters most frequented by enemy shipping. Prizes had to be brought to an English port, where, before anything was sold or landed, they must be inventoried and valued, or 'appraised', under the supervision of the local vice-admiralty officers. These were responsible for forwarding the inventory and appraisement to the Admiralty Court in London within six weeks. One-tenth of the value of every prize was to be paid to the Lord Admiral. In 1589 the practice of adjudicating prizes in the Admiralty Court was begun, and new rules were added to the bond in this connection. Should he break any of these rules the promoter might be called upon to pay to the Lord Admiral the sum stipulated in the bond— £1,000 at the beginning of the war, rising to £3,000 within a few years. It soon became customary to take such bonds from the captain and master of each ship.[2]

Such was the chief instrument by which the Admiralty Court sought to exercise some control over reprisal men. Some offenders were duly prosecuted and forfeited their bonds, but by and large

[1] H.C.A. 13/28, 12 Nov. 1590; H.C.A. 14/27, no. 149.
[2] The full text of a bond is printed in *E.P.V.*, pp. 178-9.

the sanction did not have the desired effect. All the evils concerned—attacks on neutral commerce, breaking of bulk before inventory and appraisement, evasion of tenths and customs—continued and flourished. Neutral vessels and neutral goods aboard enemy vessels were so frequently captured that the Privy Council and the Lord Admiral had to deal with an unceasing stream of complaints from foreign merchants and their governments, and suits for the recovery of spoil occupied a great part of the time and energy of the Admiralty Court. But foreigners found it difficult to obtain even partial restitution. The Italian merchant Filippo Corsini, for example, in representing the claims of a number of Italian merchants, some of them resident in Portugal, to two very valuable cargoes captured in 1590, had strong backing from the governments of Florence and Venice. He obtained a court order for the arrest of the goods in question, but found that one of the cargoes had been adjudicated good prize within eleven days of its arrival at Weymouth and had been distributed far and wide long before the sequestration order reached the town. The adventurers had of course been forewarned. The queen and the Privy Council, for diplomatic reasons, took the matter seriously, or at any rate made a great show of doing so; Dr Caesar was told, 'We would have this cause so uprightly used as the duke of Florence, whom the Queen's Majesty favoureth greatly, may not have any just cause to complain of lack of favourable justice.' His response was to reaffirm his adjudication of the Weymouth cargo, and to divide the other between the captors and the Italians. To Caesar's intense chagrin the Privy Council pronounced this sentence, given early in 1592, unsatisfactory, and the issue was now reconsidered by an *ad hoc* tribunal consisting of the Lord Treasurer, the Lord Admiral and Lord Buckhurst. Their judgement was more favourable to the Italians, but was of little practical help to Corsini and his friends, who were unable to lay their hands on the goods. Those in possession were so successful in prevaricating that in April 1593 Corsini was still complaining that he was being 'led about in a ring without end'. He made no secret of his opinion that Caesar was corrupt, and the latter brought a successful action for slander against him in January 1593.[1]

The truth of the matter was that Caesar was in no position to deal out even-handed justice. In the Corsini case the English parties interested in the capture included Sir Walter Raleigh, Sir

[1] For further details about this case, and source references, see below, pp. 115–16, 132.

George Carey, Henry Seckford (Groom of the Chamber and Keeper of the Privy Purse), the great London merchant Thomas Myddelton and, above all, Lord Charles Howard, Baron of Effingham, the Lord High Admiral of England. Powerful men like Carey, who was closely related to the queen and to the Lord Admiral, did not hesitate to invoke the 'goodwill' of the judge in return for benefits usually unspecified. Thus Carey began a civil action in 1591 by writing to Caesar; 'Sir, I received by my servant Burgley a very kind and friendly message from you, in assurance of your unfeigned goodwill to me, and your desire to find return of the like. If you shall examine the course of my life, and believe what you shall find most true, my deeds have ever accompanied my words and my friendship was never professed where not firmly performed, until cause was apparently given to the contrary; your goodwill towards me shall never die unrequited to the uttermost of my power, but have usury paid in double measure. Now Sir, you shall further understand that I have a very poor prize come into Dartmouth, and Mr Watts a very rich one. . . .'[1] The patronage of the great was something no man in Caesar's position could reject or scorn without grave danger to himself, and it required stronger character than his to rise above the prevailing sycophancy of the official world. He cultivated his noble friends, preserved their correspondence with loving care and by judicious use of influential contacts manoeuvred himself into a well-earned niche in the Jacobean establishment.[2]

But if Caesar could be influenced, he could also be—and more frequently was—ignored. Here was the main reason for the difficulties of foreigners in the matter of restitution, the contrast between 'the daily contentment which poor strangers receive by my judgements and orders in causes of justice, and their extreme complaints against the want of execution of the same'.[3] The weakness of the authority of the High Court of Admiralty, which lay at the root of its failure to control the privateers, was well appreciated by the judge, who also understood its immediate causes.

In the first place constant political interference undermined the prestige of the court. When his judgement in the Corsini case was

---

[1] Additional MS 12506, f. 285.
[2] Already Master of Chancery, Master of Requests and M.P. in Elizabeth's time, he was knighted in 1603 and made successively Chancellor of the Exchequer, Privy Councillor and Master of the Rolls. He died in 1636.
[3] Lansdowne MS 157, f. 208.

quashed by the Privy Council, Caesar bitterly protested to Burghley: 'Whensoever your lordship shall be resolved hereafter that any sentence of this court is unfit (for causes in policy and state to your good lordship best known) to be executed, it may please your lordship that the same may be done in court of justice by appeals, to the end that these extraordinary courses contrary to law be not hereafter an utter overthrow of the whole profession of civil law within this land,' tending to the discredit both of the court and of himself as judge.[1] But the work of the court inevitably affected questions of international significance, and the interference of the Privy Council therefore continued. Again, the jurisdiction of the court was constantly under fire. Some porttowns such as Weymouth claimed independent admiralty jurisdictions of their own; and the common lawyers fought a running battle of prohibitions against the extremely large claims of the Admiralty Court.

One of Caesar's main grievances was that the Lord Admiral frequently took action without reference to the court's own orders, 'which, being crossed or clean displaced by private warrants or letters (things in truth not warranted by the law), are so blunted and disgraced in the opinion of the people, that they, being freed from the sharp warrants of the law, do become careless of the Judge and of the Lord Admiral . . . and use those private warrants as they list, and when they list, rather as props to their disordered affections than as means for the furtherance or execution of justice', all of which 'hath bred so general contempts in this land as the like have not been seen in former times of peace'.[2] The Lord Admiral's attitude in prize and spoil cases was naturally influenced by his private interest as the recipient of tenths of all prizes; but he was also personally a promoter of privateering ventures, and in cases which directly affected his pocket he did not hestitate to instruct the judge accordingly. In March 1603, for example, he wrote to Caesar: 'and as touching certain Barbary ducats brought home by Captain Canyon long since and delivered unto my servant Robert Bragg, I must entreat you to forbear granting any attachment against him for the same, because if they be to be restored I myself must make satisfaction for them, who received them of Bragg'. And he adds the postscript: 'You yourself have told me that in these cases of coin there ought to be no restitution because

---

[1] Lansdowne MS 140, f. 85.   [2] Additional MS 12505, f. 269.

the same is without mark.'[1] In the same year one Captain Tom-
kins, having made spoil of certain Venetian goods, insured himself
by presenting a substantial portion of his booty to Howard. The
Venetian ambassador, seeking justice for his countrymen, was
naturally indignant at being referred to Howard and pointed out
that 'it was the Admiral himself who had part of the plunder in
his hands, and what is more he admitted it'. His report continues
acidly: 'Further I remarked that I was the minister of the Republic,
accredited to the Crown and not to the Admiral, and while I
could drink at the fountain of justice I need not go seeking turbid
water in brooks.'[2]

The vice-admirals and their officers were likewise interested
parties. The vice-admirals of Hampshire, Devon and Cornwall,
and Dorset were respectively Sir George Carey, Sir Walter
Raleigh and Lord Thomas Howard, three of the greatest privateering promoters. Lesser officials like Robert Bragg and Stephen
Ridlesden were as deeply involved. The local customers, like John
Young of Chichester and Thomas Heaton of Southampton, were
in the same business. Such men handled the administration of
prizes, and it is little wonder that the whole coast from Chichester
westwards was a hotbed of illegal privateering and prize-disposal.
In proposing to make a special circuit there in 1591, Caesar particularly asked for the full support of the queen, since 'in doing of
justice I should assuredly reap the illwill of many (some perhaps
far greater than myself)'.[3] He repeatedly complained of the negligence and corruption of the local officials. One Lazenby, for
example, was granted for six months the right to all enemy goods
taken by English ships sailing without letters of reprisal, and it was
reported that at Falmouth the agent of the vice-admiral 'did make
demand of the said commissioners [executing Lazenby's grant]
of the sum of five hundred pounds for the said Mr Payne, vice-
admiral there, and that he in respect thereof should suffer them,
the said commissioners, to proceed'.[4]

The official admiralty machine was an important sphere of
patronage, and, as the appointments were made from the centre,
the friends, relations and dependants of Lord Charles Howard
had first pick. Carey, vice-admiral of Hampshire, was his brother-
in-law; Sir Richard Leveson, son of the vice-admiral of Wales,

[1] Additional MS 12505, f. 50.
[2] R. C. Anderson (ed.), *The Book of Examinations, 1601–2*, pp. xxi–xxv.
[3] Lansdowne MS 157, f. 46.   [4] H.C.A. 13/29, 6 May 1591.

was his son-in-law; another son-in-law, Sir Robert Southwell, held the vice-admiralty of Norfolk and Suffolk; Edmund Carey, another brother-in-law, was vice-admiral of Lincolnshire; William Howard, the Lord Admiral's brother, became vice-admiral of Yorkshire. The admiralty was almost a family concern. Lesser appointments left room for the friends of the family and of central officials like Stephen Ridlesden.

Above all, corruption was inevitable when officials were unpaid. The vice-admirals were expected to make a profit out of fees and perquisites, and it has been justly observed that 'throughout the sixteenth and seventeenth centuries the admiralty was looked upon mainly as a source of profit'.[1] In the circumstances it was too much to expect local officers not to connive at piracies, smuggling and the like. Nor could the vice-admirals be expected to pass on to the Lord Admiral the one half of their profits due to him. They were supposed to return twice-yearly accounts, but, as the Lord Admiral complained in 1591, 'most of them have seldom or never accounted at all since they first had their offices'.[2]

The net result of these abuses can be read between the lines of a document of 1601 entitled 'Remembrances for Mr Burrage the Lord Admiral's solicitor'.[3] Among other things requiring to be done the author notes: the indictment of all who have taken ships to sea since 1585 without letters of reprisal, or have disposed of prizes before adjudication; the arrest of all unauthorised men-of-war; the enforcement of the statutes concerning the duties of vice-admirals; and the signing and sealing by the Lord Admiral of all compoundings or pardons for faults, fines and forfeitures. Such good resolutions had been made before, but their occurrence towards the end of the war in a kind of programme of reform indicates a more than usually disturbing financial situation in the admiralty, resulting from failure to enforce the law. For efficiency and profit were, as Caesar never tired of telling Howard, interdependent. Lack of funds prevented the institution of a regular judicial circuit, without which it was impossible, in Caesar's view, to bring to order 'such great personages who dare do and speak whatsoever them listeth, and make most small account as well of commandments from me as of letters of assistance from your lordship and the other lords, the sequel whereof being like to

---

[1] R. C. Marsden, 'The Viceadmirals of the Coast', *E.H.R.*, XXII (1907), 468–77 and XXIII (1908), 736–57.

[2] H.C.A. 14/28, no. 65, 25 Oct. 1591.   [3] Lansdowne MS 145, f. 15.

prove dishonourable and dangerous to this estate'.[1] Caesar himself could do little about these matters, though he frequently avowed in his nagging letters to the Lord Admiral that he had beggared himself by subsidising the Admiralty Court.

But the essence of the weakness of the admiralty machine lay in its historical character: it was, not only in the eyes of the Lord Admiral, but in the eyes of the queen, the great courtiers and everyone else, at once a department of state under the authority of the Crown and a private province or liberty of the Lord Admiral. When Caesar proposed reforms in the admiralty, he called them 'good counsel for the bettering of his [the Lord Admiral's] estate'.[2] The High Court of Admiralty was his court, and the judge, like all the other officers, was his servant. The organisation and personnel were entirely his responsibility, and to him accrued the profits of justice and the perquisites of wreck, piracy confiscations, tenths of prizes and the rest. Consequently his authority was coolly disregarded by powerful men and local powers, and contemptuously dismissed for what, in large measure, it really was—a private concern making a profit out of the public. In 1589 it was reported that 'there is much grudging that there are not more on the Narrow Sea to restrain the Dunkirkers. The common people lay the fault on the Admiral, who, they say, for his private gain from letters of reprisal, hinders war being proclaimed'.[3]

Yet in time of war this was clearly one of the most vital departments of state, and the loss of authority and effective control over the coasts meant a serious weakening of the central government, both in relation to its subjects and in relation to foreign powers. There took place a certain disintegration of power. Worse still, while control deteriorated and the possibility of any substantial taxation of privateering receded, the queen herself joined in the scramble by lending her ships and money for expeditions in which the motive of plunder was scarcely secondary. Hawkins' policy of systematic blockade was distorted and diluted into a spasmodic treasure hunt, and the long-term interests of the monarchy were sacrificed in favour of immediate saving. Instead of controlling and taxing its subjects, the Crown entered with them into a race for private profit, a race it utterly failed to win, for the great naval and semi-official expeditions were on the whole unprofitable.

Some contemporaries hoped for a stronger policy. A suggestion

[1] Lansdowne MS 157, f. 210. [2] Lansdowne MS 157, f. 430.
[3] *Cal. S.P. Dom. Eliz., Addenda, 1580–1625*, p. 274.

for a twenty-five per cent tax on prize-goods was made in 1585,[1] and Dr Julius Caesar's letters show considerable grasp of the issues. But none of the proposed remedies was seriously adopted, and it is doubtful whether anything short of a complete reconstruction of the admiralty could have solved the problems. Something like an administrative revolution was required, but vested interests were strong enough to prevent even minor reforms.

[1] Lansdowne MS 157, f. 450.

Chapter 3

MEN AND MATERIALS

John Hagthorpe's statement that in the 'queen's time' there were 'never less than 200 sail of voluntaries and others' on Spanish coasts may have been an exaggeration, but such evidence as we can pull together shows that it was not such a wild one as might be imagined. As Table 1 indicates, no less than 236 Eng-

Table 1. Privateers Operating 1589–1591

(classified according to port of origin and tonnage burden)

port of origin	1–49 tons	50–99 tons	100–149 tons	150–199 tons	200–299 tons	300 tons & over	unknown tonnage	total
London	9	20	7	6	6	5	17	70
Southampton and neighbours[1]	2	8	3	0	1	0	11	25
Dorset ports[2]	4	6	1	1	0	0	15	27
Devon and Cornish ports[3]	6	12	2	0	2	0	23	45
Bristol and Bridgewater[4]	3	12	3	2	0	0	9	29
Other ports[5]	2	4	0	0	0	0	4	10
Port unknown	3	7	0	0	2	0	18	30
Total	29	69	16	9	11	5	97	236

[1] Includes three Chichester ships, five of Portsmouth, five of the Isle of Wight and twelve of Southampton.

[2] Includes one Poole ship, eleven of Lyme and fifteen of Weymouth and Melcomb Regis.

[3] Includes one each from Exmouth, Tavistock, Northam and Padstow, two from Falmouth, four each from Topsham and Dartmouth, eight from Barnstaple and twenty-three from Plymouth.

[4] Includes five from Bridgewater and twenty-four from Bristol.

[5] Includes one each from Dover, Chester, Carmarthen and Barry and two each from Lynn, Yarmouth and Rye.

lish vessels are known to have been privateering at one time or another during the three years 1589–91. If we assume, as we legitimately may, that the list is incomplete, and that many of these vessels made more than one voyage in this period,[1] it is fair to

[1] Tables 1 and 2 are based on the Appendix to this book, which certainly does not constitute an exhaustive list of privateering voyages for the years concerned,

conclude that at least 300 voyages—a hundred a year—took place. Table 2, giving a total of 86 known voyages for 1598, tends to confirm this estimate, since again there is good reason to believe that the actual number was considerably larger.[1] A glance at the beginning of the war gives a similar figure. In the months

Table 2. Privateers Operating 1598

(classified according to port of origin and tonnage burden)

port of origin	1–49 tons	50–99 tons	100– 149 tons	150– 199 tons	200– 299 tons	300 tons & over	unknown tonnage	total
London	1	2	1	4	13	6	16	43
Southampton and neighbours[1]	3	2	0	0	0	0	4	9
Dorset ports[2]	1	0	0	0	0	0	9	10
Devon and Cornish ports[3]	0	1	0	0	0	0	10	11
Bristol and Bridgewater[4]	0	0	0	2	0	0	1	3
Other ports[5]	0	0	0	0	0	0	1	1
Port unknown	0	0	1	0	1	2	5	9
Total	5	5	2	6	14	8	46	86

[1] Includes one of Portsmouth and eight of Southampton.
[2] Includes four of Lyme and six of Weymouth and Melcomb Regis.
[3] Includes seven of Plymouth, two of Barnstaple, one of Penzance and one of Dartmouth.
[4] All of Bristol.   [5] One of Arundel.

from June 1585 to March 1586 letters of reprisal were issued for 88 ships,[2] and there were undoubtedly others which sailed with special authority from the queen or the Lord Admiral. It has sometimes been asserted that privateering declined towards the end of the war, but there seems to be no authority or evidence for this. Essex's Islands fleet in 1597 comprised, according to Monson, 170 ships, the great majority of them privately owned, and Raleigh on the same occasion spoke of his squadron being accompanied by 20

since the source materials are inadequate for such a purpose. The 236 ships of 1589–91 made 271 traceable voyages: i.e. in relatively few cases can we trace more than one voyage made during the three years. The list of course excludes royal vessels and plain pirates, though it includes vessels combining trade and prize-taking in the same voyage.

[1] The absence of a number of privateers mentioned in the records for 1597 and 1599 is suggestive.

[2] H.C.A. 25/1 (4). Lists for the early months of the war are to be found in Lansdowne MSS 115 and 129 and H.C.A. 14/23, no. 213.

voluntary barks of the West Country.[1] Thomas Wilson at the very end of the war referred to 'the infinite number of men-of-war that were and ever are roving abroad in the Indies and Spanish dominions, to get purchase, as they call it, whereby a number grow rich',[2] and the growing spate of complaints about the depredations of Englishmen on all and sundry in the last few years of the war creates the impression of a plague of marauders. In sum, we may be reasonably certain that at least a hundred ships a year sailed on reprisal throughout the war and that the figure sometimes rose considerably above this—perhaps as high as two hundred.

Before leaving Tables 1 and 2 we may observe certain outstanding features of the geographical and tonnage distribution of privateering, though such incomplete figures as we have do not warrant any refinement in deduction. First, the large share of London in the business is clear, even if we allow for the probability that Devon and Cornwall set forth a higher proportion of unlicensed or unrecorded ventures. Furthermore it would appear that London's share was growing. Counterposed to London were the ports westward from Chichester round to Bristol, the long southwestern leg of England. The rest of the coastline played no significant part in setting forth privateers. One other salient point is the decline in Bristol's activity. In respect of size it is safe to say that small vessels of under a hundred tons burden formed a clear majority in the early years of the war, but had sunk to a minority by the end; and that the dominance of Londoners among the larger privateers is even more marked in 1598 than in 1589–91.

The great majority of Elizabethan privateers were essentially no different from the common run of merchantmen of that time. Merchantmen most of them were in fact, converted for purposes of warfare simply by the addition of a few guns and a great many men. Often a ship would make an ordinary trading voyage one year and a reprisal voyage the next; some combined trade and plunder in the same venture; others, like a number of Bristolmen, opted for privateering probably because their normal commerce was interrupted or restricted by the war. There was not much variation in such vessels, except in their capacity, which ranged from about thirty to something over three hundred tons burden.

---

[1] *Monson's Tracts*, II, 40.
[2] F. J. Fisher (ed.), 'The State of England (1600). By Sir Thomas Wilson', *Camden Miscellany*, XVI (1936), 36–7.

This was calculated by multiplying the keel length, the beam and the depth in hold, and dividing by a hundred, the result signifying the capacity of the ship in terms of casks of Bordeaux wine. The deadweight, or 'tons and tonnage', was calculated by adding one-third to the burden. Such, at any rate, were the rules for measurement given by the queen's shipwright, Matthew Baker. In practice the Elizabethans nearly always used round figures to the nearest five or ten tons, and nearly always referred to the burden rather than the deadweight. Figures given in different sources for the same ship often differ widely and it is obvious that exactitude in this matter was not considered important. The standard rig was three-masted: fore, main and mizen masts with a bowsprit, carrying six sails, forecourse, foretop, maincourse, maintop, lateen mizen and spritsail. The general appearance is familiar: the small forecastle, set just behind the stem, the low 'waist' somewhat forward, and the long, rising superstructure aft. The rake forward and aft was about as much as the beam, and probably these ships were therefore rather less tubby than the usual pictorial representations suggest. There were probably two decks in the main hull—a lower or gun deck and an upper deck, but these evidently did not run continuously from bow to stern, but were stepped up or down wherever this was found necessary or desirable. The reconstructed Pilgrim Fathers' *Mayflower*, embodying the results of much painstaking research, gives, we may reasonably assume, a fairly accurate picture of a typical late Elizabethan merchantman.[1]

At the extremes of this largely undifferentiated mass of shipping, however, it is possible to discern some degree of specialisation. Conditions at sea in wartime and the popularity of privateering favoured the pinnace on the one hand and the large, fighting merchantman, on the other. The term 'pinnace' was then a vague one. It might, in its broadest sense, indicate any ship of up to some eighty tons burden accompanying a considerably larger ship, and here it is essentially the auxiliary function of the vessel which is implied. In a more particular sense a pinnace was a sailing vessel of up to about thirty tons, equipped with oars. There appears to have been no radical difference in build or in armament between a pinnace in this sense and an ordinary small ship, but the former had the advantage in manoeuvrability, for its oars made it especially useful in the decisive operational moments of a cruise, when

[1] See R. C. Anderson, 'A Mayflower Model', *Mariner's Mirror*, XII (1926), 260–3.

the chance of taking a prize arose. It was often easier to approach and board the enemy from an oared pinnace than from a vessel relying solely upon sail. Without a pinnace or a boat, a powerful ship of reprisal could well lie frustrated to leeward of a tempting prey; harbours and shoaled waters often provided natural refuge for a hunted vessel, which might even run itself aground, and in such circumstances the pursuers needed some sort of light craft to negotiate the shallows and cut out or bring off the prize. In Christopher Newport's voyage of 1596 his fellow captain Michael Geare, once they had safely arrived in the West Indies, sailed off in the pinnace and made a highly successful cruise, leaving the ship of war, the *Neptune*, to spend fruitless weeks looking for him off the coast of Cuba. On his return Newport and his merchant partners brought an action against Geare on the ground that the departure of the pinnace 'was the overthrowe of the viadge & cause that the shipp came home without purchase, For that the said pinnace was the hope of the viadge, because such purchase as was to be hoped for was to be had furth of harbors with the said pinnace, where the shipp could not goe'.[1] Here in the Caribbean, of course, so much inshore work was involved that almost every expedition included at least one pinnace. Some captains in West Indies ventures carried pinnaces aboard the main ship in parts and assembled them in some convenient place in the sphere of operations, thus avoiding the danger of losing a small vessel in the rough ocean seas. Elsewhere, perhaps, pinnaces were not so vitally necessary, but it was a common practice in plunder voyages for one large ship and one small to proceed in company.

At the other extreme the period of the Elizabethan war with Spain witnessed a significant growth in the number of large and well-armed merchantmen of the two, three and four hundred ton class. In the latter half of the sixteenth century, and more especially in its last twenty years, English merchants and ships were breaking into some of the lucrative, long-distance routes of world trade. Here were needed ships capable of carrying and defending rich and bulky cargoes, intimidating African tribesmen, inspiring the respect of Eastern potentates and holding their own with jealous European rivals. Above all, on long voyages the regular toll of disease made essential an ample supply of men, and therefore of victuals. Hence again the demand for larger vessels, and such, built with an eye to fighting as well as trading. were many of the

[1] H.C.A. 13/32, 23 June 1597.

ships sailing to the Levant, to Barbary and the further coasts of Africa. Typical were the Levant Company's *Merchant Royal* and *Edward Bonaventure*, both of which were employed in 1591 in the first English attempt to breach the Portuguese monopoly of the Cape route to the East. The war itself not only increased the need for such vessels, but opened fresh opportunities for their use, and most ships of this type participated at one time or another in privateering, if only by taking a prize in the course of a normal trading venture. There is no reason to suppose that in design these ships differed much from ordinary merchantmen, though possibly some of them carried a fourth mast, or bonaventure mizen, stepped abaft the mizen. But in privateering mere size brought considerable advantages: the larger ships could carry more victuals and men and more and heavier guns. Thus they could make longer voyages, attack larger prey and defend themselves against most comers. Some of them showed up well fighting alongside the queen's ships in 1588 and on other occasions.

Ships built especially for privateering were a minority among men of reprisal. The Lord Admiral's private vessels, the earl of Cumberland's and one or two of Raleigh's are obvious examples, and some merchants owned men-of-war. Thomas Heaton's *Bevis* of Southampton was a privateersman plain; the Glanvilles of London appear to have had the *Neptune* built specifically for Christopher Newport's Caribbean cruises. Another distinct group were the converted prizes—Sir George Carey's *Commander*, for example, William Grafton's *Our Lady* and Lord Thomas Howard's *Flight*. The names of ships are unfortunately no guide to their function. The *Concord*, the *Amity*, the *Affection*, the *Samaritan* and the *Truelove* were just as much fighting ships as the *Seadragon*, the *Flying Dragon*, the *Golden Dragon*, the *Green Dragon*, the *Lions* of varying hues, the *Panther*, the *Ferret*, the *Eagle*, the *Black Falcon*, the *Tiger*, the *Scorn*, the *Discontent* and the *Wildman*. Some names are peculiarly suggestive—the *Wheel of Fortune*, the *Hazard*, the *Poor Man's Hope* and the *Why not I?*

In respect of armament the Elizabethan privateers may be considered in four classes. First, there were a few large private ships built primarily for fighting—the earl of Cumberland's *Red Dragon*, for example. These were as heavily armed as the capital ships of the navy, carrying a double tier of heavy battery guns in the hull— a proper broadside. The remainder were built for trade and probably carried much, if not all, of their ordnance in the waist or the superstructure. This meant that even the large merchantmen privateers of the two, three and four hundred ton class rarely carried anything heavier than a demi-culverin, weighing about 2,500 pounds. This was a $4\frac{1}{2}$-inch gun, about ten or twelve feet in length, which fired a 9-pound shot and had a point-blank range of 400 paces and a random range of 2,500 paces. In range this was as good as any naval gun, though in battery power it could not vie with the 20-, 30- and even 60-pounders that made up the broad-side of a man-of-war.[1] Nevertheless it was a comparatively effective piece and was evidently much in favour at this period. The more formidable merchantman privateer might carry eight or ten of them and occasionally one or two culverins—guns of much the same type firing an 18-pound shot. The ordnance of John Chidley's *White Lion* (340 tons), for example, comprised ten demi-culverins, backed by twelve lesser pieces.[2] The *Golden Dragon* of London (about 150 tons) is fairly typical of the third class—ships of middling strength. She carried only two demi-culverins, backed by seventeen lesser pieces (3-, 4- and 5-pounders).[3] The fourth class—ships of under a hundred tons—usually relied exclusively on the lesser pieces, sakers (5-pounders), minions (4-pounders), falcons (3-pounders) and falconets (2-pounders) being the most common. The *Black Dog*, for example, of some fifty–seventy tons, undertook a West Indies venture with a minion and three falcons.[4] The *Catherine* of Weymouth, a very successful little privateer of thirty-five tons, had but two falcons and two falconets, weighing about 2,500 pounds in all.[5]

The better-armed ships of the first three classes undoubtedly found their superior fire-power an important asset. It enabled them to attack large merchantmen with confidence and even to defend themselves successfully against men-of-war. 'Plying the enemy with shot', 'giving them our broadside' and similar phrases con-stantly occur in contemporary accounts of privateering actions. The gunfire could be deadly. Even the little *Dolphin* of Southamp-

---

[1] The importance of the culverin type of gun is much stressed by Professor Michael Lewis, the leading authority on naval artillery in this period, in his book *The Spanish Armada*, pp. 71–80, and in 'Armada Guns, A Comparative Study of English and Spanish Armaments', *Mariner's Mirror*, XXVIII (1942) and XXIX (1943).

[2] *E.P.V.*, pp. 74–7.   [3] *E.P.V.*, pp. 230–3.   [4] *E.P.V.*, pp. 56–8.

[5] K. R. Andrews, 'Appraisements of Elizabethan Privateersmen', *Mariner's Mirror*, XXXVIII (1951), 76–7.

ton, a mere 30-ton bark, brought a caravel prize near to sinking by several hours of peppering with falcon shot.[1] In the actions with the carracks *Madre de Dios* and *Cinco Chagas* the gunfighting was prolonged and bitter. One of the best demonstrations of the persuasive powers of a privateer's broadside was given by Cumberland's *Anthony* in the harbour of Puerto de Caballos in 1594. A well-armed flagship and six other substantial vessels were taken after a night of bombardment.[2]

However, the advantage of the larger ship in this respect should not be exaggerated. Privateers did not often meet enemy warships, much less challenge them, and the majority of prizes were of the middling and lesser sorts of merchantmen, easy prey to any privateer. What is more, there was little to be gained and much to be lost by inflicting serious damage on an intended prize. In privateering operations generally close fighting was more important than bombardment, and the attackers relied mainly on their secondary armament, consisting of quick-firing guns such as fowlers, murderers, port-pieces and bases, together with considerable numbers of muskets, harquebuses and calivers. These and the lesser artillery—sakers, minions, falcons and falconets—poured shot into the enemy with the object of wounding or killing the crew. Then followed the inevitable boarding with sword, dagger and pike. Sometimes the prize surrendered before this, and the boarding parties merely took possession; more often this was the decisive phase of the action.

For in the last resort it was manpower that mattered, and by all accounts this was one thing the privateers never lacked, at least at the outset of their cruises. They were almost invariably overcrowded—a proportion of one man to two tons burden was lower than usual—and the readiness of owners to cram their ships with men was only exceeded by the eagerness of seamen to serve in such ventures. The attitude of the promoters is easily understood: the more men they could ship, the stronger the boarding parties would be, and the more prizes could be manned home, or turned into auxiliary privateers; as for the extra expense, it would only amount to the cost of extra victuals, for privateering crews as a rule received no wages, and the same one-third of the total haul of

---

[1] G. H. Hamilton (ed.), *Book of Examinations and Depositions, 1570–94*, pp. 149–151.

[2] *E.P.V.*, pp. 241, 252–3, 281–3.

prize-goods would be allocated to the crew irrespective of their numbers, so that the effect of overmanning was simply to reduce the share of each individual sailor. What remains, on the face of it, something of a mystery is that seamen notoriously preferred these ill-conditioned and disease-ridden voluntary ships to those of the queen. 'It is strange', wrote Monson, 'what misery such men will choose to endure in small ships of reprisal, though they be hopeless of gain, rather than serve her Majesty, where their pay is certain, their diet plentiful, and their labour not so great. Nothing breeds this but the liberty they find in the one, and the punishment they fear in the other.'[1]

The seaman's life aboard a privateer was nasty, brutish and short. His diet at the beginning of a voyage might consist of bread or biscuit, oatmeal or peasemeal, salted beef or pork, fish, butter, cheese and beer, but even then gave no defence against scurvy, that 'plague of the sea and the spoil of mariners'. In any case before long the food would go bad and the beer sour. Dysentery—the 'bloody flux'—was inevitable in the filthy conditions which prevailed, and especially common when the ships reached warmer climates or captured cargoes of wine. And in spite of the readiness of privateers to rob other vessels of provisions, the crews sometimes simply starved to death, as did most of the men in John Chidley's *Robin*. In these respects the overcrowded and undisciplined crew of a privateer was likely to suffer more than that of a royal ship. But since the causes of disease were not understood, the freedom associated with privateer service acted only as an attraction to sailors.

For while in Elizabeth's navy discipline was, by eighteenth-century standards, extremely slack, in the privateers it was almost non-existent. Mariners had long been men of skill, accustomed to respect, to a voice in the conduct of the voyage and to a fair chance of becoming masters, or even owners. With the expansion of the merchant marine and royal navy during the sixteenth and seventeenth centuries and with the simultaneous growth in the proportion of large ships, the independent position of these craftsmen of the sea was gradually being undermined and the profession diluted with unskilled men. But in the last quarter of the sixteenth century the operation of these factors was temporarily offset by the great demand for seamen, above all for voyages of plunder, where brute force would inevitably tend to assert itself. The results were

[1] *Monson's Tracts*, II, 237.

observed by Richard Hawkins: 'Mariners are like to a stiff-necked horse which, taking the bridle betwixt his teeth, forceth his rider to what him list, maugre his will.'[1]

Drunkenness and disorder aboard ship became common, uncontrolled violence and lawlessness at sea developed by the end of the war into a general menace to commerce, and attempts to impose discipline met with mutiny. It remained normal in privateers to consult the crew in any important matter. Their consent was necessary in cases of consortships arranged at sea, and they often compelled captains to change the course or conduct of the whole voyage. When Captain Grafton, for example, suggested to his crew that they should sail with the earl of Cumberland, they vetoed the proposal on the ground that a small ship like theirs would get little or no share of the prizes.[2] In Cavendish's last voyage it was his 'insolent mutinous company' that determined his return.

Quarrelling and brawling were common enough, but when it came to pillage and the sharing of prize-goods the sailors often got completely out of hand. Monson's suggestion that they were 'hopeless of gain' is very wide of the mark, for here indeed was the main attraction of this type of service—the prospect of loot. 'As for the business of pillage,' wrote Boteler, 'there is nothing that more bewitcheth them, nor anything wherein they promise to themselves so loudly nor delight in more mainly.'[3] By 'pillage' was meant the customary right of the victorious crew to possess themselves immediately of goods and valuables not belonging to the cargo proper. These included all items found above deck, together with any personal belongings of the crew and passengers of the prize. There were certain rules about what constituted rightful pillage and about its division among the captors: for example nothing above the value of forty shillings was supposed to be counted as pillage, except items of clothing; again every man was supposed to bring what he found to the mainmast, where it would be shared according to rank, the chief officers of the privateer being entitled to certain special perquisites in addition to their share of the whole. Thus the captain took the enemy captain's chest and the best piece of ordnance, the master had his counterpart's chest and the best cable—and so on. It is quite obvious, however, that these were only customary rules that could not cover every contingency nor

[1] J. A. Williamson (ed.), *The 'Observations' of Sir Richard Hawkins*, p. 12.
[2] H.C.A. 13/30, 23 Aug. 1592.   [3] *Boteler's Dialogues*, pp. 39–40.

be enforced with any precision.[1] There was bound to be a great deal of latitude and in any case at such times even the best of crews might deteriorate into a gang of robbers. In the heat of the boarding it was every man for himself, and the stage of fighting merged insensibly into the stage of 'rifling' the prize. This was the moment the sailor longed for, his chance to fill his pocket; the moment for brawls and mutinies, like the 'great turmoil' on board the *Examiner* in 1591 'betwixt the captain and the company, for that he charged the company they had robbed him'.[2] When Carey's *Swallow* took a prize in the same year 'the Captain of the Swallow and others of the Swallow's chief men were all that day until eveninge on board their prize pacifying of brauls that were on board amongst the company'.[3]

Very often, moreover, the company took a hand in the disposal of the cargo proper before it could be inventoried and legitimately divided. This practice, known as 'breaking bulk', was very likely to lead to trouble between the captain and the crew because it was officially forbidden, and the captain, who had given his bond not to break bulk, would be held responsible. Thus on a London privateer, the *Tiger*, commanded by a Dutchman, one of the crew 'heard William Ivey the master, at sea near the Burlings after the taking of the said ships, set the captain at nought, and when the captain blamed him for breaking bulk and making spoil of the goods, the said master in this examinate's hearing said shite on thy commissions, we have nothing to do therewith; we know what commission our owner master Holliday hath given us and that they would follow. . . . The said Captain Barnestrawe was not regarded by the Englishmen, but greatly reviled and called copper-nose and that he was fitter to drink ale than to be a captain'. The master's mate and the quartermaster threatened to cast him over-board, and one of them struck him with a dagger.[4]

Breaking bulk usually took place when the prize or prize-goods had been brought to a convenient place for their disposal and sale. The 'embezzlement' of part or all of the goods would now proceed. The goods would be landed with or without the connivance of customs and admiralty officials, and thus at one stroke the queen would be cheated of her customs duties, the Lord Admiral

---

[1] Trinity House laid down a ruling about the distribution of pillage in 1594 (Pepys MS 2870, Miscellanea, vol. 2, p. 101).

[2] H.C.A. 13/28, 23 Dec. 1590.

[3] *E.P.V.*, p. 150.   [4] H.C.A. 13/29, 7 Dec. 1591.

of his tenth and the promoters of the two-thirds share due to them. The fate of the cargo of the great Portuguese carrack the *Madre de Dios* is well known; John Bird, one of the merchants interested, angrily wrote, 'It is not tolerable to let such spoil be made. There is no good order used any way to encounter the thievery of these lewd fellows.'[1] Recognised smuggling centres like Mead Hole in the Isle of Wight, 'a place not accustomed for merchants to make sale of goods and merchandize in of his knowledge, but rather such as make sale there are suspected to have some evil by the goods they there sell',[2] were to be found not only on the south and western coasts, where they were most notorious, but also in Ireland which, largely beyond the reach of English law, presented magnificent opportunities. As the Lord Admiral put it in 1589, 'Sundry prizes taken at sea by virtue of letters of reprisal are daily brought into the realm of Ireland and sea coasts thereof and there vented and sold and no allowance of the tenths of the said prizes due to me by virtue of my office of Lord Admiral for the most part made or yielded to my use.'[3] Milford Haven and other places in Wales afforded similar facilities. The disposal of cargoes in Barbary grew so common that Dr Caesar thought he would 'open a gap of great profit' to the Lord Admiral by confiscating the good behaviour bonds of those who resorted there.[4] In less remote parts the business was carried on less openly, but continued more or less unchecked: 'There are divers and sundry ships, goods and merchandizes,' it was officially complained, 'as well by reprisal as otherwise brought into the river of Thames and places adjoining, whereof is no intelligence given into Her Majesty's High Court of the Admiralty.'[5]

Most of the sailors profited little from such dealings, for they were obliged to pass on their booty as quickly as possible, and so made poor bargains. Thus one merchant boasted 'that he had bought fifty hundred [weight] of Master Watts' ginger at Plymouth of the mariners for xxviii[s] or xxx[s] the hundred, and that he never made so good a voyage all the days of his life'.[6] Jewels, gold, perfumes and spices from the *Madre de Dios* and many another rich prize were sold at ridiculous prices, and the money thus gained was quickly spent on drink and women.

On the other hand if the crew obeyed the law and took only

[1] Lansdowne MS 70, f. 206.   [2] H.C.A. 13/28, 8 Dec. 1590.
[3] H.C.A. 14/26, no. 67.   [4] Lansdowne MS 157, f. 442.
[5] H.C.A. 14/26, no. 44.   [6] H.C.A. 13/30, 29 April 1592.

their rightful one-third of the cargo, they were still at a disadvantage. They seldom had facilities for storing or finding buyers for such goods as hides, unrefined sugar, logwood or indigo, and they were usually obliged to accept what the owners and victuallers were prepared to give them for their thirds. In fact it was customary for the promoters to calculate the value of the third, divide it among the crew according to rank, and pay them what was due in cash, either directly or through the captain. The sharing of the third was a complicated business, partly because it involved so much arithmetic, the various members of the crew being entitled to varying numbers of shares and half shares, and partly because there was no standard scale of sharing. The customary rules were, as usual, rather vague and flexible, and this led to disputes. It was this uncertainty that led Trinity House to lay down an official scale,[1] but as it would have meant a reduction of the two or three shares normally taken by the rank and file to a single share each, it is unlikely that it was adopted in practice. At this stage captains and promoters were not in a position to enforce unpopular measures and would hardly have dared to infringe the customary rights of the sailor to this extent.

On the whole it is clear that the financial attractions of privateering were greater than those of the queen's service. In the latter the men were paid ten shillings a month, whereas a single share in a successful privateering cruise would amount to four or five pounds, giving the ordinary seaman twelve or fifteen pounds for a few months' service, quite apart from what he might gather by way of pillage or embezzlement. Of course there was no certainty in it, and privateers sometimes came home with nothing to show for the voyage. But the incentive was there, and it is hardly surprising that sailors—always inclined to be penniless, happy-go-lucky spendthrifts—chose to take their chance in a privateer. After all, they had nothing to lose but their lives, and who can blame them for valuing themselves at more than ten shillings a month?

In such circumstances landlubbers took to privateering in considerable numbers. Long before the war, in 1571, Sir Henry Radcliffe reported from Portsmouth: 'The farmers and honest inhabitants with some of the constables of the sea-coast adjoining came to me making their moan that they could not be sure certain of any servant they had for they would openly say that why should they serve for five nobles or forty shillings a year and might make

[1] Pepys MS 2870, Miscellanea, vol. 2, p. 101.

their share at sea within one week four or five pounds.'[1] During the war the situation grew far worse. Runaway servingmen made their way to the ports to take ship and Monson maintained that 'the numbers of sailors and seamen are increased treble by it [privateering], to what they are in the navigations of peaceable voyages'.[2]

Yet it would be wrong to conclude that the privateers were manned with the riff-raff of Elizabethan England. The evidence of numerous Admiralty Court depositions, which normally begin with a statement of the witness's name, place of residence, occupation and age, often giving his place of birth, shows that the privateer crews were in the main recruited from men born and bred in the ports of southern England, from Bristol round to the Wash. The largest group by far hailed from the Thames, and especially from St Katherine's by the Tower, Wapping, Ratcliffe, Limehouse and Rotherhithe. There must have been many like Gideon Sanders, aged thirty-four in 1592, then living in the Isle of Wight, but having lived for the greater part of his life, when he was not at sea, in London. He had been at sea since he was eight or ten years old and had made a hundred voyages in his time, both in trade and warfare.[3] Or Nicholas Dockerey of London and Wapping, aged fifty, who had been at the taking of prizes in Queen Mary's time and now, in 1592, was still a regular reprisal man.[4] Others, like James Bratholt, gunmaker of London, aged twenty-five, or Noe Baily, barber-surgeon of London, aged twenty-two, made their first sea-voyage in a privateer, and that long after the beginning of reprisals.[5] These depositions also show that many merchant seamen took ship fairly regularly in privateers after 1585. Those who were asked questions about their experience of the sea frequently referred to several ventures in which they had sailed and some of them would mention the queen's ships as well. Again there was a noticeable and natural tendency to form a connection and continue in the same ship, or at least under the same captain or in the service of the same owner for several voyages.

The materials of a privateering venture, like those of any business enterprise, cost money, and no satisfactory analysis of privateering can be made without some attempt, however laborious, to estimate the financial commitment involved in fitting out ships of

[1] S.P. Dom. Eliz., lxxviii, no. 15.   [2] *Monson's Tracts*, IV, 21.
[3] *E.P.V.*, pp. 155–6.   [4] *E.P.V.*, pp. 149–51.   [5] *E.P.V.*, pp. 146–8.

reprisal. Unfortunately information on this aspect of the subject is not ready to hand in easily manageable form. Accounts for each venture must have been kept at the time, for the 'joint stock' nature of the organisation made some sort of record of investment essential, but such accounts have not survived, as far as we know, for any of the purely private expeditions. We must therefore proceed indirectly.

The ships, equipment and provisions for a voyage were normally supplied by a variety of individuals. Most of the principal adventurers were shipowners. Small vessels were quite often the property of one man; larger vessels were usually part-owned by two or three persons, and occasionally by more, though there is no case known of more than eight part-owners. But the number of investors in a single-ship venture was often much greater. Small contributions of money, victuals and other provisions to the value of a few pounds each were common in the smaller enterprises, and these investors would often be seamen or local tradesmen such as bakers, butchers and brewers. Many ventures were thus financed on credit, the supplier of the goods being given a 'bill of adventure' to the value of his contribution. A wide distribution of shares was probably less typical of the larger sort of expedition. At the end of the voyage what was in fact a 'terminable joint stock' would be wound up by the apportioning of the prize-goods. The Lord Admiral was entitled to a tenth, and the queen to her customs duties, normally levied at the rate of five per cent; of the remainder one-third was supposed to go to the owners of the ships, one-third to the victuallers and one-third to the crew. The owners and victuallers would divide their part of the proceeds as shareholders. Occasionally unspent victuals or even money shares would be ploughed back into the next voyage.

The chief items of expense were the ships, their armament and ammunition, victuals, other provisions, and repairs. The estimates which follow are based mainly on naval records, modified by miscellaneous scraps of information relating to privateering ventures.[1]

[1] For this account of costs the following have been of most value: Laughton, *Defeat* (especially I, 129, 312, 339; II, 156, 200–3, 288); Oppenheim, *Administration* (especially pp. 128–9, 159–60); Corbett, *Spanish War* (especially p. 90 and appendix A); M. Lewis, 'Armada Guns, a Comparative Study of English and Spanish Armaments', *Mariner's Mirror*, XXVIII (1942), 41–73, 104–47, 231–45, 259–90; *Cal. Salis. MSS*, VI, 132, 285–8; X, 405; XII, 607. For detailed references to H.C.A. and other source materials see mv Ph.D. thesis, pp. 63–72.

The value of ships varied chiefly according to size and condition. Ships of under a hundred tons burden might be worth anything from 10s. to £3 a ton, while larger vessels ranged from £1 to £5 a ton, the higher figure representing in each case the approximate price of new ships. Armament was an expensive item. The cast pieces were almost always of iron and were valued according to weight, the rate being about 10s. a hundredweight. As we know the approximate weights of the various types of guns in use, we can, with the representative sample of privateer armament given in Table 3 arrive at reasonable estimates for different classes of ship. Gunpowder cost about £5 a hundredweight, and for the normal privateering cruise a ship with 10,000 pounds of ordnance would require about eight hundredweight. Shot was valued at about 12s. a hundredweight and we know the

Table 3. Estimated Cost of the Armament of Various Privateers

(in £ sterling)

ship's burden	value of cast pieces	value of powder	value of shot	value of muskets, pikes, etc.	total
350[1]	299	240	71	175	785
250[2]	294	240	61	125	720
200[3]	202	160	39	100	501
160[4]	133	106	26	80	345
150[5]	89	71	17	75	252
120[6]	45	36	10	60	151
100[7]	54	43	12	50	159
80[8]	57	45	12	40	154
45[9]	16	13	4	23	56
40[10]	26	21	6	20	73
35[11]	11	9	3	18	41

[1] The *Merchant Royal*, with 2 periers, 4 culverins, ten demi-culverins and six sakers, weighing in all 59,800 pounds (see M. Lewis, 'Armada Guns').
[2] The *Edward Bonaventure*, 4 culverins, 9 demi-culverins, 8 sakers, 4 minions, weighing 58,900 pounds (*ibid.*).
[3] The *Minion*, 7 demi-culverins, 10 sakers, 4 minions, weighing 40,300 pounds (*ibid.*).
[4] The *Bark Rawe*, 4 demi-culverins, 8 minions, 4 sakers, weighing 26,600 pounds (*Cal. Salis. MSS*, VI, 132).
[5] The *Bark Hawkins*, 4 demi-culverins, 4 sakers, weighing 17,800 pounds (M. Lewis, *op. cit.*).
[6] The *Primrose* of Poole, 2 sakers, 4 minions, 1 falcon, 2 falconets, weighing 9,100 pounds (Laughton, *Defeat*, I, 129).
[7] The *Pansy* of London, 2 sakers, 5 minions, 3 falcons, weighing 10,800 pounds (Laughton, *Defeat*, I, 339).
[8] A ship of Rye, 3 sakers, 4 minions, 3 falcons, weighing 11,300 pounds (*Cal. Rye MSS*, p. 86).
[9] The *Bark Way*, one minion and 3 falcons, weighing 3,200 pounds (Andrews, 'Appraisements of Elizabethan Privateersmen').
[10] The *Fortunatus*, one saker, 2 minions, 2 falcons, weighing 5,200 pounds (*ibid.*).
[11] The *Catherine* of Weymouth, 2 falcons, 2 falconets, weighing 2,200 pounds (*ibid.*).

approximate weight of the types of shot used for the various pieces and roughly the amount of shot required. Table 3 includes estimates of costs of cast pieces, powder and shot. It also indicates an allowance for calivers, muskets, harquebuses and the powder and shot for them, as well as for match, cartridge canvas and weapons such as pikes, at a total rate of 10s. per ton burden.

The official victualling rate for the queen's ships was 14s. per man per month. Such evidence as we have for privateers indicates cheaper victualling, presumably because there was much less room for corruption and swindling in a small and private venture where the victuallers were directly involved as shareholders, and because privateers often supplemented their stores from prizes and may have counted on doing so. As to quality, though navy victuals were unfavourably compared with those of merchantmen, there is not sufficient evidence to conclude that privateering promoters treated their crews any better. Bearing all this in mind, we have put the victualling rate at 13s. per man per month. It was usual to victual for six months. Additional provisions, such as candles and wood, cost about 30s. a month for every fifty men.

By far the most uncertain item in expenses was the cost of repairs and replacements after a voyage. This might in some cases amount to the original cost of the ship, or might be negligible. We have estimated refitting after every six months' cruise at an average ten per cent of the ship's value.

We now have more or less complete, though by no means precise, estimates for the setting forth of various classes of privateer, and these are summarised in Table 4 (p. 49). It will be noted that no allowance is made for wages, since in such ventures the crew usually sailed for their 'thirds' only. If the peculiarities of individual ships and the rough character of the figures in Table 4 are taken into account, available contemporary estimates of the total costs of privateering ventures will be seen to bear out the conclusions embodied in the two right-hand columns. The *Galleon Oughtred*, of 500 tons, was said to be worth, fully equipped, £6,000. Chidley's *White Lion* (340 tons), after extensive repairs, represented a total capital outlay (including some expense on wages for the crew) of over £4,000. The *Elizabeth* of London (140 tons), victualled for eight months, was valued at £800. The mayor and aldermen of Southampton estimated that it would cost £500 to prepare, man and victual a 100-ton ship for war service, but in this case wages and perhaps extra ordnance would have

Table 4. Estimated Cost of Privateers Equipped for Six Months
(in £ sterling)

ship's burden	number of men	value of ship	value of guns[1]	value of powder, shot, etc.	value of victuals	value of other provisions	cost of repairs	total cost of fitting out	total investment
350[2]	175	1750	387	398	683	32	175	1288	3425
200[3]	100	800	252	249	390	18	80	737	1789
100[4]	50	300	79	80	195	9	30	314	693
50[5]	30	150	36	37	117	5	15	174	360
30[6]	20	90	20	21	78	4	9	112	222

[1] This column represents the value of cast pieces together with that of pikes, muskets, calivers and harque-buses, the latter being calculated at half the figure given in the fifth column of Table 3. The other half of that figure represents powder and shot for the muskets, etc., as well as cartridge canvas, etc., and is therefore in-cluded here in the column headed 'value of powder, shot, etc.'.

[2] The armament figures are taken from those given for the *Merchant Royal* in Table 3.

[3] The armament figures are taken from those given for the *Minion* in Table 3.

[4] The armament figures are taken from those given for the *Pansy* in Table 3.

[5] The armament figures are taken from those given for the *Fortunatus* in Table 3, since this was at least as strongly armed as most ships of fifty tons.

[6] The armament figures are taken from those given for the *Catherine* in Table 3.

E

been required. For furnishing the *John* of Chichester, 60 tons, with victuals, powder, shot and some artillery for two months, John Young asked £242, including £30 payment for hire. The 25-ton *Lizard* was valued, with her victuals, ordnance and furniture, at £200 or £270. Clearly the actual expenses for any particular ship might vary considerably from the estimates in Table 4, but by and large they do give a reasonable indication of costs.[1]

These figures hold certain important implications for the economics of privateering. In the first place it is noticeable that large ships required a far greater total investment per ton burden than medium or small ships. This progressive rise in costs, however, does not occur in the fitting out expenses, which are between £3 and £4 per ton burden for all classes, but in the basic capital outlay for the ship and her guns, which rises from £3 or £4 per ton burden in the lesser privateers to £6 in the larger. Secondly, well over half the fitting out expenses went on victuals, and if the ship carried soldiers or was victualled for more than the usual six months, as was the case in the more ambitious ventures, this would raise the total cost of the venture considerably. Thirdly, the column of estimates for the total costs of fitting out gives a rough indication of the returns the promoters would require to make a 'saving voyage': briefly, that share of the prizes which finally came into the hands and pockets of the promoters would have to be at least equal to the cost of fitting out. Thus if we know the tonnage of a privateer and the value of the prizes she took, we have the basis of a rough estimate of the profitability of the voyage, provided that we can also calculate the approximate share of the promoters in the prizes.

The share of the promoters, however, varied greatly from one venture to another, and we can approach some satisfactory generalisation only by an artificial classification of the ventures according to the main types of promoter—the amateur, the professional and the great merchant. These categories, which we have adopted in the following chapters, are neither exhaustive nor mutually exclusive, and are merely used for the convenience of analysis.

---

[1] Oppenheim, *Administration*, p. 168; *E.P.V.*, pp. 79–80; H.C.A. 24/59, no. 15; *Cal. Salis. MSS*, IV, 120; *A.P.C.* XIX, 26; H.C.A. 13/33, 26 Jan. 1598/9, 4 Feb. 1598/9.

Part II

VENTURES AND VENTURERS

PRELUDE

Sir Thomas Sherley, 1602[1]

A true discourse, of the late voyage made by the Right Worshipfull Sir
Thomas Sherley the yonger, Knight: on the coast of Spaine, with foure
Ships and two Pinnasses: no lesse famous and honourable to his Country,
then to him selfe glorious and commendable. Wherein is shewed the taking
of three townes, *Boarco, Tavaredo* and *Fyguaro*, with a Castle and a Priorie.
Written by a Gentleman that was in the Voyage.
London. Printed for Thomas Pavyer, and are to solde [*sic*] at the signe of the
Cat and two Parrets, neere the Royall Exchange, 1602.

A true discourse of the late voyage made by the Right Worshipfull
Sir Thomas Sherley the younger, Knight; on the Coast of
Spaine, with foure Shippes and two Pinnasses; no lesse famous
and honourable to his Country, then to himselfe glorious and
commendable. Wherein is shewed the taking of three townes,
Boarco, Tavaredo, and *Fyguaro*, with a Castle and a Pryory. Written
by a Gentleman that was in the voyage.

Forasmuch as heretofore sundry rumours and reports have beene
spred abroad of the taking of Gyblaltar, and Aymounte in Spaine,
by Sir Thomas Sherley the younger. It is not altogether impertinent
to make the truth knowne of the said voyage, as well for the better
satisfaction of all such as are desirous to be resolved of the truth, as
also for the incouraging of other Gentlemen, desirous to honour
their country with their travailes, and to win perpetuall fame and
credit to themselves, by shewing their valour upon the common

---

[1] The only known copy of this pamphlet was acquired by the British Museum in
1959 (See R. A. Skelton, 'An Elizabethan Naval Tract', *British Museum Quarterly,*
XXII, 51–3). Until then the only known references to the voyage were Sherley's letter
to Cecil (*Cal. Salis. MSS*, XII, 78), in which he begged Cecil to invest £100 in the
venture, referring to an earlier and evidently vague promise; the mayor of Southampton's letter to the Privy Council, 8 April 1602 (*Cal. Salis. MSS*, XII, 99),
reporting Sherley's departure from the Isle of Wight; Sir Thomas the elder's letter to
Cecil, 11 April 1602 (*Cal. Salis. MSS*, XII, 103), defending his son against suspicion of piratical intentions; and John Chamberlain's letter to Sir Dudley Carle-
ton, 27 June 1602 (*Cal. S.P. Dom. Eliz., 1601–3*, p. 209), quoted below, p. 66.

enemy of God, and their Country, and on such as are the Generall disturbers of all tranquility and peace in Christendome.

This young Knight (having made provision of foure Shippes and two Pinasses: to wit, the Dragon, whereof himselfe was Captaine, and Admerall: the Lyon, whereof was Captaine a young Gentleman called Mr. Tho*mas* Sherley Vice-admeral: the George, whose Captaine was Captaine Flood and Reare-admirall: the Virgin commaunded by Captaine Nichols: the Katherin by Captain Povye: and the Nan by Captaine Cobden:) having I say sufficientlye provided, munition, and furnished these sixe Sips [*sic*], with Marriners, victuals, and all other necessaries fit for his pretended voyage, with 900. Land men, to the great charge of the sayd Sir Thomas and others his friends: The Ships for want of commodious windes lay long at Hampton and the Cowes before they could put to Sea.

Thursday being the first day of Aprill 1602. the whole fleete put to sea from the Cowes about seaven of the clocke in the morning, the winde being North-west: the next day we were a thwart Dartmouth, the weather faire, and the winde North-west.

Satterday the third day, the winde scanted at South, wee met with sixe saile bound for Rochell, whereof 4. were English, and the other two Dutch Ships.

Sunday the fourth day, we had the winde South untill it was noone, and then it came to the West North-west. The same night Captaine Cobden absented himselfe with ye Nan, not bidding the Admiral adieu. The 5 day was faire weather, but the winde opposite at South-West.

Tewsday the sixth day, was a mighty storme at South South-west, and the same night we lost the company of the Lyon.

Wednesday the 7. day, the storme continued, and the same day the Virgin spent her Rudder, & the Dragon tooke a leake, where-by our Admirall was forced to put Roome.

Thursday the 8. day of April, the fleete put in at Falmouth, the storme continuing with great extreamity, and contrariety of windes untill the 17. day, mean while our Admerall went to Plimmouth to relieve some wants.

Friday, being the 9. day, the Lyon came into Falmouth ex-treamely weather-beaten, & discharging a peece to salute the Castle, the same brake and killed two of her men, hurt divers others, tore her deckes, and brake her Maine-yard.

Friday the 18. day, our Admerall sent the Katherin to Plim-

mouth for the Nan: the same night the winde came faire at north
& north northeast, but our Admiral attending ye returne of the
said two Pinnasses until the 20. day at noone, the wind scanted:
& the 21. day was so great a tempest at Southwest, that we were
forced to put in at Plimmouth.

On Thursday being the 27. day, our Admiral discovered a
faction sturred by foure of his Land Captaines: to wit, Captaine
Alley, Captaine Goare, Captaine Fitzhuse, Captaine Dalby, and
a Leifetenant: which at the first our Admiral appeased (as he
thought) but afterward, on Fryday following, the fire was againe
kindled, so that they forsooke our Admirall: whether that it was
that they had been sore weather-beaten, or unwilling to endure
any further tryall of such a voyage, or any other dislike I know
not, but how soever it was, 400. of our men (by their ensample)
forsooke the Admirall also: but himselfe (not any thing at all
therewith dismayed) proceeded with a stoute resolut[ion], according to the first intent.

Satterday being the first of May at midnight, the winde came
faire, but Sir Thomas could not get his men aboord untill two of
the clocke after midnight. The third and fourth dayes the winde
Northwest with faire weather. The fift day was calme, wee met
with Roswell the Marchant in a Shippe of Dover laden with
Spaniards, which had bin taken, and were againe sent into
Spaine. Our Admirall (listing his companies) found he had left
40 of his men a shoare such as had no intent to follow the Captaines which had forsaken the voyage. All this night the winde
was Southwest with a bon gaelle, until Thursday the 5. day about
noone, and then it came into the North and by West: the 7. 8. &
9. daies faire weather. The 10. day we spake w^t a man of Roane,
whom (after some conference) wee suffered to depart in peace:
wee doubled the Cape in the after noone, where Roswell with his
Spaniards departed from us.

On Tewsday the 11. day wee entended to have landed at
Avero, but finding the difficultie thereof, by reason of the bar, we
forbore, and turned our purpose to *Boarco*, a towne bigger then
Plimmouth.

Thursday the 13 day, faire weather: this day wee hulled all day
within sight of land, and about 12 of the clocke in the night we
landed 400. men in a sandy Cave [*sic*], halfe a mile from the
towne, with such silence, that our Vauntguard, and Sir Thomas
himselfe being on shoare two houres at the least, before the rest

came, the towne tooke no allarum: about 3. of the clocke in the
morning we entred the towne, and tooke it without any resistance.

Friday the 14. day, about 9. of the clocke in the morning, there
appeared certaine bandes: whereuppon one of the Captains
(whome Euphoniae gratia I spare to name) possessed the companies in such a feare (I know not upon what vain immagination)
that they retyred from the towne some half mile, so that our
Admeral had much to do with many perswasions to cause them
to returne, wherby they of the town had gained sufficient time to
carry and convay away their best goods: and at his comming
back, ye enemy was growne much stronger upon the hils. Then
Sir Thomas drew out 5 Auncients with some 200. men: to wit,
his own, Captaine Vachans, Capt. Carpenters, Captaine Sherleys
and Captaine Catesbyes, and made a stand with the Colours,
sending Captaine Povy, Captaine Catesby, and Captaine Rigges
with 40. shot and 20. pykes, to skirmish with the enemy. At the
first encounter the enemy fled: the said Captaine (chasing them a
mile and a halfe) found a Castle on the Sea side, which upon the
first attempt they forced and tooke: from thence they marched
halfe a mile further, to a smal town called Tavaredo, wherein was
great store of wheate, wine & fish: the same night we retired to our
ships.

Satterday the 15. day in the morning we landed againe a mile
from Tavaredo with 250. men, 500. at the least of the enemies
looking on while we marched to Tavaredo; where (after guardes
set upon all the advenues of the Towne) Syr Thomas sent Captaine Povie, Captaine Ruggs [sic], and Captain Carpenter, to
discover the Countrey, accompanied with some 60. souldiers,
(Captaine Syms being left in the Towne, to see fish and wine
shipped for our provision) Syr Thomas himselfe with Captaine
Sherley, and Captaine Hawkins, and 40. souldiers, went to a
Pryorie which stood halfe a mile from the Towne, but when they
came thither, they found the same abandoned, and nothing left,
but bookes and pictures onely.

The Captaines before named which were sent to discover,
marched two miles to a Towne called Fyguaro, which they tooke,
the Earle thereof with all his neighbours being fled. Our Vauntguard was here much engaged, environed with 300. men in
Armes. They sent to our Admirall to relieve them, which he
accordingly accomplished with 60. men, whereof Captaine
Sherley, accompanied with Catesbie and Hawkins, marched in

the Vaunt with 30. men, and Syr Thomas with Captaine Androwes in the Reare, with other 30. But for their retrait, M.Kevet with 20. men was left beside the Manasterie, to make the same good. With these few men Captaine Povie was relieved with a good retrait, skirmishing perpetually, and ever beating the enemie, whose forces continually encreased, and yet we carried away such needfull provision as we found in Tavaredo, notwithstanding we were continually vexed with allarums by great troups both of horse and foote, yet would the enemy never make good any bravado, but still fled at the first encounter.

About three of the clocke there came one to Syr Thomas with a flagge of truce, whose request was to forbeare to fire Tavaredo. But he was answered that all the three places should be fyred, if within one houre they did not deliver 20. hostages, which should undertake for the ransome of the three Townes, to be paide the next day by noone. The Agent returned within his houre, offering to bring Hostages the next morning. But our Admirall (not a little moved) returned him with a scornefull and sterne visage in stead of an answere, and then (after we had carried aboord such provision as we thought good, and suffered our men to pillage what they could) we began to fire the Towne. At which very instant there came a Gentleman to Syr Thomas, called Don Johan de Pyna, who offered five hostages for the ransome of the Townes. Syr Thomas was contented, so that himselfe would then remaine for one, and that the other foure should be with him within halfe an houre. Don Johan stayed, but the rest refused to make good his word, saying that the other foure should come in the morning. By this time the Countrey was growne very hotte, for which way soever we looked, we might behold armed troupes, of 1000, or 500. in a company at least, by all mens judgement between 3. and 4000. men in view, so as our Admirall with his company was now besieged. Whereupon we marched three miles along the Sea side, sounding our Drums all the way, and our boats following as neare the shore as they could, the enemie notwithstanding his great multitude, not once daring to offer any alarum or other impediment while we thus marched from him.

By two of the clocke in the morning our men were all boated, though with small profit, yet not without great honor, Syr Thomas refusing to enter into the last boate, untill hee had seene the last man in before him : and (his ship lying farthest out) he was thereby in great danger to have bene drowned, for a myst rising, dimmed so the light which was hanged out of his ship, that the same could not be discerned, the winde being most boysterous with a great storme, his boate rowed two miles into the Sea, and there rode two houres untill five of the clocke, that the myst began to breake up.

Sunday the 16. day in the morning, the Inhabitants of Boarco wrote very submissively unto Syr Thomas, humbly entreating him that he would no more land his people to vexe poore miserable men. This afternoone Don Johan de Pyna made a writing to the admiral, declaring (that upon the earnest request of al the inhabitants of the Countrey) he was come unto him as their Orator, whereupon Sir Thomas set him free on shore, and departed thence.

Monday, we had the winde at West with faire weather.

Tuesday the 18. Wednesday the 19. faire weather, the winde North-east. This day we determined to goe to the Iles of Canares, to take Garrechico.

Thursday the 20. day, the said enterprise was found to be full of difficultie, by reason that we understood that the plague reigned there extreamly, and therefore we altered our purpose, and determined to attempt Aymounte. This day and the next the winde blew very high at North North-east.

The 21. day we met with a Fleete of Danes, whom (after some speeches & examinations) we suffred as friends quietly to depart, and the same night we doubled the Cape S. Vincent. Saterday the 22. calme.

The same day was spent in consulting, and labouring to prevent many disorders which hapned in our former landings.

Sunday the 23. day, the wind was East. Monday the 24. calme weather. Tuesday the 27. day, we met with Captaine Jolliff, who reported unto us that the Queenes ships had met with the Spanish Fleete.

Wednesday the 28. day, (the winde being at North) wee stood backe againe for Aymounte. Friday about 10. of ye clock in the night, we anchored at the Barre foote of Aymounte, and had that night attempted the Town but for two impediments. The one was, for that the Lyon (wherein were 3. of the land companies, being a most Lee-ward Cart) anchored so farre off, that her men could hardly reach the Towne before day.

The other was, for that the Virgin struck upon the Barre, and could not be gotten off before day, by reason whereof we discovered ourselves before we could land, wherefore on the Munday following we determined to attempt Algufero, a Towne and way betweene Lagos and Aymounte.

Tuesday being the first of June, and Wednesday the second, we had faire weather, the winde for the most part at North. Thursday morning about 7. of the clocke, we landed two miles to the Westward of the Towne, and marched directly unto the enemy, making many shewes by the way, but durst not once offer to fight with us, neither did we profer any skirmish, because we had an other errant. But being approached the towne, we found it to be the strongest small peece [*sic*] that ever we had seene; for it is scituate upon a Rock, which containeth no more ground than the circuite of the towne, having 3. walles one within the other. Notwithstanding Sir Thomas desirous to try his fortune, if perhaps any good successe might have happened according to his desire, sent Captaine Vachan and Captain Norris with 30. shot and 20 pikes, to entertain a skirmish on that side the Towne where all his men were enbattailed, whilest Captaine Povie and Lieftenant Huggens were appointed to discover the Towne round, but they found it of like strength every where, and exceedingly well manned: for all the gentlemen of the country thereabouts were drawne thither for the defence thereof. Whereupon we retired, but by the way we entertained divers small skirmishes with the enemie, who offered many braves, but would endure nothing: in which fight we lost one man, and an other was hurt. But afterwards by conference upon exchange of prisoners, we were credibly enformed, that our Ordenance had shrewdly torn that side of the towne toward ye Seaward, and killed many of their men, besides sundry which we had slain & hurt in ye skirmishes.

Our Admirall (being returned from this place) called all the Captaines and Maisters to counsell, and finding that the allarum was so hot in Spaine and Portugall, all along the Sea coast, were without all hope to do any present good there: resolution was taken to goe to Gratiosa, to repaire our victualles, and to refresh our men, whereof many were sicke.

Satterday and Sunday we had faire weather. Munday the 7. day, was a great storme at Northwest, which continued Tuesday, Wednesday, Thursday, and Friday, being the 11. day, at what time ye storme had brought us to the Northwards of the Burlings.

Saterday the 12. day, the wind being at South-west, we appointed to go to ye Iles of Bayon to water (all hope of Gratiosa being cut off) and so intended to have taken some small towne there for our refreshing.

Sunday the 13. day faire weather, the wind was at south south-west: the next day so likewise. And then we were within sight of the Island, but so far Lee-ward, that we could not fetch them: neither was it ill for us, for our Admirall (examining our strength) found more the*n* three parts of our me*n* to be extreamly sick, & our drink almost consumed, for he had but foure tuns of Beere left in his own ship for 260. men, whereof 190. at least were grievously sicke.

Hereupon by generall advice and consent of all our Captaines and Maisters, on Tuesday being the 15. day of June, we directed our course for England. The 16. day we chased a ship into the Groyne, and the next day 5. other ships into the same place, the night following being exceeding stormie, with a south-west wind, the Lyon, the George, and the Dragon, lost each of them a boate, and the Lyon spent her top Mast.

Thus after a tedious and unprofitable voyage (though famous and honourable to our English nation) the ships arrived at Hampton the 10. day of June, 1602,[1] not without good boote and pillage, gotten by the Marriners and souldiers. For which the Almightie God (the chiefe governour and directer of all things in this world) be blessed & praised. Amen.

---

[1] 20 June 1602, more probably. It had indeed been a tedious and unprofitable voyage. The weather may have been bad and sickness inevitable, but natural diffi-culties cannot be blamed entirely for the dismal failure. Sherley either had no particular objective or else had not the determination and powers of leadership to go through with what he had planned.

Chapter 4

THE AMATEURS

In warfare as at court the pursuit of fame and honour was rarely divorced from more material considerations, and those most deeply influenced by the knightly ideal were nearly always the most in need of money. When Essex risked the Queen's anger by departing secretly on the Portugal expedition in 1589, he wrote: 'If I speed well I will adventure to be rich; if not, I will not live to see the end of my poverty.' He was then in debt to the extent of £23,000.[1] In Elizabeth's day young men of good family were expected to live up to their rank, to spend freely; a gentleman who cautiously counted the cost would soon be left behind in reputation. Those who gained distinction often found it expensive in other ways, for the service of the Queen was apt to be unrewarding. Landed gentry who busied themselves in London to the neglect of their estates would soon find their real incomes declining as prices rose. This was a favourable time for money-lenders.

In circumstances of this sort there was always a temptation to gamble, and to men fed upon notions of chivalry one form of gambling seemed especially attractive—the sea venture. Sir William Courtenay wrote to the Earl of Rutland in November 1585: 'I am therfor to desier your Lordship's favor that I may with all spede have your licence in the sale of such things as I mean to depart with, to ridd myself out of debt and so flie a hundred villanies I find myselfe disposed unto. I will endevor to sell so much betwen this and the next terme as shall release me of this bondage, which, without your assistance, I can make no assurance of. Which don, you shall see I will either recover it againe or lose my selfe. My case permit no delay nor my vexed mind can recover no ease till I ether be able to purche [i.e. capture] so much more or honorably end my life.'[2]

Similarly Thomas Fenner informed Walsingham in 1589 of his losses and of his intention to employ the remainder of his fortune in a journey to the Indies. Fenner was a professional seaman and a

---

[1] J. E. Neale, *Queen Elizabeth*, p. 306.   [2] *Cal. Rutland MSS*, I, 183.

man of solid ability; we do not know whether his projected
voyage took place, though he did take out letters of reprisal for
four ships to sail under his command with the financial backing
of the London merchant John Bird.[1] Whatever may have
happened, with such leadership and support the venture stood
every chance of success. But in this respect it stands apart from the
gambling operations of the amateurs. These were seldom content
with ordinary privateering objectives; some great and memorable
achievement was more often envisaged, which would bring resounding fame and wealth—or else ruin. The scale of such expeditions was proportionately grandiose and expenses were high.
The ships were victualled for twelve months or more; soldiers in
some numbers were taken, and for long voyages of this sort the
mariners expected an advance of wages. Merchants rather lent
their money than invested it directly in this type of enterprise, and
the gentleman promoter would have to bear the greater part of the
cost himself, perhaps with the help of one or two more of his own
kind. Unbusinesslike methods and lack of the necessary knowledge and contacts made these ventures even more expensive than
they would have been in professional hands. Finally, though they
knew little or nothing of the sea, those who aspired to fame would
further prejudice success by taking personal command.

The tragi-comic history of the Sherley brothers provides a
striking example of this type of venture.[2] Their father, Sir Thomas
Sherley of Wiston, Sussex, was appointed Treasurer at War in
the Low Countries in 1587. It was an unenviable position for an
honest man of little or no financial ability, and within a few years
he was brought face to face with ruin. By 1596 'he owed the queen
more than he was worth'.[3] Meanwhile his second son, Anthony,
born in 1565, had become a soldier. He had fought bravely at
Zutphen where Sidney met his death, and in 1591 had gone with
Essex to Normandy, where he conceived an enormous admiration
for the earl and resolved to make him 'the pattern of my civil life,
and from him to draw a worthy model of all my actions'.[4] For his

[1] *Cal. S.P. Dom. Eliz.*, *1581–90*, p. 610; H.C.A. 25/3 (9), 21, 30 Jan. 1590/1.

[2] B. Penrose, *The Sherleian Odyssey*, gives a general account. See also the *D.N.B.*;
E. P. Shirley, *The Sherley Brothers*; I. A. Wright, 'The Spanish Version of Sir
Anthony Sherley's Raid on Jamaica, 1597', *H.A.H.R.*, v (1922), 227–48; R. C.
Anderson (ed.), *The Book of Examinations, 1601–2*; *Principal Navigations*, x, 266–77;
and above, pp. 53–60.

[3] Quoted in E. P. Shirley, *op. cit.*   [4] *D.N.B.*

services in this campaign Henry IV made him a knight of the order of St Michael, but in accepting this honour from a foreign prince Sir Anthony incurred the queen's displeasure. On his return he was thrown into the Fleet and compelled to renounce the knighthood, though in fact he continued to be known as Sir Anthony for the rest of his life. Two years later his connection with Essex was cemented by his marriage to Frances Vernon, a first cousin of the earl.

The marriage was not a happy one, and it was said that Sir Anthony was driven by his wife 'to undertake any course that might occupy his mind from thinking on her vainest words'.[1] The actual course he took, however, was determined partly by the family bankruptcy and partly by his ambition to achieve some notable feat of arms. Consequently he projected, with the patronage of Essex, an expedition to capture the Portuguese island of São Thomé off the Guinea coast. No expense was spared—and he even descended to cheating his already penniless father, who complained bitterly to Cecil: 'After wounding my estate by his voyage he has now the more undone me in my present desperate state by thus cozening me of money which I am no way able to repay.'[2]

No less than eight ships were bought from Thomas Heaton, the customer of Southampton, an important shipowner and privateering entrepreneur. In the *Bevis*, a new ship of 300 tons and the flagship of the expedition, Heaton probably retained a half share, as he did in the *Black Wolf* (150 tons); but the rest—the *Galleon Constance* (250 tons), the *George* (200 tons), the *Archangel* (180 tons), the *Mermaid* (100 tons), the *Swan* (alias the *Double Flyboat*, 250 tons) and the *Little John* (80 tons)—were sold outright. Three other vessels, the *George Noble* (140 tons), a galley and a pinnace, were also acquired. This powerful fleet, manned with a force of nine hundred soldiers and sailors, was reduced in strength even before the expedition got under weigh, for three ships (the *Archangel*, the *Swan* and the *Mermaid*) and five hundred soldiers were handed over to Essex at Plymouth for the Cadiz venture. Thus depleted, Sir Anthony had to change his plans. He had originally intended to attempt Madeira on the way to São Thomé,

---

[1] *Sidney Papers*, I, 359, Rowland Whyte to Sir Robert Sidney, 7 November 1595.
[2] *Cal. Salis. MSS*, VII, 526. Anthony had borrowed money from his father and made off to sea without fulfilling his promise to repay it. His father asks Cecil to 'let him be stayed till he has made delivery either of the money or of the jewels. For this indeed is wickedness to add to the affliction of his poor aged parents'.

but now, leaving Plymouth in May 1596, he set course direct for the Guinea coast.

July found him still short of his objective, his men dying like flies and himself at death's door. Despairing of reaching São Thomé, Sherley turned north to the Cape Verdes and with characteristic foolhardiness took the town of Santiago against great odds and eventually retired with heavy losses and nothing to show for them. Sickness pursued them across the Atlantic as they made for Dominica. Over a month was required here for the survivors to recover their strength, and the much reduced force then proceeded by way of the Main to capture Santa Marta. Again nothing but victuals resulted, save the opportunity for the general to challenge a relieving force of seven hundred Spaniards 'to defend their towne like men of worth'—a challenge they refused.[1]

The only real success of the voyage came in January 1597, with the virtually unopposed occupation of Jamaica's single settlement, La Villa de la Vega. Victuals—a large quantity of meat and bread—were the main outcome of the forty days they spent on the island, but Sherley's men, by now crazy for loot, also took every scrap of movable property of any value. When they took a camp in which some of the Spaniards had made themselves a refuge, they left nothing 'but empty and broken chests and wool which was emptied from the mattresses—for the sake of the ticking'.[2] After Jamaica, Honduras. But Trujillo proved too strong, even though Sherley had now the consortship of Captains William Parker and Michael Geare; as for Puerto de Caballos, it was easy enough prey, but proved to be 'the most poore and miserable place of all India'.[3] Frustrated, 'our General reserving unto himselfe his silent inward impatience, laboured to doe some memorable thing,'[4] and now sailed into the Golfo Dulce with Parker and did his best to march across the mountains of Guatemala to the South Sea. Even the inevitable failure of this wild adventure did not daunt him. He now planned to revictual at Newfoundland and 'so to depart for the streits of Magellan, and so by his very good policie would have concluded his voyage in the East India'.[5]

Fortunately at this stage the other ships deserted him and he was

---

[1] *Principal Navigations*, x, 266–77.

[2] Wright, 'The Spanish version of Sir Anthony Sherley's Raid on Jamaica, 1597', *H.A.H.R.*, v (1922), 227–48.

[3] *Principal Navigations, loc. cit.*   [4] *Ibid.*   [5] *Ibid.*

obliged to return home, 'alive but poor'.[1] It is some measure of the man's resilience that he almost immediately set off with Essex on the Islands voyage. Here again, of course, glory escaped him as it escaped his master, but in 1598 another chance of fame and fortune presented itself. He was invited by Essex to lead a company of English volunteers to Ferrara, to intervene in a dispute there. However, when he arrived he found the dispute had been settled, and accordingly he moved on, with the aid of money raised on Essex's credit, to Persia, in an attempt, entirely unofficial, to establish diplomatic and commercial relations with the Shah. As this freelance endeavour failed to win the approval of the queen, who forbade him to return to England, his travels thenceforth were prolonged—and as unrewarding as ever. They took him to Venice, to Prague, to Morocco, and wherever he went he left behind him a trail of unpaid debts and worthless promissory notes. Eventually he arrived in Spain and here at length in the country of Cervantes he perhaps found his spiritual home, for here he stayed, though with no more luck than before. He managed to impose himself on the king of Spain so far as to obtain a commission to organise a fleet against Spain's Mediterranean foes, the Turks, the Moors and the Dutch. The expedition, which sailed in 1609, achieved nothing against Philip III's enemies, but inflicted considerable damage on neutral merchantmen. Sherley was dismissed in disgrace.

In 1619 Sir Francis Cottington, English ambassador in Madrid, reported: 'The poor man comes sometimes to my house, and is as full of vanity as ever, making himself believe that he shall one day be a great prince, when for the present he wants shoes to wear.'[2] In 1625 he was said to be styling himself 'Earl of the Holy Roman Empire' and to be in receipt of a pension of 2,000 ducats from the king of Spain, 'which in respect of his prodigality is as much as nothing.'[3] He was also described as 'a great plotter and projector in matters of state, and undertakes by sea stratagems, to invade and ruinate his own country'.[4] He died in poverty some time after 1635, pathetic to the end.

His elder brother, Sir Thomas, began badly by offending the queen. He secretly married Frances Vavasour, and for this worst of crimes he was expelled from the court and imprisoned in the Marshalsea. He took to privateering in 1598. In his first attempt

[1] Sir R. Cecil to Lord Borough, July 1597, *Cal. S.P. Ireland, Eliz., 1596–7*, p. 361.
[2] *D.N.B.* [3] *D.N.B.* [4] *D.N.B.*

F   A.E.P.

to organise an expedition he was ruthlessly cheated by his lieutenant and in the end could only manage to set forth one ship, the *Dragon*. With her he took four substantial Lübeckers, but his own ship was badly mauled and forced into the Île de Rhé, where Thomas had to borrow money to get home. To add to his misfortunes the Lübeckers were declared not good prize and duly released. Later in the same year he tried again and this time took seven prizes. This was probably a profitable venture, but he was still in difficulties.

As Ferdinando Gorges reported to Cecil: 'I never saw poor gentleman in a more miserable state, afflicted with extremity of sickness, destitute of honest and trusty servants, and matched with an unruly rout of mariners.'[1] He was being sued for debt in 1599.

The following year he again took prizes and it looked as though this persistent privateering might win him solvency. But the gambling spirit in him seems to have been aroused. In 1602 he assembled a fleet of six Southampton ships for a raid on the Spanish coast, a full account of which is printed above. The result was thus sarcastically noticed by John Chamberlain in one of his news-letters: 'Sir Thomas Sherley is returned with his navy royal, and yesterday with his Lieutenant General Colonel Sims, posted to the Court, as though they had brought tidings of the taking of Seville or some such town, whereas God knows they have but sacked two poor hamlets of two dozen houses in Portugal, the pillage whereof he gave to his army, reserving to himself only two or three peasants to ransome, of whom when he saw he could raise nothing, he would not bring them away for shame.'[2]

Desperate now, he staked what was left of his fortune in a final gamble and departed in September 1602 for the Mediterranean. As he wrote in explanation to Lord Burghley, Sir Robert Cecil's brother: 'I am a man unknown to your Lordship, but a gentleman, a knight, and a household servant of the queen's; my father is a man of good living, but something cast behindhand by hard fortune. I am his eldest son, and since his disgrace I have travailed to get my living by my sword and the labour of my hands, in handling which course I have thrust into the Straits with two ships which are wholly mine own.'[3] He managed to acquire an Italian commission to make war on the Turks, but the venture

[1] Quoted by Penrose, pp. 31-2.
[2] *Cal. S.P. Dom. Eliz., 1601-3*, p. 209. See above, pp. 53-60.
[3] Quoted in E. P. Shirley, *The Sherley Brothers*, p. 12.

was disastrous. His consort deserted him and took to piracy, like many English men-of-war in the Mediterranean at this stage. Sherley was now left with one ship, the *Dragon*, and a mutinous crew. In January 1603 he decided to keep his men busy by attempting the seizure of the island of Zea. Unhappily for him the islanders counter-attacked and Sherley, deserted by his own men, was captured. Now, while his men made off in the *Dragon* and turned pirate, poor Sherley suffered incarceration in the worst Turkish dungeons, and it was not until 1605 that he was released on the belated intercession of James I. The rest of his life he spent in poverty and distress. He was imprisoned for debt in 1612 and eventually sold his family seat to retire to the Isle of Wight as keeper of the royal park.[1]

Another amateur was John Chidley, a young gentleman of Devon, born in 1565 into an old and well-connected family.[2] Like others, Chidley was inspired by Drake's famous circumnavigation to venture by the Magellan Straits into the South Sea and return via the East Indies. He was not driven by poverty or disgrace to undertake this gamble, but in many other respects his experience was remarkably like Sir Anthony Sherley's. In financing the voyage he obtained the help of a number of investors, including several merchants, but essentially it remained Chidley's own project, in which he and his chief partner, Francis Manby, held the decisive large shares. Both sold the greater part of their estates for the adventure. Three ships—the *Wildman* (300 tons), the *White Lion* (340 tons) and the *Delight* (alias the *Robin*, 120 tons)—and two pinnaces (one of them called the *Wildman's Club*) made up about 800 tons of shipping—a formidable force for a private venture. Expenses in the fitting-out were excessive. The *Robin*, which was acquired from the Bristol shipowner William Walton, was probably worth far less than the £900 bill of adventure that Chidley gave for her; and the 25-ton *Wildman's Club*, which had been Paul Bayning's *Susan's Handmaid*, cost the astounding sum of £600. The *White Lion* alone, fully furnished and victualled, represented a capital outlay of four or five thousand pounds, and if the other vessels were as lavishly provided the whole expedition must have cost well over £10,000.

[1] 'Having sold Wiston, married a whore and spent all, he came to end his days miserably in our Island.' [Francis Bamford (ed.), *A Royalist's Notebook. The Commonplace Book of Sir John Oglander Kt. of Nunwell* (1936), p. 182.]
[2] Chidley's venture is analysed and documented in *E.P.V.*, pp. 59–85.

The fleet left Plymouth on 5 August 1589, Chidley commanding the *Wildman*, Thomas Polwhele the *White Lion* and Andrew
Merrick the *Robin*. This last was separated from the fleet some-
where between Cape Blanco and the coast of America. Nevertheless she kept her course to the Magellan Straits and only turned
back after six weeks of encroaching despair, having lost thirty-
eight out of a complement of ninety-one, the remainder threaten-
ing mutiny. Finally only six remained alive to bring the ship to
the coast of Normandy, where she was wrecked for lack of an
anchor. Meanwhile the other ships were faring little better. Disease
spread through the force, and in November, off the Guiana coast,
Chidley and Polwhele both died. Soon afterwards Benjamin
Wood, a notable seaman in his time, brought the *White Lion*
home. The *Wildman* and her *Club* then made for Trinidad, where
the crews stayed some time recruiting their healths, and here it was
that a few of them, led by Abraham Kendall,[1] stole away with
the pinnace, sailed it to Barry in Wales and there sold it. The
Wildman herself returned last, about midsummer 1590, and
the disasters of the sea now gave place to salvage operations in the
Admiralty Court, where investors set forth their financial claims
against the dead man's widow.

Chidley, the Sherleys and their compeers were the wild men of
privateering, conforming to a recognisable type with its own
peculiar behaviour pattern. Another such was 'that famous and
valiant Englishman, Edward Glenham, Esquire' of Benhall in
Suffolk, who sold his family seat to attempt the capture of St
George's Island in the Azores with two ships under his own
command. When he failed he turned to piracy.[2] These ventures
also had very marked economic characteristics. The cost of such a
gamble as John Chidley's was so great that no ordinary haul of
plunder would make the voyage. Chidley's initial outlay amounted
to well over £10,000, and probably at least £5,000 went on
victuals, munitions, stores and wages. Let us suppose Chidley had
captured goods to the value of £10,000; suppose that his ships
had returned intact; suppose that the sailors had embezzled
nothing, and that the young gentleman had been able to sell his

---

[1] The navigator (see *E.P.V.*, p. 62).

[2] *D.N.B.* (art. Glemham [*sic*]); H.R., *Newes from the Levant Seas* (London,
1594). Lansdowne MSS 140, ff. 80, 86, 93, 95, 97, 99, 100, 102; 142, f. 40 (copy
of his bond for good behaviour); Lansdowne MS 134 (indictment for piracy
1594); *Cal. S.P. Dom. Eliz.*, ccxlii, nos. 19, 129, 130.

cargoes at a good price. Even in these unlikely circumstances the crews' fair pillage and thirds and the dues payable to the customs and admiralty would have reduced the return available to the shareholders to under £6,000 in prize goods and £5,000 in shipping. In effect, Chidley required an ideally smooth voyage and £10,000 worth of plunder to show even a small profit. In practice, as Chidley learned to his cost, amateur voyages were usually anything but smooth, and the adventurers were not likely to see their money again unless some unusual slice of luck befell the ships. The trouble with these knights of the sea was that they would not content themselves with a modest effort. Vainglory prompted them to plan their ventures on the grand scale, with well-furnished men-of-war and soldiers. Sir Anthony Sherley's 1596 expedition of eleven ships would have been worth, fully equipped, about £15,000 according to our table of costs; but Sherley took soldiers to swell his numbers and inflate his victuals account, and probably had to pay some advance wages to his sailors, which would have brought the initial expense considerably above £15,000. Of this something over £6,000 would have been laid out on stores, the ships and guns having a value of about £9,000. But if Sherley was cheated by his lieutenants in the way his brother was the cost of his venture must have come nearer to £20,000. This burden would have been shared to some extent by fellow-adventurers like Thomas Heaton, but this did not alter the painful truth that Sherley would require about £20,000 in prizes (gross) to meet his bills and make a small gain. The project was by no means insane, of course; if he had taken São Thomé and two or three good prizes, as there was reasonable hope of doing with such a large fleet, he might well have realised a handsome profit. But the risk was great, especially with an amateur in command, and in the event Sherley ruined himself. The chances were ten to one that he would.

But they did not always fail. Thomas Cavendish, another Suffolk man, achieved the greatest success—and yet he ran true to type. His famous circumnavigation venture was organised on much the same lines as Chidley's—he sold and mortgaged much of his land to raise several thousands and persuaded his friends to invest smaller sums. As luck would have it, they were well rewarded, at a rate of 200 per cent profit. Cavendish was undoubtedly wealthy on his return in 1588, but he was no millionaire, and when it came to fitting out his second expedition in 1591 he once again had to sell and mortgage manors and to rely on others for at least £2,000 of the capital. Even then the supplies were unusually deficient in quantity and quality, and this amateurishness in the preparations was more than anything the undoing of the voyage. Luck was not with Cavendish this time, and his weakness as a leader emerged all too clearly. Though repeatedly asked to do so, he made no provision for rendezvous in case the ships were scattered; he abandoned his flagship after developing fancied grievances against the company and his own following of gentlemen; and he finally seems to have lost touch with the rest of the fleet through his own carelessness. While Captain John Davis persisted nobly with the task of navigating the Straits of Magellan, faithful to the point of disaster to his general's instructions, Cavendish floundered about the Atlantic and died cursing his men as deserters.[1]

In sum such efforts contributed precious little to the waging of war on Spain. Even in the sphere of privateering itself the activities of the knights errant were of no great weight. But we must admit one important exception—the earl of Cumberland. He had much in common with the gentleman amateurs we have considered, but his enterprises were undertaken on such a scale and with such persistence that they had an appreciable influence on the sea war. His fleets were often comparable in striking power to squadrons of the royal navy, and there was scarcely a year during the war when he had no ships at sea. 'I have spent in sea journeys, I protest, £100,000' he wrote in 1600—and this was probably no exaggeration.[2] But what most distinguishes Cumberland's venturing from that of lesser amateurs is the change it undergoes in form and intent in the closing years of the century.[3]

George Clifford, third earl of Cumberland, having succeeded to the title in 1569, attained his majority in 1579, entered into one of the richest inheritances of the country and naturally assumed a

---

[1] *Purchas*, XVI, 151–77; *Principal Navigations*, XI, 290–347; 389–416. Gwenyth Dyke, 'The Finances of a sixteenth century navigator, Thomas Cavendish of Trimley in Suffolk', *Mariner's Mirror*, XLIV (1958), 108–15.

[2] G. C. Williamson, *George, Third Earl of Cumberland*, p. 240.

[3] A valuable study of the finances of the earl of Cumberland is contained in the unpublished London Ph.D. thesis by R. T. Spence, 'The Cliffords, Earls of Cumberland, 1579–1646: a study of their fortunes based on their household and estate accounts'. I am much indebted to him for some of the detail upon which the following interpretation is based.

prominent place at court. Here, 'an extreme love for horse races, tiltings, bowling matches and shooting and that such and hunting and all such expensive sports did contribute the more to the wasting of his estate,'[1] so that by 1586 he was seriously in debt, though the main body of his estates was as yet unimpaired. His first privateering venture in 1586 was undoubtedly undertaken in the hope of meeting these debts—an extension of his gambling operations to a new and larger sphere. But in projecting this voyage for the South Seas he aimed as much for fame and honour. As Fuller picturesquely put it, 'his fleet may be said to be bound for no other harbour but the port of honour, though touching at the port of profit in passage thereunto.' However, since there appeared to be some contradiction between the pursuit of honour and the pursuit of profit, Fuller added, 'I say, touching, whose design was not to enrich himself but impoverish the enemy.'[2] But it was also a matter of honour for a nobleman to pay his debts, and in asserting, as he did repeatedly, his disdain for profit, Cumberland deceived himself. When it came to counting gains and losses and staking claims he was as eager as any man.

Neither profit nor honour came from this first venture.[3] It was towards the end of June, 1586, that the *Red Dragon* and the *Bark Clifford*, of 260 and 130 tons respectively, set out from Gravesend under the command of Robert Withrington and Christopher Lister. Accompanying them went the *Roe* and Sir Walter Raleigh's pinnace the *Dorothy*. Cumberland did not sail himself, but gave strict instructions that they were to make for the Straits of Magellan and not turn back unless they had taken £6,000 worth of prizes. In the absence of the earl, however, counsels were divided and faint hearts ruled the day. The ships turned back at 44° S, without making any serious attempt to reach the Straits. Cavendish, who had left England some three weeks later than Cumberland's men, debouched into the South Sea with a much smaller fleet at the very moment the rival expedition was turning northwards to Brazil. Here at Bahia a few worthless prizes were taken and considerable time and life wasted in pointless fighting with the Portuguese. September saw them home empty handed, and the earl's plight was worse than ever. Nor did a second ven-

[1] Williamson, p. 17.
[2] Thomas Fuller, *The Worthies of England* (ed. Freeman, 1952), p. 660.
[3] Williamson, pp. 27-35; *Principal Navigations*, XI, 202-27.

ture in 1588 improve the position.[1] An expensive voyage in the queen's *Golden Lion* resulted in one small prize, which can hardly have met the original costs, let alone the damage caused to the *Lion* by a severe storm. In 1589 the earl's debts stood at £6,800.

Now at last his luck turned. In the summer and autumn of 1589 the Azores teemed with English privateers, and there was little the Spanish could do, after their devastating losses the previous year, to drive off their enemies or convoy home the merchantmen from America and the East. It was a magnificent opportunity, and Cumberland, commanding in person the queen's *Victory* and three of his own ships, provided a nucleus for the raiding forces.[2] The voyage was successful, though far less so than it might have been with a little more luck and better judgement. The earl himself had next to no experience and had to rely on his vice-admiral, William Monson, and his flag-captain, Christopher Lister. It is not clear who was at fault, but the fleet was ill supplied and had to spend much of the time flitting from island to island in search of drink, instead of operating a systematic plan of interception. As a result the Portuguese carracks from India and several valuable West-Indiamen slipped through. The English took only one rich prize—Monson said it was worth £100,000—and even that was lost in Mount's Bay, so nearly home. Nevertheless, the numerous minor captures made the venture well worth while, and Cumberland wrote to his wife that he hoped to discharge all his debts.

These gains were to some extent offset by losses in the next two years. The *Robert* and the *Delight*, at sea in 1590, may have earned their keep,[3] but a large expedition in 1591 to the coast of Spain, with one of the queen's ships and four others, again under the earl's command, achieved little, apart from the seizure of some contraband and the loss of the untrustworthy and malignant Monson, who was now taken prisoner.[4] In this venture Cumberland was undertaking a task which should have been allotted to the royal navy—the blockade of the Spanish coast.

[1] Williamson, *George, Third Earl of Cumberland*, pp. 38–40.
[2] *Monson's Tracts*, I, 226–37; *Principal Navigations*, VII, 1–30; Williamson, pp. 41–64.
[3] See below, pp. 248, 250.
[4] *Monson's Tracts*, I, 269–76; Williamson, pp. 70–82; see below, p. 262. The contraband proved good prize (H.C.A. 14/28, no. 84) and a Brazil sugar-man was returned to Portsmouth (Lansdowne MS 67, f. 146).

In 1592 Fortune smiled again. In the Azores Cumberland's ships, in the company of others, captured the great Portuguese carrack the *Madre de Dios*, laden with a huge cargo of jewels, spices, silks and other precious goods.[1] The earl himself stayed at home this time, entrusting the command of his five ships, totalling 1,160 tons burden, to John Norton. In the Azores Norton consorted with Sir John Burgh, who was leading a strong fleet equipped by Raleigh, the queen, the City of London, Sir John Hawkins and others, and the combined force was joined by other ships. In the long and bitter fight for the carrack Cumberland's men played their part and were, as consorts, entitled to a proportion of the spoils. But when it came to dividing the plunder no rules were observed. On the night of the capture the mariners ransacked the cargo, pocketing most of the jewels and other valuables. Then, while Sir John Burgh in the *Roebuck* escorted the carrack to Dartmouth, the rest ran into port wherever they could to sell their pillage. Thus of a cargo worth perhaps half a million there remained a mere £140,000 for the adventurers. Elizabeth, who was a shareholder to the extent of some ten per cent, eventually took about half the returns and awarded Cumberland £36,000. The earl considered this shabby treatment, and made his feelings known. Half the net returns would probably have been his fair share according to established consortship rules, since in ships and men his fleet made up nearly half the combined force at the time of the action, and his men, unlike most of the others, had sailed for 'thirds' and not for wages. At first he evidently expected a handsome profit and wrote to his wife concerning the prize, 'the spoil in her hath been unreasonable, yet there is so much left as I will have make me a free man.'[2] In the end, however, the £24,000 remaining after his mariners had been paid off would have left him some £5,000 clear of his original expenses, and this had to be shared with fellow adventurers. A paltry reward indeed—and yet he certainly fared better than Raleigh, whom the queen mulcted without mercy. The scramble was no more dignified among the adventurers than among the seamen, and by jungle law

---

[1] C. Lethbridge Kingsford, 'The Taking of the Madre de Dios, Anno 1592' in *The Naval Miscellany*, vol. II (Navy Records Society, XL) prints five reports; there are also accounts in *Principal Navigations*, VII, 105–18, *Purchas*, XVI, 13–17, *Monson's Tracts*, I, 278–86, *E.P.V.*, pp. 201–4, and Williamson, pp. 83–112.

[2] Williamson, p. 111.

the lion took the largest share, leaving nothing in this case to the jackal.[1]

For his next venture in 1593 the earl borrowed two of the queen's ships and fitted out three of his own together with a pinnace.[2] In a short voyage they took two Leaguer prizes as well as a cargo of sugar and large quantities of contraband powder and ammunition. Monson, who had been released from captivity in Spain and sailed in this voyage, says that the French prizes alone 'did more than treble the expense of the voyage', but this, like many of his statements, is questionable. However, before returning from this brief outing, Cumberland detached two of his own ships and a pinnace for a raid on the West Indies. Under James Langton's leadership they gathered substantial booty at La Margarita and along the Santo Domingo coast, and the final triumph of the voyage was the capture of six ships lying at Puerto de Caballos to collect the treasure from Guatemala and Honduras. Langton missed the treasure, but came away with the choicest of the Spanish wares laded into the enemy flagship. Purchas describes the whole venture as 'the most gainful which he made before or after', but Cumberland himself remarked, 'what wealth soever the Indies afforded, Spain was the gulf that swallowed it up.'[3]

The five years since the Armada had seen at the most three moderately profitable cruises—those of 1589, 1592 and 1593— and it is very likely that the greater part, perhaps all, of these gains were cancelled by the dead loss of the 1591 expedition. Excellent opportunities and reasonably good luck had certainly compensated for deficiencies in management; that Cumberland nevertheless failed to make privateering pay was due to the scale and organisation of his ventures. The queen's ships undoubtedly cost far more to fit out than merchantmen of equivalent size, and Cumberland not only occasionally borrowed the queen's ships, but also used comparable men-of-war of his own. He disdained to send a fleet to sea without a flagship of at least 500 tons burden, which would cost at least £500 a month in wages and victuals. Even still, strict costing cannot account for the huge sums he

---

[1] Raleigh, however, scarcely expected anything, since he was then in disgrace with the queen, and in any case owed his entire fortune to her.

[2] *Monson's Tracts*, I, 297–302; Williamson, *George, Third Earl of Cumberland*, pp. 113–25; *E.P.V.*, pp. 236–83.

[3] Williamson, p. 117.

spent—£19,000, for example, on 1,200 tons of shipping in the 1592 expedition. In this case he hired his 'admiral', the *Tiger*, for £300 a month—an unusual initial expense—and wasted three months at Plymouth waiting for a wind. Nevertheless it is hard to see how he can have spent £19,000 on his five ships. On this voyage his men sailed for shares, not wages, so that some 600 men for eight months would have cost him £3,360 at the official victualling rate. Other supplies would not normally amount to more than £2 a ton burden for such a cruise—£2,400 in this case. Even supposing the *Tiger* was hired for twelve months, we would still not reach £10,000. If he completely rerigged and refurnished all his five vessels with new guns and small arms, the earl would have been hard put to it to dispose of another £9,000. It can only be assumed that he, like the queen (at least before Hawkins took over the navy), was ruthlessly cheated. This fatal combination of lavishness and carelessness was characteristic of the amateur ventures, and more than anything else doomed them to financial disaster. Nor can it be imagined that Cumberland and his kind were any more businesslike in the disposal of prize cargoes; in this matter they were more or less at the mercy of the big merchants who commanded the market—the members of the Grocers' Company, for example. Thus in spite of comparatively favourable fortune at sea, Cumberland's debts rose from £6,800 in 1589 to £11,200 in 1594. Of course privateering was only one item among many contributing to the deficit, but it was probably the largest. And the next four years were to see these debts doubled again, for the same principal reason.

A marked and significant change now appeared in the organisation of Cumberland's expeditions. Hitherto he had frequently used the queen's ships together with his own. Henceforth he co-operated increasingly with some of the great London merchant promoters of privateering, employing their ships and their capital and borrowing from them on a large scale. His enterprises thus became more syndicated and the Londoners' interest rapidly developed, until in 1598 it was the controlling one. This is an excellent illustration of the growth in the power and influence of the great City entrepreneurs in the field of privateering. Even more remarkable was the way in which Cumberland's own ideas of national maritime expansion were moulded by this contact, so that he became a champion, in words and deeds alike, of their policy of combining sea war with commercial penetration of the enemy's empire.

For the 1594 cruise Cumberland employed, in addition to his own *Sampson*, two powerful London merchantmen—the *Royal Exchange*, of 300 tons, owned by William Holliday, Thomas Cordell and William Garraway, and the *Mayflower*, also of 300 tons.[1] It was perhaps at this date that there began his close financial association with Cordell of the Mercers, a Levant Company merchant and shipowner and a great promoter of privateering and East India ventures. He was one of the earl's chief creditors from 1595. These ships, together with the pinnace *Violet*, which belonged to yet another London privateering merchant, Bartholomew Matthewson, made first for the Burlings to patrol the Iberian coast, and thence to the Azores. Here they encountered the homeward-bound, 2,000-ton carrack the *Cinco Chagas* (the *Five Wounds*). A desperate battle ensued and in the end the carrack took fire and blew up. It would have been a far richer prize than the *Madre de Dios*, and the English came very near to forcing her surrender. As it was, they could only console themselves with the thought that King Philip had lost some 2,000,000 ducats of cargo, a valuable ship and many valuable men. A little later another carrack was sighted and challenged, but the force was now too weak and demoralised to tackle another of these formidable monsters. The few small prizes taken in this voyage can have done little to offset the original cost and the considerable damage suffered by the ships.

In 1595 Captain Langton set forth with the newly-built *Malice Scourge*, a very powerful ship of some 600 tons, the *Alcedo*, the *Anthony* and the *Frigate*—all of them Cumberland's own vessels except the *Alcedo* of 400 tons belonging to the London merchant John Watts.[2] He had no better luck, however, and returned with little to show for what must have been a great expense. 1596 saw no important expedition, but in 1597 two more failures followed—a short and unrewarding trip by Cumberland himself in the *Malice Scourge* and the queen's *Dreadnought*, and an equally fruitless venture by Captain Francis Slingsby in the *Ascension*, which belonged to William Garraway.[3]

The last and greatest of the earl's expeditions was the famous

[1] Williamson, *George, Third Earl of Cumberland*, pp. 126–39; *Monson's Tracts*, I, 309–11; *Principal Navigations*, VII, 118–22.
[2] Williamson, pp. 140–52; *Monson's Tracts*, I, 341.
[3] Williamson, pp. 168–73.

voyage of 1598 to Puerto Rico.[1] Twenty vessels were provided, with a total of some 4,600 tons burden; fifteen ships, a pinnace, two frigates and two barges. Of these Cumberland owned four ships, the pinnace, the barges and one of the frigates, making 1,200 tons burden, the rest being contributed by London merchants, among whom the chief investors were Sir John Hart, Paul Bayning, John Watts, Thomas Cordell, William Garraway and William Shute. With the exception of Sir John Hart, these were key men in the privateering and shipping world. Articles of agreement between Cumberland and ten persons representing the City of London were made out for the regulation of the conduct of the voyage and the disposal of prizes. The ten included the five above-mentioned merchants and John More, Leonard Holliday, James Lancaster, Thomas Allabaster and Robert Walden. It is interesting that Watts, Cordell, Bayning, Shute and Allabaster all lent money to, or bought property from the earl, while Garraway and Allabaster are found acting on his behalf two years later in the sale of the *Malice Scourge*. Clearly the London merchant interest dominated this venture, and its influence was shown in the choice of objective if, as seems probable, the original purpose was to capture Recife. This was the great centre of the Brazil sugar trade which had provided England, by way of prizes, with a booming sugar industry since 1585, and in 1595 Watts, Bayning, More, Shute and others had sponsored James Lancaster's successful raid on the port—a soft and succulent spot in Philip's empire and an obvious target for the commercial magnates, who even before the war had attempted to tap its wealth.

However, by the time the expedition sailed in March 1598, some six months after the commission was granted, rumours of the objective had reached Philip's ears and he had taken some measures to strengthen Pernambuco's defences. Cumberland therefore decided to attack the city of San Juan de Puerto Rico instead, and to establish there an English base for further attacks on Spanish colonies and shipping. He left too late to intercept the West Indian treasure fleet on his way out, and was just too soon to capture the carracks outward bound from Lisbon, but his presence at the mouth of the Tagus instilled such terror that the carracks did not sail. They were unloaded and then sent with other

[1] The main authorities are Sloane MS 3289; *Purchas*, XVI, 29 *et seq.*; Williamson, pp. 174–218; *Monson's Tracts*, II, 204–25; there is also some valuable material in the Seville archives.

ships to escort the homeward bound carracks from the Azores. As it happened Cumberland missed these too, but he had at least succeeded in causing a serious interruption in the normal schedule of the East India trade. More important still, Spain sent orders to stay the West Indies fleet at Havana. In sum the earl had already inflicted severe damage on the enemy before he left European waters—and without striking a blow.

At Puerto Rico itself he struck swiftly and hard. It was an excellently conducted operation and completely successful, though it must be admitted that there was no very serious opposition once the English had shown their determination to go through with the assault. It was only after the capture of the town and the surrender of the enemy fort that difficulties began. The English casualties in battle had been negligible, but within three weeks of the capture of the town the earl had lost two hundred out of twelve hundred men from dysentery, and another four hundred were ill. With disease spreading at this rate it was obvious that the 'key of the West Indies' could not, after all, be kept. Lading his ships with a rather disappointing haul of sugar, hides, ginger and ordnance, he sailed home. No ransom was obtained from the Spanish because they realised as well as Cumberland that his departure was forced. Nine prizes were taken in the course of the venture and the total returns were estimated at £16,000. Almost certainly this was not a saving voyage, but Cumberland was not displeased with the result. He saw it as the beginning of good policy and hoped that it would be followed up by a double offensive against the trade of the East and West Indies. The stoppage of the carracks, he realised, could eventually so weaken the Portuguese hold on the East Indies as to open the way for English merchants, 'drawing a perpetual trade that will not only enrich our country, but breed numbers of men to strengthen the walls of our realm'. As for the West Indies, the earl was so impressed by his easy success at Puerto Rico that he boldly offered to tackle Panamá and Havana with a like force and so 'overthrow all his trade in the Indies'. Cumberland was no original thinker, and the inference to be drawn from the long and somewhat muddled letter including the passages quoted[1] is that he had come to see the long-term interests of the nation through the eyes of the great London merchants who were now his partners and creditors. The sale of the *Malice Scourge* to the

[1] Williamson, *George, Third Earl of Cumberland*, pp. 220–5.

East India Company two years later made thus a fitting end to his maritime career.

'I have done unto her Majesty,' he wrote, 'an excellent service and discharged that duty which I owe to my country so far as that, whensoever God shall call me out of this wretched world, I shall die with assurance I have discharged a good part I was born for.'[1] Heavily in debt, he now tried to recoup his losses by retrenchment and reform. But it was too late. The greatest knight errant of them all had spent his fortune in the merchants' cause. In return they lent him money at interest. All he got from them in the end was a glimmering of their view of England's future—the true marriage of trade and plunder. A pious and patriotic man, he confused these with God and glory.

Cumberland was not the only nobleman who went in for privateering, but he seems to have been the only one who, as he put it, threw his land into the sea. Some others, like Charles and Thomas Howard and Sir George Carey (Lord Hunsdon from 1596), being deeply involved in the prosecution of the sea war, had what may rather be considered a professional interest. Privateering was speculative for them, as for any promoter, but the expeditions they fitted out were on nothing like the scale of Cumberland's and were not (with the exception of one or two of Carey's) concerned with anything grander than the taking of prizes. Moreover they were themselves closer to the business, less vulnerable to fraudulent servants. Others again, though undoubtedly amateurs, limited their interest to an occasional dabble —Sir Robert Dudley and the Earl of Hertford are examples.[2] Sir Robert Cecil, too, was an amateur, but gained the advantages of a professional by collaborating with the Howards.

The economic effects of these incursions of landowning elements into the most speculative kind of business enterprise were limited. The amateur promoters were for the most part not ordinary country gentry, but men connected with the Court. The money that was raised for privateering by land sales and mort-

<hr />

[1] Williamson, p. 224.

[2] For the Howards and Carey see ch. 5. For Dudley's expedition see G. F. Warner (ed.), *The Voyage of Robert Dudley into the West Indies, 1594-5* (Hakluyt Society, 2nd Ser., LXXI). Hertford owned the *Phoenix* of Portsmouth, which was privateering in 1590, 1591, 1592 and 1593 [Harleian MS 598, ff. 8, 19; Lansdowne MS 142, f. 115; H.C.A. 25/3 (9), 12 Jan. 1592/3], and the *Frances*, privateering in 1590 and 1591 (Lansdowne MS 67, f. 177; 157, f. 30; H.C.A. 13/29, 3 Feb. 1591/2).

gages made up only a small part of the capital invested in privateering and an almost negligible fraction of the wealth represented
by land itself. The amateurs lost far more than they gained, but
their losses can hardly have had any appreciable effect on the
landowning interest as a whole. Some merchants who associated
themselves too closely with amateur enterprises—Thomas Heaton,
for example—burnt their fingers, but many more gained at the
expense of the amateurs by lending them money, or selling them
ships and provisions.

The voyages of the amateurs attracted attention and publicity
out of all proportion to their real importance, helping to create for
posterity a false impression of the general character of privateering.
In fact professionals and merchants played a far larger part and
their ventures were much more humdrum and much more
successful.

Chapter 5

THE PROFESSIONALS

The term 'professional' is a loose one in this context, covering a range of persons from the Lord Admiral at one extreme to the humble skipper with a part-interest in his ship at the other. What distinguishes the professional promoter is that, whether captain, shipowner, official or simply 'man of war', he understood the business and was a part of it, though the extent of his commitment to privateering might vary a great deal.

The purest form of professional venture was that of the seaman commanding his own ship, and here its advantages in economy, discipline and forcefulness are to be seen most clearly. The captain would of course depend upon merchants ashore for his victuals and supplies, but he could make his own bargains and at least ensure that the ship was adequately fitted out. As for the crew, he would pick them himself. Embezzlement and excessive pillage, which caused the most serious wastage of other promoters' profits, would be reduced to a minimum, and in any case, as captain, he would get the lion's share of legitimate pillage. What is more, in addition to his owner's third of the final returns he would take his captain's share of the crew's third. But in the last resort the success or failure of a venture depended upon what happened at sea. Sheer luck, though a big factor in any voyage, could be circumscribed and conditioned by human skill and determination, qualities the seaman owner-captain was more likely to possess than some, and more likely to exert to the full than others.

The *Catherine* (or *Little Catherine*) of Weymouth, owned by Robert White of that port, was a small vessel of thirty-five tons. In 1590 she was valued at £86 19s. 11d., with all her masts, sails and tackle, two falcons and two falconets (3-pounders and 2-pounders respectively), four calivers and some powder and shot. This was an appraisement made in connection with an Admiralty Court action, and was probably on the low side, but even supposing that the ship and guns alone were worth £100 and that victuals and other necessaries would cost £150 (see Table 4, p. 49), she could be set forth for an initial outlay of £250. In this same year under the owner's personal command she took two Brazilmen, the Lord Admiral's tenths of these being valued, respectively, at £146 10s. 4d. and approximately £200. Pillage would already have been taken before the assessment of tenth, but customs dues had still to be deducted. Let us suppose that the Lord Admiral's share was actually his full tenth and therefore that the cargoes were together worth £3,465. After payment of tenths, customs and the crew's thirds, White probably received, as owner, victualler and captain, some £2,000, most of it clear profit.

The following year he brought in another Brazilman, the Lord Admiral's share being rated at £285, and White's gain was probably about £1,600. In 1592 White evidently sold the money-spinning *Catherine* to one Peter Neville, who forthwith brought in yet again a Brazilman, this time to the value of £4,239. But the record haul was still to come. In 1595 Neville (who presumably had made voyages in 1593 and 1594) captured a West-Indiaman with cochineal, hides, sugar, cassia fistula, blockwood and taffeta, China silk, pearls, emeralds, gold rings, 68½ ounces of gold chains, sapphires, topazes and other precious stones, as well as £777 17s. 0d. in rials of plate. The Admiral's tenth of the hides, sugar, cassia fistula and blockwood was valued at a mere £84; unluckily we do not know how much the rest was worth—certainly it would be reckoned in thousands. As for Robert White, he appeared in 1592 as the owner and commander of the *Catherine White*, or *Great Catherine*. His success with the small privateer had obviously decided him to increase the stakes. With this larger vessel he continued prize-hunting until 1598 at least, and there is no reason to suppose that he stopped then, since he was still acquiring substantial prizes: we know of one in 1592, two in 1595 and two in 1598. As the man prospered he gradually retired from personal command, entrusting the ship to others, in particular to a certain John White, who was regularly master from 1595, though only once in full command. Robert by this time was in his late forties. He had been on reprisal since 1587 at least, and had captained his *Little Catherine* in the Narrow Seas in '88. A mere mariner, he pushed his fortunes so far as to became mayor of Weymouth and Melcomb Regis in 1593-4.[1]

[1] H.C.A. 24/58, no. 66; Harleian MS 598, ff. 7, 9, 12, 17, 18, 22, 23, 33, 36,

The career of William Parker of Plymouth provides a good example of that combination of skill and daring so characteristic of the professional owner-captains. He was already a captain in 1587, serving with Drake in the Cadiz expedition. He next appears in the *Richard* of Plymouth, belonging to the merchant Richard Hutchins, which Parker commanded in 1590 and 1591, bringing home several prizes. The next two years saw him in the West Indies, again in the *Richard*, but it was in 1594 that he made his first big *coup* (in the same ship) with the capture of Puerto de Caballos in Honduras, a feat he repeated in 1595. The following year he served in the second Cadiz expedition, this time as captain of the queen's *Rainbow*, but in November he departed once more for the Caribbean, now equipped with his own ship, the *Prudence* of Plymouth, and a bark called the *Adventure*, sailing 'at his own charges'. After a rather fruitless consortship with Sir Anthony Sherley, Parker went on alone into the Bay of Mexico and, in an exploit worthy of one of Drake's disciples, captured the town of Campeche. Then, as the captain himself tells us: 'The multitude of the Spaniards which fled upon my first assault by ten of the clocke in the morning assembling together reneued their strength, and set furiously upon me and my small company. In which assault I lost some sixe of my men, and my selfe was shot under the left brest with a bullet, which bullet lieth still in the chine of my backe. Being thus put unto our shifts wee devised on the sudden a newe stratagem; for having divers of the townesmen prisoners, we tied them arme in arme together, and placed them in stead of a baricado to defend us from the fury of the enemies shot. And so with ensigne displayed, taking with us our sixe dead men, wee retired with more safetie to the haven, where we tooke a frigat which rode ready fraught with the kings tribute in silver and other good commodities, which were presently to bee transported to S. Juan de Ullua, and brought the same and our Periago or Canoa to my ship, which lay in two fadome water sixe leagues from the towne, being not able to come any neerer for the sholds upon that coast.'[1] Later the bark *Adventure*, with her captain and thirteen men, was taken by two frigates of war manned out from Campeche; the English had taken rich booty, but they had paid heavily for it.

45; H.C.A. 13/27, 10 Feb. 1587/8; H.C.A. 13/101, 30 Jan. 1593/4; Laughton, *Defeat*, II, 329.
[1] *Principal Navigations*, X, 277–80.

Parker's greatest success, however, came in 1601 with his sensational raid on Porto Belo at the very heart of the Spanish Empire, the details of which are related in a later chapter. By 1602 Parker owned not only the *Prudence*, but the *Penelope* and the *Perce*, both of which were at sea taking prizes that year under other captains. Parker himself evidently intended another West Indies raid in 1602, but was detained on government service. It would appear, however, that he made another voyage to Honduras and Campeche at or after the end of the war, committing acts which the Spaniards denounced as piracy, though in 1605 he was cleared of all the charges against him. In this case his status and connections probably helped, for Parker was evidently of the minor gentry and by now an eminent person in Plymouth. He seems, moreover, to have had a close connection with Raleigh, who referred to him in 1596 as 'sometime my servant', and who obtained from him a valuable Spanish rutter of the West Indies. In 1606 he was one of the founding members of the Virginia Company, which indicates his arrival in the English as well as the North American 'establishment'. Nevertheless the salt was in his veins and in 1617 he accepted an appointment as vice-admiral of an East Indies expedition, in which voyage he died at Bantam in 1618.[1]

Parker epitomises all that was best in the minor Elizabethan sea-gentry. Different again were the captains who rose from humble beginnings in the merchant service. Generally we know very little about such men, because they rarely sailed in the queen's ships and therefore have not attracted the attention of naval historians. Captain Christopher Newport is a case in point. To those interested in early North American history he is known as the admiral of the Virginia Company fleets in the first six years of the colony's life, the seaman after whom was named the town of Newport, Virginia. It is also know that he made a West Indies voyage in 1592, since this exploit is chronicled by Hakluyt. What is not generally realised is that Newport was plundering West Indian shipping and coastal settlements year after year from just after the Armada campaign right up to the end of the war, and that he continued to sail thither for trade after the war. In fact his career was remarkable and he may well be taken as a prototype of those men of the merchant service who went in for privateering.

---

[1] *E.P.V.*, pp. 219–24, 308–25; see below, pp. 178–80; *Cal. S.P. Dom. Eliz., 1601–3*, pp. 81, 85, 137, 140; *Raleigh's Works* (ed. Oldys and Birch), I, 518; H.C.A. 14/35, nos. 212, 252; H.C.A. 14/36, no. 41.

He was born in 1560, but the first record of him does not occur until 1580. In this year he sailed in the *Minion* of London in one of the first English ventures to Brazil. It was an unfortunate voyage, marred by jealousies and factions among the merchants and the sailors and finally ruined by the hostility of the Portuguese authorities. At Bahia a quarrel broke out between the master, Stephen Hare, and some of the crew, who complained of the shortage of victuals. Hare, who was involved in all the lamentable squabbles, lost his temper and swore 'that if one of them called Abraham Cocke would not rule his tongue, he the same master would make him longer than ever god made him'. Cocke apparently took this threat seriously, for he and two other discontented seamen, one of them being Newport, lost no time in going ashore. Here they remained while the *Minion* beat a hasty retreat in the face of armed attack by the Portuguese.

In 1582 Newport's name is mentioned in a list of Harwich shipmasters, and this probably indicates that he served his apprenticeship here. Thus like Drake he went through the finest training any seaman could have, so that the handling of a ship on a difficult coast or in bad weather became second nature to him. This reference to him may not indicate that he had already returned from Brazil, but the next item of news is unequivocal—he made his first marriage in 1584, to Katherine Procter. Three years later he was master's mate in a privateer called the *Drake*, owned by the London merchant John Watts, and sailed in the company of Sir Francis Drake to Cadiz. After the destruction of the Spanish ships, Newport's privateer, among others, remained prize-hunting on the coast of Spain. Now and henceforth Newport is designated 'of Limehouse, mariner', and in the service of the London merchants he rose rapidly. In 1589 he was master of the *Margaret* of London in a privateering cruise, and in the following year he achieved his first major command as captain of the *Little John* in the fleet set forth by John Watts for the West Indies and Virginia. Newport himself did not reach Virginia on this occasion. Off the northwest coast of Cuba he and his men were attempting the capture of two Mexican treasure ships when, along with many more of the English, he was wounded, his right arm being 'strooken off'.

After this he was sometimes referred to as 'Captain Newport of the one hand', but the loss certainly did not deter him. The next four years saw four successive voyages to the West Indies, still in

the service of the London merchants, and by 1595 he had commanded two major expeditions and established a position in the
front rank of privateering captains. The ship he had sailed since
1592 had been the *Golden Dragon*, belonging to Henry Cletherow
and John More, and now in 1595 he made one more voyage in
her, his only voyage to the Mediterranean. This was a trading
venture, but Newport was presumably equipped with letters of
reprisal, as many southward-sailing merchants captains were, for
he returned with two Spanish prizes.

In 1590 he had contracted a second marriage, and now in 1595
he set the seal on his success by a third marriage—to Elizabeth,
daughter of Francis Glanville, one of the leading London goldsmiths. The result was a privateering as well as a matrimonial
partnership. In 1596 Newport set forth with a new ship, the
Neptune, a formidable man-of-war, the major shares in which were
held by Francis and Richard Glanville and the captain himself. It
was the first of a long series of West Indies ventures for this ship,
six of which were led by Newport in person. Time and again he
raided towns—La Yaguana, Puerto de Caballos, Tabasco and
others—returning laden with loot. No other English captain is
known to have frequented the Caribbean to this extent—not even
Drake—and after the war Newport went twice again in trade.
When he was chosen by the Virginia Company, at the age of
forty-six, to command its first expedition in 1606, Newport must
have been an obvious choice, and to describe him as 'a mariner
well practised for the western parts of America' was not only
ambiguous geography but something of an understatement. He
served his new masters well, and his unrivalled experience of the
Atlantic and West Indian waters did much to secure the precarious foothold of the English on North American soil. He did
his best to bring some harmony into the troubled affairs of the
early settlers, but in 1611 he left this service at length because he
was dissatisfied with the supply arrangements for the plantation.
Finally he undertook three voyages for the East India Company,
in the last of which, on 15 August 1617, he died at Bantam. His
will shows him to have become a man of considerable position
and possessions.[1]

[1] P.C.C. 92 Meade. He left a widow, two sons and two daughters, bequeathing
to them his 'dwelling house' on Tower Hill with its adjoining garden, a £400 share
in the East India Company and an interest in the Virginia Company. He is referred
to as one of the six masters of his Majesty's Navy Royal. For his career in general see

Another Limehouse hero was Michael Geare, who began his privateering career at the age of nineteen at the outbreak of the war. According to his own statement, made in February 1592, he had gone to sea on reprisal every year since reprisals began, first making two voyages in the *Marlyn* of Sir George Carey's, then (1588) a West Indies venture in John Watts' *Drake*, a cruise in the *Examiner* (1589) and two more West Indies ventures in the *Little John* (1590 and 1591). These last two ships each belonged in part to John Watts, and Geare's progress in the service of this great privateering magnate marched almost step by step with Newport's. He did not become a master until 1589, and in 1590 actually served as master under Newport. Then, while Newport took up with another London syndicate, Geare achieved his first command as captain of the *Little John* in 1591. On this voyage he emerged as a tough fighter, none too scrupulous in securing for himself an ample share of the proceeds, either by the main force of pillage or by clever smuggling operations. The eight single shares to which he was entitled as a captain were admitted to be worth ten pounds each, and in fact were probably worth fifteen or twenty; add to that the legitimate pillage and the various valuables he was suspected of having embezzled, and it is more than likely that Geare made several hundred out of this one venture. It is not surprising that in 1592 he appears as part-owner of a privateer called the *Michael and John*. His partner was now John Stokes, who had been Watts' partner in the *John* the previous year. It looks, therefore, as if Geare bought Watts' share and had the ship re-named accordingly. The *Michael and John* was for the next three years sailing under Geare's command in successive and successful plunder ventures. In his fourth and last voyage in her, in 1595, he visited the West Indies again, losing his pinnace in a severe fight with several enemy vessels on the Havana coast, but returning as usual well laden. More West Indies ventures followed; with Newport in 1596, with David Myddelton in 1601-2 and again with Newport in 1602-3. In nearly every voyage that he made Geare was accused of sharp practice in the matter of appropriating prize goods, and by the end of the war he was rich. Soon he was Sir Michael Geare and an Elder Brother of Trinity House; and after his death his house in Three Colt Street, Stepney, called the

K. R. Andrews, 'Christopher Newport of Limehouse, Mariner', *William and Mary Quarterly*, XI (1954), 28-41, and the *Dictionary of American Biography*. His West Indies voyages are described in *E.P.V.* (*passim*) and ch. 8 below.

Dagger House, after the dagger that used to hang outside, was conveyed to the Corporation of Trinity House, with instructions to distribute from the rent five pounds yearly among the poorest decayed seamen and seamen's widows of the hamlet of Limehouse.[1]

What enabled Geare and Newport to become promoters in their own right was their skill as mariners, fighters and leaders. In Newport's case it was actually his marriage into the Glanville family that gave him a ship, but he certainly could not have contracted such a marriage had he not acquired some property and social standing already. What is interesting is that Newport remained essentially a sailor to the end of his days. The long-term trend in shipping was in fact producing a new sort of captain— responsible, well-to-do, allied in interest to the owners, but seldom an owner himself. Abraham Cocke, Newport's shipmate in the Brazil voyage, likewise became a successful privateering captain, but though he married the daughter of an important shipowner he never, so far as we know, became a shipowner himself.[2] In smaller ships and in the smaller world of the outports it was more common for a seaman to make his way to the position of a merchant shipowner, but in the long run the future lay with the larger ship and with great mercantile enterprises like the East India Company. Privateering did enable some skippers, like Geare, to make their pile and retire into comfortable respectability, but many others, even though they had done well by plunder, were attracted by its ample opportunities and rewards into the East India service. Newport, Parker and some of their contemporaries thus formed the first generation of what might be called the managerial element in England's major trades.

[1] *E.P.V.*, pp. 160-1, 330-7 for his career up to 1595; see below, ch. 8, for his later voyages.

[2] Cocke settled down in Brazil and did not return to England until 1587, when he was captured in a small Portuguese merchantman by Cumberland's men near the River Plate. In 1589 he went back to the River Plate with two ships of John Watts. In 1590 he led Watts' West Indies and Virginia expedition. In 1592 he commanded Cumberland's *Sampson* and probably gained as much as any sailor from the *Madre de Dios* pillage. In 1593 he went again to the River Plate and there presumably perished. He had married the daughter of William Bygate. [Andrews, 'Christopher Newport of Limehouse, Mariner', *William and Mary Quarterly*, xi (1954), 28–41. *Purchas*, vi, 367–70; xvi, 6; xvi, 230; *Roanoke Voyages*, pp. 579–716; *Monson's Tracts*, i, 278–96; Foster, *Lancaster's Voyages*, p. 41; H.C.A. 25/3 (9), 19 March 1592/3; R. T. Spence, 'The Cliffords, Earls of Cumberland, 1579–1646', unpublished London Ph.D. thesis, 1959.]

In the promotion of private maritime warfare a rather more important part was played by the leading officers of the royal navy. The distinction between the royal navy and the aggregate of private shipping which embodied the sea-going force of the nation was not yet sharply defined. The royal navy had practically no regular personnel and relied upon such sea-faring commercial people as the Winters, Hawkinses and Fenners for organisation and leadership. Men who had grown up in the tradition of aggressive trade naturally assumed the leadership of the nation's maritime forces in all phases of the struggle, official as well as unofficial, and their position in the official sphere gave them special opportunities and advantages in the unofficial. Such was their influence that even naval men without their background readily joined in.

Thus most of the men associated with the queen's ships were also privateering promoters, from the Lord Admiral downwards. Lord Charles Howard had the *Charles*, the *Disdain*, the *Lion's Whelp*, the *Great Delight*, the *Truelove*, the *White Lion* and the *Cygnet* as his private men-of-war. There is evidence that he expended money on their fitting out, not only to accompany the queen's ships in large expeditions, but also occasionally for purely private ventures.[1] His kinsman, Lord Thomas Howard of Bindon, one of the leading naval commanders of his day, was almost as active. He had an interest in the *Lion's Whelp*, and in 1592 set forth a West Indies expedition of four ships under Benjamin Wood.[2] The treasurer of the navy, Sir John Hawkins,

---

[1] Lawrence Stone, in his contribution to *Essays in the Economic and Social History of Tudor and Stuart England* (ed. F. J. Fisher), pp. 92–4, gives a most interesting picture of the privateering partnership of the Lord Admiral and Sir Robert Cecil, showing not only that it was highly profitable but also that the partners were often able to shift much of the burden of costs on to the Exchequer, having their ships fitted at royal expense. In addition to Stone's references, see, for the *Charles*: Harleian MS 598, ff. 61–2; Lansdowne MS 67, f. 171. The *Disdain*: Harleian MS 598, ff. 56–8; Lansdowne MS 67, f. 171; H.C.A. 13/27, 14 Aug. 1589; H.C.A. 13/28, 12, 19 Nov. 1589, 18, 22 Dec. 1589, 13 Jan. 1589/90; H.C.A. 13/29, 1, 11 Feb. 1591/2. The *Lion's Whelp*: Lansdowne MS 70, f. 106; H.C.A. 13/28, 28 Jan. 1590/1; H.C.A. 14/27, nos. 21, 25, 50; H.C.A. 13/33, 29 Nov. 1598, 14 Feb. 1598/9, 21 March 1598/9; H.C.A. 14/33, no. 153; see below, p. 176. The *Great Delight*: Lansdowne MS 67, ff. 171, 177; H.C.A. 13/29, 2 March 1591/2. The *Truelove*: H.C.A. 13/33, 6 July 1598, 11 Aug. 1598, 26 Sept. 1598; H.C.A. 14/33, no. 237. The *White Lion* and the *Cygnet*: *Monson's Tracts*, I, 139. Cecil was also interested in the *Darling* of Southampton: *S.P. Dom. Eliz.*, cclxviii, no. 95; cclxxi, no. 90; Marsden, *Law and Custom*, I, 325–9.

[2] *E.P.V.*, pp. 173–83.

found time to build a fine galleon, the *Dainty*, which played an
important part in capturing the *Madre de Dios*, and in 1593 she
sailed under Richard Hawkins in his famous South Sea venture.
Sir John also set forth the *Bark Bond*, the *Bark Hawkins* and a pinnace called the *Fly*, and had a share in Humphrey Fones' *Elizabeth* of Plymouth (there were several *Elizabeths* of Plymouth, for a
reason not far to seek, and they were therefore often referred to as
the *Elizabeth Fones*, the *Elizabeth Fishbourne*, etc.).[1] Nevertheless
the Hawkins family did not contribute as much to private warfare
after 1585 as they had done in earlier days, and the same may be
said of Drake. Sir Francis took two ships of his own—the *Thomas*
and the *Francis*—on his great West Indies cruise in 1585, and
again took the *Thomas* with him to Cadiz, but this seems to have
been the extent of his purely private venturing.[2] Both Hawkins
and Drake were putting their money as well as their energy into
national enterprises, and when they fitted out a ship of their own it
usually went with a royal fleet or a fleet in which royal ships took
the lead.

Lesser figures, such as Sir Henry Palmer,[3] William Winter
junior and John and Robert Crosse,[4] were now at least as interested in privateering as Drake or Hawkins. Perhaps the most
typical naval promoters were the Fenners of Sussex—merchants,
shipowners, naval captains and privateersmen. Like the
Hawkinses, they made their first fighting appearance in the
sixties, encroaching on the Portuguese monopoly of West African
trade. The voyage of Thomas Fenner in 1564 to Guinea was followed by the better-known venture of George and his brother
Edward to the Cape Verde Islands and the Azores. These were
ostensibly trading ventures, but on the former occasion Thomas
was summoned before the Admiralty Court to explain his
acquisition of quantities of sugar and brazilwood out of a Portuguese merchantman, and in the second voyage George and
Edward with three ships and a pinnace successfully fought off a
fleet of seven Portuguese men-of-war. In the crisis of the early
seventies Thomas was at sea in the newly-built *Bark Fenner*,

---

[1] J. A. Williamson, *Hawkins of Plymouth*, pp. 325–6; Laughton, *Defeat*, ii, 337;
Corbett, *Spanish War*, pp. x, xx, 45; H.C.A. 25/1 (4), 5 Oct. 1585; H.C.A.
25/3 (9), 24 Feb. 1589/90.

[2] Corbett, *Spanish War*, xi, xx, 45.   [3] *E.P.V.*, pp. 209–18.

[4] Winter: Harleian MS 598, f. 17; G. C. Williamson, *George, Third Earl of
Cumberland*, pp. 178–9. Crosse: *Monson's Tracts*, i, 213; Lansdowne MS 67, ff. 146,
171, 183; Harleian MS 598, f. 24; S.P. Dom. Eliz., cclxii, no. 86.

making private war on Spaniards under a commission from William of Orange. His kinsman George was also plundering Flushingers and Spaniards, and one of the Fenners was said to have reached the Azores and the West Indies in 1572. In 1584 Edward and his nephew William obtained a commission from the Portuguese pretender Dom Antonio, and in the *Galleon Fenner*, in the company of the notorious pirate John Challice, pillaged various French vessels and a rich Portuguese sugarman. An indictment for piracy resulted, and it was not until 1598 that Edward was officially pardoned, his nephew having meanwhile given his life for the queen in the Lisbon expedition. When the war began the *Galleon Fenner* sailed under William Fenner in legitimate reprisal action in 1586. George and Edward, for their part, fitted out the Lord Admiral's *Disdain* in 1589, bringing in at least two prizes, and Thomas and Edward combined with the London merchant John Bird to prepare a substantial expedition of four privateers in 1591. Edward, as owner-captain of the *Peregrine* of Portsmouth, also took part in the spoil of Pernambuco in 1595. Apart from all this private enterprise, naval service occupied much of their time. No less than six Fenners commanded royal ships at various times during the war, and in the Armada campaign the four stalwarts mentioned had charge of four of the chief men-of-war.[1]

Such men made up the backbone of England's sea-power. The Fenners came from Chichester and its neighbourhood, and here was to be found a small knot of men bound up together in all the ambiguous business of prize-mongering. John Young, the customer of Chichester, an old sea-dog who had seen service in Mary's reign, was at the centre of it all. Like the Fenners, he obtained a commission of reprisal from Dom Antonio and set

---

[1] K. R. Andrews, 'Thomas Fenner and the Guinea Trade, 1564', *Mariner's Mirror*, XXXVIII (1952), 312–14; *Principal Navigations*, VI, 266–84; H.C.A. 25/1 (3), 11 Dec. 1572; H.C.A. 24/44, no. 96; H.C.A. 1/39, 17 March 1572; *Cal. S.P. Spanish, Eliz.*, II, 429, 432, 434, 438, 464; Lansdowne MS 144, f. 351; S.P. Dom. Eliz., clxxvii, no. 46 and cclxviii, no. 6/7; H.C.A. 1/42, 30 March 1585, 24 July 1585; H.C.A. 13/28, 9 Dec. 1589; *Monson's Tracts*, I, 177, 185, 196; Marsden, *Law and Custom*, I, 246–7; Lansdowne MS 144, f. 319; H.C.A. 14/23, no. 13; H.C.A. 14/26, no. 128, H.C.A. 13/28, 12, 19 Nov. 1589, 18, 22 Dec. 1589, 13 Jan. 1589/90; H.C.A. 13/27, 14 Aug. 1589; H.C.A. 25/3 (9), 21, 30 Jan. 1590/1; see below, pp. 211–12; Laughton, *Defeat*, II, 325–6; J. S. Corbett, *Drake and the Tudor Navy*, II, 13, 159; see also numerous references to the Fenners in *Monson's Tracts*.

forth his ship the *White Bear* in 1582 under the command of the
pirate John Storye. In the following year his name is linked with
George Fenner's in a spoil case. In 1584 he was interested in the
voyage of George Somers to Lisbon and the Canaries in the *Lion*
of Chichester, and a year later he and Somers obtained letters of
reprisal for the *Bark Young*. Another associate was John Crooke of
Southampton, owner of the *Primrose*, the *Marigold* and the *John
Evangelist*, all fitted out as privateers in 1585. In 1587 Young was
part-owner of the *Bark Way*, another privateer, and in the Armada
campaign he had four ships in service, one of which—the *Bear
Young*—he saw drift in flames into the midst of the Spanish fleet
off Calais. The *John Young* was out on reprisal in the three years
following, and in 1590 Sir George Carey, Crooke and Young
combined to send the *Bark Young* to the West Indies and possibly
to the Virginia coast. Young was something of an expert on naval
tactics and wrote a treatise on the subject, but his experience of the
privateering world must have been even more impressive, for in
1597 he was appointed special adviser to the Lord Admiral and
Dr Caesar in prize causes.[1]

Somers was likewise a professional, mixing naval service with
private enterprise, as did George Raymond, another Chichester
man. Raymond was captain of the *Lion* of Chichester in 1585 and
evidently the chief adventurer in her voyage that year with Grenville for Virginia. Raymond was separated from his admiral on
the way out, and after setting thirty-two men ashore on the island
of Croatoan, went on to Newfoundland, where he met Bernard
Drake in the *Golden Riall* of Topsham. Drake, Amyas Preston
and others had originally fitted out this ship to follow up Grenville, but had been diverted on the queen's orders to round up
enemy fishing vessels off Newfoundland. A Brazilman had been
taken on the way out, and Preston had returned with the prize.
Raymond and Drake now consorted together and on the way
home took a rich haul of Portuguese sugarmen and French fish.
Of these Raymond had his share and must have made a good

---

[1] S.P. Dom Eliz., cclix, no. 48; H.C.A. 13/25, 15 Aug. 1584; H.C.A. 1/43,
27 Oct. 1583; H.C.A. 13/25, 17 April 1584, 5 June 1584, 1 April 1586; Lansdowne MS 115, f. 196; H.C.A. 25/1 (4), 2, 16 July 1585; Harleian MS 598,
ff. 1, 4; Laughton, *Defeat*, II, 287, 326–7; H.C.A. 13/28, 15 Nov. 1589; H.C.A.
24/57, nos. 38, 67; H.C.A. 13/29, 19, 29 Nov. 1591, 28, 31 Jan. 1591/2; H.C.A.
14/28, no. 195; *E.P.V.*, pp. 86–94; *Monson's Tracts*, IV, 202–27; Lansdowne MS
157, f. 256.

profit, but Preston had to sue for his rightful portion of Drake's share. In the next year, 1586, Raymond and Somers were joint adventurers in the *Swiftsure* of Chichester. 1587 saw Raymond at Cadiz with Sir Francis Drake, while Preston went privateering in the *Eleanour* of Weymouth. Both of course served against the Armada. Then in 1589 their paths crossed again. Preston this year sailed with Cumberland to the Azores, and among the numerous privateers thronging those islands was Preston's own *Julian* of Lyme, under the command of George Somers. The *Julian* and her pinnace were sailing in company with the *Swiftsure* of Chichester, now owned outright by Raymond, and the *Unicorn* of Barnstaple, owned by the merchant William Morcomb, and together these ships took two very rich prizes, worth some £30,000. Another court case ensued, in which Preston and Somers were allied against Raymond and Morcomb. Raymond meanwhile was at sea in the queen's ship *Scout*, but also had an interest as part-owner and victualler in the *Blessing* of Portsmouth, one of Thomas Heaton's privateers. In 1590 two more of Raymond's ships were out on reprisal—the *Penelope* and the *Swallow*—and all these ventures yielded substantial prizes. He was thus a successful promoter as well as a noted seaman when he set out on his famous East Indies voyage in 1591, and in his own *Penelope* took precedence over James Lancaster in the *Edward Bonaventure* and Samuel Foxcroft in the *Merchant Royal*. On the way to the East, just past the Cape of Good Hope, the man and the ship disappeared for ever. As for Preston and Somers, their careers were steadier. They made an important voyage together to the West Indies in 1595 and together rose to very near the top in the queen's service in the later years of the war. Both achieved knighthood and played a part in the foundation of Virginia.[1]

The shifting contacts and alliances of the Chichester men illustrate well the composition of the privateering interest and the role of the naval element in it. The Chichester men were connected chiefly with Portsmouth, Southampton and the Isle of Wight, and this complex of ports made up a substantial privateering

---

[1] *Roanoke Voyages*, pp. 121, 158, 165–6, 171–3, 179–80, 234–42; H.C.A. 13/26, 6, 8, 11 May 1587; Corbett, *Spanish War*, p. 141; *E.P.V.*, pp. 377–98; H.C.A. 24/57, nos. 17, 196; H.C.A. 13/28, 18 March 1589/90; Harleian MS 598, ff. 3, 9; Lansdowne MS 145, f. 115; H.C.A. 13/29, 10 Feb. 1591/2; H.C.A. 14/27, nos. 23, 50; H.C.A. 24/58, no. 64; H.C.A. 13/28, 28 Jan. 1590/1; see below, pp. 169–70.

base, second only to London in importance, but connected with London in many ways. Merchants of course provided many of the ships and much of the capital, but the professionals were themselves sometimes merchants as well as sailors, or else were closely linked with merchant families by marriage.

Perhaps nothing illustrates this professional and mercantile alliance and the fusion of private and national enterprise better than the Cadiz expedition of 1587. Its leader was the personification of the link between private and national enterprise, but not only Drake was there: Flick, Towerson, Lancaster, Barrett, West, Fishbourne, Broadbent, Hallett, Raymond, Newport, Parker, Fenner, Crosse, Foxcroft—every one of them was a privateer captain and several were merchants. Eleven of the ships—the *Merchant Royal*, the *Speedwell*, the *George Bonaventure*, the *Margaret and John*, the *Edward Bonaventure*, the *Salomon*, the *Thomas Bona-venture*, the *Little John*, the *Susan*, the *Drake* and the *Post*—were set forth by a syndicate of London merchants led by Cordell, Watts, Bayning, Boreman, Lee and Flick. Of the rest four were Plymouth ships, two belonged to the Lord Admiral and six to the queen. All but one or two of these, apart from the queen's, made privateering voyages on other occasions. As for their merchant backers, Cordell, Watts, and Bayning ranked with Raleigh and Cumberland among the greatest of the privateering promoters. What is more, the original intention of the Londoners was to capture the outward bound Portuguese carracks, and their most immediate benefit from the raid was the carrack *San Felipe* with a cargo worth over £100,000. The Cadiz expedition was, looked at from one angle, a matter of national self-preservation; from another, it was privateering writ large.[1]

Finally we can hardly avoid including here those who had a vital interest in the official and unofficial aspects of the sea war, but were neither seamen nor merchants. Eminent among these was Sir George Carey, who as captain-general of the Isle of Wight, vice-admiral of Hampshire, brother-in-law of Charles Howard and kinsman of Queen Elizabeth, exerted enormous influence in the Solent area from 1582, when he took up his post at Carisbrooke Castle. He was of course responsible for the defence of the area in any case, but as a champion of the war party he made himself also

[1] Corbett, *Spanish War*, pp. xvii-l, 97-299; H.C.A. 25/2 (5), 13 March 1586/7.

the moving spirit of its offensive operations, which consisted mainly of privateering expeditions. From the very beginning in June 1585 he was agog for action, writing to Walsingham, 'If only there be a secret sufferance of her Majesty's subjects to take some revenge upon the king and his, then will I make suit by you and other my good friends to be admitted amongst the number of such adventurers as either will lose part of what they have or get more from the King of Spain. In the meantime if I may have your word, it shall be warrant sufficient for me to prepare what by myself or friends I may against him.' What friends? The very next sentence, pleading for Flud the pirate to be allowed to go to sea, leaves us in no doubt.[1]

And Carey's deeds were as good as his words. Two small ships of his—probably the *Muscat* and the *Marlyn*—took what is said to have been the first prize of the war. William Monson, who sailed in this venture, described the bloody fight: 'In the month of September 1585, and about eight a-clock in the evening, being upon the coast of Spain with two small ships aforesaid, we met and boarded a Spanish vessel of three hundred tons burden, well manned and armed. All our men with one consent entered her, and were left fighting aboard her all night, the seas being so grown that our barks were forced to ungrapple and fall off. The Spaniards betook themselves to their close fights, and gave two attempts by trains of powder to blow up their decks on which we were, but we happily prevented it by fire-pikes. Thus continued the fight till seven in the morning, when the Spaniards found the death and spoil of their men to be so great as they were forced to yield. When we came to take a view of our people we found few left alive but could shew a wound they received in that fight. The spectacle, as well of us as of the Spaniards, was woeful to behold; and I dare say that in the whole time of the war there was not so rare a manner of fight, or so great a spoil of so few men on both sides.'[2] But if it was difficult in the taking, this Biscayner, with her cargo of Newfoundland fish, was even more troublesome to dispose of. For she was claimed by Stephen Damaskette and others, Frenchmen, who took the case to the Admiralty Court. Carey, who was never diffident about using his influence, wrote more than once to Dr Caesar about the matter, referring to Caesar's 'friendly favouring of my rightful cause, for which your courtesy assure yourself I will not be unthankful'. He went on to complain pitifully of his lot,

[1] S.P. Dom. Eliz., clxxix, f. 84. [2] *Monson's Tracts*, III, 43–4; V, 174.

hoping presumably to excite the judge's sympathy as well as his cupidity: 'My unhappy ships are returned of their second setting forth without returning to me the value of £10. The cause was the bad dealing of the masters and company who in nothing followed my direction, so that I protest unto you since my first embarking into these sea causes I have disbursed about 1200 pounds and never received 10 in return, for my Spanish prize was reported to have in fish accompting the ship to the value of £960, whereas-from I sent my Lord Admiral £100, paid to the mariners their shares £300, and only had for all the fish, of Mr Eaton, £300. . . . The ship I only have towards all my charges, which I esteem not at £200, and that the French would by cunning draw from me.'[1]

But Carey was already at loggerheads with the French over the matter of a cargo of linen cloth that had been captured by Captain John Clarke, sailing in Raleigh's *Roebuck* early in 1585. Clarke had evidently handed over the prize to the pirate John Challice, who had rendered up the vessel itself to its French owners, but distributed its cargo to a most interesting set of buyers. Some of course was taken ashore at Weymouth for Raleigh's use, but the rest seems to have been handled by Sir George Carey, his steward George Bland and his agent George Somers, with the willing collaboration of Thomas Heaton, customer of Southampton, and John Young, customer of Chichester. What is more, the customer of London, Thomas Smythe, was one of the buyers. He sent his man Martin Parker down to Southampton and over to Carisbrooke Castle, and Parker himself admitted having paid Carey £238 and Young £30 for nine and a half packs of linen cloth. Parker was even alleged to have told Challice 'that he retained to master customer Smith of London and dwelled at the sign of the three doves in Newgate market, and desired him that if he came on the coast with any good prizes, to send him word, and he would repair unto him and bring ready gold and pay him on the hatches for whatsoever he dealt, for that as he said he did it for his master'.[2] These scandalous proceedings, which included smuggling done by and for customs officers, were all revealed when certain French merchants laid claim in the Admiralty Court to the goods so dis-

---

[1] Lansdowne, MS 158, f. 56. For the Damaskette case see Additional MS 11405; Lansdowne MS 158, ff. 54, 62; Lansdowne MS 143, f. 406; H.C.A. 13/25, 17 Dec. 1585.

[2] *Roanoke Voyages*, pp. 153–5. See also H.C.A. 13/26, 15, 22 June 1586, 7, 21 July, 1586.

posed. What the poor Frenchmen presumably did not realise was that one whom they might have supposed beyond reproach— Caesar himself—had already been bribed by Challice on Carey's advice. Carey's letter to Caesar about this is amazingly frank. 'Sir, after my hearty commendations. Whereas I am informed that one Martin Parker is entered into great trouble for buying certain cloth in this island, by the means of a bankrupt vermin and a caterpillar named Fewilliams, in respect it is a matter wherewith I was partly acquainted, and that the concealment of my knowledge therein may breed question of my good or bad dealing, I have thought good hereby to impart unto you the whole state of the cause, that you may answer in my behalf and some ways relieve the poor man.' There follows a wholly unconvincing account of how it came about that he had allowed the goods to pass from Challice to Parker. But the sting is in the tail : 'You may remember that I wrote upon Challice's first offer of his service to me, that I had persuaded him, for your hereafter good friendship to him, to present you with two packs of cloth, which he yielded unto, but after occasion to spend more money than he expected, would have deferred the presenting of them to you until his return, which I would not permit, as having advertised you thereof before, but he desired you would be content with £50, which you were to receive of the money paid by Parker to my own use. Declaro I protest I shall not receive 10s, but let not that knave Fitzwilliams cosen you and discredit me.'[1]

All this happened in 1585, though the court proceedings in both cases took place mainly in 1586. At this time Carey's attention was still probably focused on the Channel and the waters southward to the Spanish coast. In 1587, however, he launched out in another direction, setting forth the first of three or possibly four western ventures. For this enterprise he fitted out three ships— the *Commander*, the *Swallow* and the *Gabriel*—the first of these being that same Biscayner which had caused him so much trouble and which he had grossly under-valued in his letter to the judge. Monson says that she was reckoned the best ship of war we had—a devious sort of boast on his part, since he had been present at her capture. One of Carey's retainers, William Irish, led the expedition, which visited the West Indies and Virginia. In 1588 Carey may have contributed a ship to John Watts' West Indies venture, and in 1590 he sent Irish again to the Caribbean.

[1] Lansdowne MS 158, f. 62 (10 Oct. 1585).

In both cases there may well have been the intention of visiting Raleigh's colony, and these two voyages, along with the first, are therefore described in another chapter herein. What was evidently Sir George's last important project in privateering was his 1591 venture of three ships, again under Irish, and this also is described elsewhere in connection with West Indian voyages.

After this Carey's name continues to crop up in connection with occasional ventures—for example his *Desire* was at sea under William Irish in 1596, the year Carey succeeded to a peerage as Lord Hunsdon, but from this date no more is heard of such pursuits. Perhaps he felt it was time to settle down now that he had reached fifty. Nevertheless he will be remembered for his younger days as a crude, war-mongering magnate 'longing', as he put it himself, 'to understand what course is intended to be taken against Spain'.[1] And in the Isle of Wight it was remembered for some time that 'an attorney coming to settle in the island was, by his command, with a pound of candles hanging at his breech lighted, with bells about his legs, hunted owte of the island'.[2]

Sir Walter Raleigh, Carew Raleigh and Adrian and Sir John Gilbert were interested in privateering in the same kind of way, being closely concerned with many ventures, though no seamen themselves. Their voyages, and those of Grenville, who falls in the same category, are to be dealt with later. Admiralty officials were often active participators. In an age when the country gentry administered agrarian policy and the merchants managed the customs system, it was perhaps only to be expected that the administrators of the business of reprisal should themselves be engaged in it. Thus Stephen Ridlesden, who transacted much admiralty business directly for the Lord Admiral, was an adventurer in several expeditions. Some were merchants as well as officials—James Bagg of Weymouth, for example, who was mayor of Plymouth in 1595 and 1603, and whose son by his corrupt handling of naval business won the nickname 'Bottomless Bagg'. But his privateering investments, which included a share in the *Conclude* of Plymouth, were not so extensive as those of Robert Bragg, London merchant, servant of the Lord Admiral and collector of the latter's tenths in Devon and Cornwall. Among other ventures, Bragg backed two West Indian expeditions and

[1] Lansdowne MS 158, f. 66.
[2] *D.N.B.*, art. 'Carey'. The quotation is from Sir John Oglander. Cp. Francis Bamford (ed.), *A Royalist's Notebook*, p. 14.

played an important part in the post-war attempts to establish trade in the Caribbean.[1]

All these we have called professionals clearly played a vital part in privateering. In one way or another they all had the advantage of being on the inside of the business of maritime warfare. But at every level they owed much to merchants. Some made their way in the service of merchants, many depended on merchants for financial backing, and some of the most typical professional seamen either married into merchant families or were themselves merchants—Fenners, Hawkinses, Braggs and Winters.

---

[1] Ridlesden: H.C.A. 13/31, 25 Nov. 1594; *E.P.V.*, pp. 130, 326. Bagg: *Roanoke Voyages*, pp. 67, 624, etc., and Oppenheim, *Administration*, p. 232. Bragg: *E.P.V.*, p. 326 and below, pp. 184–5; *Roanoke Voyages*, pp. 237–8; H.C.A. 14/33, nos. 38, 39, 229; H.C.A. 13/33, 15 Feb. 1598/9; H.C.A. 13/27, 2 Dec. 1588; H.C.A. 14/35, no. 97.

Chapter 6

THE GREAT MERCHANTS

Of all the social groups financially interested in privateering the merchants were by far the most important, and among the merchants a comparatively small body of magnates, mainly Londoners, dominated the field. The participation of these great merchants in the business took a variety of forms.

Its most profitable form was the direct combination of trade and plunder in the same voyage. A famous instance of this, recounted in Hakluyt's pages, occurred in 1592. Captain Thomas White was returning from a trading voyage to Barbary in the *Amity* of London when he sighted two large Spanish ships. A considerable battle ensued, but in the end the Spaniards submitted and White brought up the Thames his two prizes, laden with 1,400 chests of quicksilver, a great quantity of Papal bulls and gilded missals and a hundred tons of 'excellent wines'. White estimated that the repercussions of this capture would lose the king of Spain £707,700, but perhaps more to the point was the value of the prize-goods to the captors, which amounted to something over £20,000. This would be shared equally, at least in theory, between the owners, the freighters and the crew, as the custom was in such cases. The sailors, who received their normal wages, thus obtained a substantial bonus, while the merchants reaped in effect a superprofit.[1]

The *Amity* was a merchantman of a hundred tons burden, but exceptionally powerful for a ship of her size. The Hakluyt narrative shows her to have carried a complement of forty-two men and

[1] *Principal Navigations*, VII, 103–5. Lansdowne MS 70, ff. 51–2 gives another account of the capture and a valuation of the quicksilver—100 tons at 2s. a pound, totalling £20,000. Normally quicksilver would sell at 3s. a pound, but it was expected that this cargo would produce a glut, since 'there cannot be uttered in the realm in one year one hundred kintalls, which cometh to five tons'. An inventory of the rest of the cargo is given in Lansdowne MS 70, f. 231. The Admiralty Court appraisement (H.C.A. 24/59, no. 67) estimated the total cargo at the ridiculous figure of £4093 6s. 9d. See also H.C.A. 24/59, no. 57; H.C.A. 13/30, 17–18 Jan. 1592/3, 3 Feb. 1592/3.

a boy—twice that required for a peacetime voyage—and to have wielded a devastating broadside. She was employed chiefly in the Barbary trade by four members of the London Grocers' Company—Henry Colthurst, Simon Lawrence, Oliver Stile and Nicholas Stile. These four, who were connected by marriage, worked regularly in partnership and were generally known as Henry Colthurst and Company. They seem to have come together about 1574 and to have remained in association for twenty years, trading to Morocco primarily, but also to Marseilles, Italy, the Levant and Spain. They were wealthy and important members of the London merchant community, belonging to the Levant as well as the Barbary Company. Lawrence died in 1594 and Colthurst in the following year, but the Stiles went on to become members of the East India Company and served in the government of the City, Oliver as sheriff in 1605, Nicholas as an alderman. All four left considerable property.[1]

In 1585 they sued in the Admiralty Court for losses sustained in Spain and were issued with letters of reprisal for the *Amity*, armed with thirteen guns and forty men and victualled for six months. Other ships of theirs were also taking prizes up to 1594, when the partnership was disrupted by the death of Lawrence. The 90-ton *Dolphin*, for example, arrived at Safi in Morocco in 1586 under Master John Giles. After he had unloaded his cargo, Giles followed a Spanish caravel out of the port and captured it. The Spanish crew escaped ashore and complained to Muley Ahmed, the king of Morocco, and as a result Giles, who refused to restore the prize, was imprisoned, while the *Dolphin*'s cargo was confiscated. Later the legality of the prize was admitted, the English goods were returned to their owners and Giles was released. The *Dolphin* sailed with the *Amity* in 1589 and they brought home two good prizes. She met her doom two years later in the Straits of Gibraltar, coming home from Marseilles under the wing of a powerful Levant Company ship, the *Centurion*. Assailed by five Spanish galleys, the *Centurion*, though undermanned, fought them off; but the *Dolphin*'s powder magazine was hit and she went down with all hands. The same owners' *Eagle*, *Passport* and *Lark* were making successful voyages in the same period, trading to the Mediterranean or Morocco and bringing home prizes.[2]

[1] Willan, *Studies*, pp. 205-10.
[2] Reprisal suit: Marsden, *Law and Custom*, I, 248-9; H.C.A. 25/1 (4), 8, 31 Jan. 1585/6; Lansdowne MS 135, f. 38; Lansdowne MS 144, ff. 353-61; H.C.A.

Here we have a special form of privateering. A merchantman
would make a trading voyage and try to pick up a prize in the
course of it. We know that some masters were instructed to spend
a certain time looking for prizes. For example, in 1598 Oliver and
Nicholas Stile combined with Thomas White (hero of the *Amity*'s
1592 voyage) and Lady Margaret Hawkins to set forth the
200-ton *Amity* (built in 1593) and the *Concord*, both of London.
The owners instructed the masters to spend three months off
the coast of Spain taking prizes, and then to go on to Barbary and
carry out their trading mission.[1] Christopher Newport in his early
days once took a ship with freight to Barbary and thence made
across the Atlantic to plunder the West Indies, but this was
unusual. The best opportunities for this kind of venture were to be
had in the normal course of the Mediterranean and West African
trades, since the routes of the English traders lay right across the
main Spanish and Portuguese shipping lanes. For this very
reason the English vessels needed in any case to be well armed and
manned, and it took little more in the way of guns and men to
make them formidable privateers. For a mere 100-ton merchantman the *Amity* may have been unusually strong, but she was
probably of average size and strength for a Barbary trader. Such
ventures were more common in the Barbary trade than in any
other. Among the members of the company Anthony Dassell,
Thomas Bramley, John Newton and Roger Ofield combined
trade and plunder in this fashion.[2]

13/26, 19 Jan. 1586/7. The *Dolphin* in 1586: Willan, *Studies*, pp. 227-9 and Lansdowne MS 144, f. 321. The *Centurion* incident: *Principal Navigations*, VII, 35-8.
For other voyages of the Colthurst ships see appendix.

[1] H.C.A. 13/33, 17 Jan. 1598/9.

[2] Dassell was interested in the voyages of the *Messenger* and the *Nightingale*
[*Principal Navigations*, VII, 90-102; Lansdowne MS 142, f. 109 (five entries);
H.C.A. 25/3 (9), 25 Sept. 1591]. Bramley, beginning with Spanish trade,
developed interests in Eastland, Brazil, Barbary and eventually East Indies trades
(Willan, *Studies*, pp. 292-5); with Ofield owned the *Samaritan*, which combined
Barbary trade and plunder in her 1590 voyage [Lansdowne MS 133, f. 24; H.C.A.
24/58, no. 73; H.C.A. 13/28, 11 Aug. 1590, 10, 12 Nov. 1590; H.C.A.
25/3 (9), 2 March 1590/1]; obtained letters of reprisal for the *Blessing of God* and the
Roebuck in 1592 [H.C.A. 25/3 (9), 22 Dec. 1591, 22 Jan. 1591/2]. Newton traded
to Spain, to the Mediterranean, Guinea and Morocco (Willan, *Studies*, p. 216 and
Principal Navigations, VI, 73); he was financially interested in the ventures of the
Minion [H.C.A. 25/1 (4), 24 Jan. 1585/6, 4 Feb. 1585/6], the *Prudence* (*E.P.V.*,
pp. 95-172) and the *Julian* (H.C.A. 24/62, no. 68; H.C.A. 13/102, 2 April
1595, 25 June 1595, 24 Jan. 1595/6, 11, 13 April 1598; H.C.A. 13/31, 11 June

Dassell was also a member of the Senegal and Gambia Company, and obtained letters of reprisal for his ships regularly from 1587 to 1593. Newton organised voyages to the Guinea coast in partnership with John Bird, and a prize was taken in at least one of these ventures. Richard Dodderidge of Barnstaple, another member of the Senegal and Gambia Company, had ships out on reprisal from the beginning of the war; his *Prudence* (110 tons and eighty men) took a prize of gold and ivory on the West African coast in 1590 said to be worth £16,000; the following year it returned two more prizes; and in 1592 it brought into Barnstaple another ten thousand pounds worth of prize-goods. The *Prudence* was obviously trading to West Africa in 1590, and probably in the other years as well. In this trade clashes with the Portuguese were inevitable, on land and sea alike, and the London and Devon men of the eighties and nineties were simply carrying on the tradition of Hawkins and Fenner.[1]

1594). In 1599 he was trading to the Canaries (H.C.A. 13/34, 11 Dec. 1599) and in 1601 to Portugal (H.C.A. 13/35, 12, 13 May 1601). He is described as John Bird's 'brother' in Lansdowne MS 157, f. 324. For their Guinea voyages see *Principal Navigations*, VI, 450–61. Jointly they set forth the *Bark Burr* in 1585–6 [H.C.A. 25/1 (4), 3, 16 Nov. 1585; H.C.A. 13/26, 3 May 1586; H.C.A. 25/2 (5), 1 Oct. 1586]; the *Golden Noble* and the *Moonshine* in 1586–7 (Harleian MS 598, f. 1; Lansdowne MSS 144, f. 442; 145, ff. 171, 324; 157, f. 320; H.C.A. 24/57, nos. 65, 87, 153–4; H.C.A. 13/26, 26 April 1588; H.C.A. 13/28, 12 Dec. 1589, 14 Sept. 1590; *Principal Navigations*, VI, 35–8; H.C.A. 13/27, 9 June 1589). The *Golden Noble* served against the Armada and in the Portugal expedition, was freighted for a Barbary voyage in 1590 and went with Cumberland's ships in 1591 (Laughton, *Defeat*, II, 326; *Monson's Tracts*, I, 183, 271; A.P.C., XX, 164). The *Moonshine* served against the Armada (Laughton, *Defeat*, II, 327) and was privateering in 1590 (H.C.A. 24/57, no. 5; Harleian MS 598, f. 6; Lansdowne MS 133, f. 24), 1591 (H.C.A. 24/58, nos. 14, 41; H.C.A. 13/29, 9 March 1590/1, 17, 20 April 1591; H.C.A. 14/27, no. 62; Lansdowne MSS 133, f. 24; 148, ff. 197, 199; 67, f. 90; H.C.A. 13/28, 13, 16 Feb. 1590/1; A.P.C., XXI, 376; *Monson's Tracts*, I, 262, 271) and 1592 (E.P.V., pp. 175–6, 180). Bird, who traded with Spain, Barbary, Guinea and Brazil, also collaborated with Watts in the early years of the war (*Principal Navigations*, XI, 26; H.C.A. 13/28, 21 July 1590; and below, pp. 105–6). Ofield was prominent in the Barbary trade and became a member of the Levant and East India Companies. He was a sugar refiner (Willan, *Studies*, pp. 194–6). He shared ownership of the *Samaritan* with Bramley (see above) and was interested in various other trade-cum-privateering ventures [H.C.A. 13/30, 24 Nov. 1592, 3 Feb. 1592/3; H.C.A. 24/62, no. 57; H.C.A. 25/3 (9), 5 April 1592].

[1] *Principal Navigations*, VI, 443; J. B. Gribble, *Memorials of Barnstaple*, pp. 438–9; H.C.A. 14/27, no. 26; H.C.A. 24/58, no. 26; H.C.A. 13/96, 11 Aug. 1591; H.C.A. 25/3 (9), 14, 15 July 1592; H.C.A. 13/30, 10 June 1592.

Several of the Barbary merchants were members of the Levant
Company—the Colthurst group, Roger Ofield, John Newton,
Richard Staper and Edward Holmeden. The last two were
interested mainly in Mediterranean trade. Neither of them, however, played a large part in the business of reprisal, and this is significant. The Levant Company men did not take to privateering
in the same way as the Barbary and West Africa merchants.
Their ships did return from trading voyages with prizes quite
often, but there is no evidence that they actually spent time looking
for spoil. When a ship was freighted with a valuable cargo from
the Levant, the owners of the goods might well grudge the
risk involved and time wasted in such diversions. In one case
merchants sued for damages caused 'by the long detaining of their
goods about reprisal causes'.[1] Moreover the Levant Company
was particularly sensitive to disturbance 'within the Straits',
which often led to trouble with neutrals and the confiscation of
English goods by way of reprisal. Many captures were made in the
Mediterranean, particularly towards the end of the war, but the
Levant Company was not to blame; its governor roundly condemned 'the outrages, rapines and robberies of our English men of
war'.[2] Nevertheless Levant Company members were among the
greatest promoters of privateering of a different kind.

Some of the Levant merchants went in for reprisal on such a
scale that it became for them a major interest alongside their normal trading activities. At least one, John Watts, made it his chief
business. His privateering ventures were so numerous and so
successful that shortly after the war he was described as 'the
greatest pirate that has ever been in this kingdom'.[3] The comment
was in a sense unjust, for Watts was no pirate; but he was perhaps
the greatest privateering promoter of his time.

John Watts was the son of Thomas Watts of Buntingford,
Hertfordshire, and was born about 1550. He was still in his teens

[1] H.C.A. 24/66, no. 191/2.
[2] Stevens, *Dawn*, p. 280. Freelance traders in the Mediterranean were less in-
hibited, so that even here the combination of trade and plunder was more usual
than unadulterated plunder, as Alberto Tenenti points out in his admirable study,
Naufrages, Corsaires et Assurances maritimes à Venise, 1592–1609 (1959), p. 39. For
English piracy in the Mediterranean Tenenti's work should be collated with E. P.
Cheyney, *A History of England from the Defeat of the Armada to the Death of Queen
Elizabeth*.
[3] Brown, *Genesis*, I, 99.

when he married Margaret, daughter of the leading London clothworker, James Hawes, who became Lord Mayor in 1574-5. Watts himself was admitted to the Clothworkers' Guild and went into business with his father-in-law and brother-in-law, John Hawes. All this suggests that Watts may well have been apprenticed to James Hawes in the first place. In any case the marriage was a most advantageous one, since it brought Watts directly into the ranks of the merchant aristocracy. Another of Hawes' daughters married Robert Lee, a future Lord Mayor, and yet another married Thomas Wilford, Chamberlain of the City.[1]

Like most young merchants Watts gained his knowledge and experience of trade as a factor. As early as 1572 he was to be found in Cadiz, and in the seventies and early eighties Spain seems to have been his main sphere of interest. He and Sir James and John Hawes were assistants of the Spanish Company at its foundation in 1577.[2]

Although a member of the Clothworkers' Company, Watts was no more tied to the business of his guild than were any of the great trading capitalists of the time. By 1585 he was trading direct to the Azores and the Canaries as well as to Spain. Thus, like the Dutch merchants, he was finding in Spain the gateway to Atlantic trade. Then suddenly crisis supervened and Watts was one of the chief losers by the Spanish confiscations of 1585. He appears to have had an interest in five of the ships arrested, and when he and his associates sued for letters of reprisal they put their losses at £15,000.[3]

Watts' career as a privateering promoter began at once. In the first two years of the war his chief partner was John Bird, since he and Watts together owned the *Emmanuel*, one of the confiscated ships. Bird was an important shipowner, who with John Newton of the Barbary Company had acquired the ships of Olyff Burr, including the powerful *Bark Burr* and *Golden Noble*. Bird thus brought in Newton as a partner, while Watts on his side was associated with John Stokes, part-owner of the *Little John*. All these ships were now sent out on reprisal, together with the *Bear*

---

[1] Harleian MS 1546, f. 108; A. B. Beaven, *The Aldermen of the City of London*, II, 45, 175.

[2] H.C.A. 13/19, 1 March 1572-3; V. M. Shillington and A. B. W. Chapman, *The Commercial Relations of England and Portugal*, appendix.

[3] H.C.A. 13/24, 2 Feb. 1579/80, 4 March 1582/3; H.C.A. 13/25, 30 March 1584, 5 June 1584, 26 Aug. 1585, 4, 9 Sept. 1585; Landsowne MS 115, f. 196.

and the *Anne Gallant*.[1] However, the connection with Bird did not last long. In 1587 Watts played a major part in setting forth the Cadiz expedition, being the owner of the *Margaret and John* (200 tons), the *Little John* (100 tons) and the *Drake* (80 tons); his pinnace the *Examiner* probably sailed in this venture too. The *Drake* and the *Examiner* remained off the Spanish coast after Drake's departure, and in company with Thomas Cordell's *George Bona-venture* and John Ridlesden's *Prudence*, they took several valuable prizes.[2] What with the profit on these and his share in the *San Felipe*, as well as earlier prizes, Watts had probably recouped his losses by the year of the Armada.

In that year Watts sailed the Channel in his own *Margaret and John*, and it was characteristic that he should be first in the race for the great galleasse the *San Lorenzo* when she lay stranded on the Calais beach. The fight for her possession was perhaps the hottest single engagement in the protracted Armada struggle, and Watts was in the thick of it. Lieutenant Tomson's account of the fighting, which Watts himself delivered to Walsingham, refers to him as being 'present at the doing of most of these things happened within these two days, not without danger enough of his person both of cannon and musket shot, whereof his apparel beareth some tokens, although it pleased God to spare his life'.[3]

But while Watts was fighting in the Channel his lieutenants were making the first of a long series of West Indies ventures. The *Examiner*, with his brother Thomas in command, went out in company with the *Drake* and two other ships in 1588. The *Harry and John* (160 tons, belonging to Henry Cletherow and Watts), the *Little John* and the *John Evangelist* made an important and rewarding voyage to the Caribbean and Virginia in 1590. The *Harry and John*, the *Little John*, the *Centaur* (140 tons) and the *Pegasus* (120 tons), these last two being also Watts' ships, scored a tremendous success in 1591. Three of Watts' men were off Havana again in 1592—probably the *Centaur*, the *Affection* (120 tons) and the *Little John*. The *Centaur*, the *Affection* and the *Jewel*

---

[1] H.C.A. 25/1 (4), 15 July 1585; H.C.A. 25/2 (5), 19 Aug. 1586, 20 Sept. 1586, 1 Oct. 1586; Lansdowne MS 145, f. 171; H.C.A. 13/25, 12–27 Jan. 1585/6, 24–26 Feb. 1585/6, 18 March 1585/6.

[2] H.C.A. 25/2 (5), 13 March 1586/7; Lansdowne MS 143, ff. 6–46; H.C.A. 13/26, 5, 11 and 31 Jan. 1587/8; H.C.A. 13/27, 7 Feb. 1588/9; H.C.A. 24/56 no. 45.

[3] Laughton, *Defeat*, I, 350.

(130 tons) all took valuable prizes in the West Indies in 1594.[1] In 1596–7 the *Centaur*, the *Pegasus* and the *Affection* were in consortship with three other vessels raiding the pearl fisheries near Rio de la Hacha.[2] In 1598 Watts was one of the main backers of Cumberland's Puerto Rico expedition, contributing by way of ships the *Alcedo* (400 tons), the *Consent* (350 tons), the *Galleon Constant*, the *Affection*, the *Pegasus* and the *Margaret and John*.[3] Meanwhile other hunting-grounds were not neglected. There is no point in attempting to list all the ventures, but it is worth noting that the *Alcedo* and the *Margaret and John* had their share of the riches of the *Madre de Dios*[4] and that Watts was one of the chief promoters of Lancaster's raid on Pernambuco in 1595.[5] Nor did his efforts slacken towards the end of the war. After 1598 the *Centaur*, the *Affection*, the *Alcedo*, the *Examiner*, the *Jewel* and the *Sonne* were still taking prizes. In nearly all these expeditions Watts was the major promoter, though there would often be one or two other shareholders of some importance, such as Henry Cletherow and John Stokes, each of whom shared the ownership of one of the vessels mentioned above. But he was not closely or permanently associated with other merchants in the business of privateering. His associates were his captains—his eldest son, John, who sailed with Lancaster in 1595 and was general of the fleet on the Spanish Main the next year and commanded the *Malice Scourge* in Cumberland's great venture; William Lane of the Clothworkers' Guild, who led Watts' men to success in 1591; and young protégés from his own household like William Craston and Stephen Michell, both commanders in the 1591 expedition. The only important Londoner to be allied with Watts in several major enterprises was Paul Bayning, whose niece married Watts' eldest son John, Bayning's godson. Nor did Watts often put money into other people's ventures—his £400 investment in Chidley's South Sea expedition is the only known case of this apart from the joint enterprises already mentioned.

Nevertheless even John Watts did not put all his eggs in one basket. The *Margaret and John* was trading within the Straits in 1590, and Watts was admitted a member of the Levant Company

[1] *E.P.V.*, pp. 40–9, 95–172, 211, 284–307; *Roanoke Voyages*, pp. 579–716.
[2] See below, p. 176. [3] See above, pp. 76–8.
[4] Lansdowne MS 73, ff. 38, 40. They were with Frobisher's squadron and therefore took no part in the carrack action, but as consorts shared in the proceeds.
[5] See below, pp. 210–12.

in 1592. In 1595 the *Jewel* was expected home from a Mediterranean trading voyage.[1] Watts was not one of the leaders of the Levant Company and during the war trade seems to have taken second place to plunder in his business operations, but his fundamental interest was still trade. The goods he acquired by privateering were very often the sort of goods he had been importing before the war; the ships he had built since 1585—the *Alcedo* and the *Consent*, for example, both built in 1595—were as suitable for long-distance trades as for war; and for a certain kind of oceanic voyaging Watts and his men had developed an unrivalled experience. It is surprising, therefore, that Watts was not elected to be one of the original 'committies' of the East India Company; his name does not even appear in the first list of subscribers. As an alderman since 1594, he was presumably a respected citizen, and we can only surmise some special reason for his non-participation. But the omission was soon remedied. After the election of the full twenty-four committies in October 1600, Watts' name was added to the list, and a little later it was 'agreed by this assembly, in respect of the great experience of Mr Alderman Watts in shipping and other directions in voyages, there may be great use of the opinion of Mr Alderman Watts in the further proceeding of this voyage. That . . . the said Mr Alderman shall be warned to all meetings and to be used as a committy in all things concerning the business'. And the following year, when Sir Thomas Smythe was imprisoned on suspicion of being one of Essex's supporters, Watts was elected governor of the East India Company in his place.[2]

With the accession of James came a knighthood, and in 1606–7 he was Lord Mayor of London. On 12 June 1607 he entertained the king at his own house adjoining Clothworkers' Hall in Mincing Lane, and James was made a free brother of the Clothworkers.[3] Thus Watts was the recognised leader of the London merchant community at the very moment when the first permanent footing was established in North America, and he played an active part in promoting the new colony. Watts had joined with Raleigh in the attempt to salvage the earlier colony in 1590, and there may have been a similar intention in their privateering

---

[1] *Principal Navigations*, VII, 31–5; M. Epstein, *The Early History of the English Levant Company*, appendix V.
[2] Stevens, *Dawn*, pp. 63, 67, 166.
[3] Cockayne, *Lord Mayors and Sheriffs*, p. 29; Thomas Girtin, *The Golden Ram: A Narrative History of the Clothworkers' Company, 1528–1958*, p. 73.

partnership of 1591. Now, while this work was resumed, Watts' son was among those who followed up Raleigh's other great empire-building project in Guiana. In 1610 his ship, the *John* of London, was trading for tobacco in the Orinoco under Captain John Moore, and it was said that England imported at least £60,000 worth of tobacco that year.[1] These were no great and gallant deeds; Watts was merely one of the great merchants who were now developing English interests in the East Indies, Virginia and Guiana. Many of the others had gone in for privateering during the war, but Watts, who made his fortune that way, seems to personify the contribution of privateering to the expansion of English commerce.

He died in 1616, a rich man and, as John Chamberlain, his neighbour at Ware, reported, 'as lusty a man of his years as I know any'. He left to his eldest son his manor of Mardocks, Hertfordshire, as well as other lands in Hertfordshire, Essex and Norfolk, his London house and adjoining shop, his jewels, plate and chains of gold and his ship the *Centaur*. Four other sons obtained lands and sums of money from £100 upwards, and his one unmarried daughter received £800 for dowry. There were various other small legacies and the usual charitable bequests.[2]

Alderman Paul Bayning's career was in many respects comparable. He was born about 1545, and in 1572 was one of a group of factors who went out in the *Primrose* of London to sell cloth and other goods to the Portuguese at Vianna and Caminha. They were probably attempting to smuggle goods into Spain as well, and for their pains were captured by two pinnaces from Vigo and subjected to some harsh treatment by the Spaniards for contravening the trade embargo then in force. On this occasion Bayning evidently had instructions to go on to San Lúcar and arrange for the lading of a cargo of oils into another ship. Bayning was one of the leading participators in the boom which followed the official resumption of normal trade with Spain and Portugal. His brother Andrew and Robert Flick, a fellow member of the Grocers' Company, were active on his behalf in the Iberian ports. At the same time Bayning took the lead in developing trade with Venice—he was one of the four Venice merchants mentioned by name when

[1] H.C.A. 13/143; C. A. Harris (ed.), *A Relation of a Voyage to Guiana by Robert Harcourt* (Hakluyt Society, 2nd Ser., LX), 1928.
[2] P.C.C. 129 Cope.

the Turkey Company merged with them to form the Levant Company.[1]

When the confiscations occurred in 1585, Bayning and a partner Robert Barker together sued for losses to the extent of £37,422. But no immediate action seems to have followed the grant of letters of reprisal, and Bayning's first known venture into privateering was his contribution to the Cadiz expedition of 1587, in which his *Susan* (260 tons) was commanded by James Lancaster. This ship was probably used in Chidley's 1589 venture, under the name of the *Wildman*, and Bayning also supplied Chidley with the *Susan's Handmaid*, which was renamed the *Wildman's Club*. Like many shipowners, Bayning named more than one of his ships after his wife, and in 1592 the *Great Susan* made her appearance, equipped with letters of reprisal. She is known to have taken prizes in 1594 and 1598.[1] Bayning played a great part in setting forth Lancaster's Pernambuco expedition in 1595 and Cumberland's Puerto Rico voyage in 1598. Having begun West Indies privateering at this late stage, he continued with the *Golden Phoenix*, which sent and brought home hides, campeche wood, pearls, gold and silver in 1599 and 1600. The *Phoenix* sailed again to the Caribbean in 1602–3, in company with the *Neptune* and the *Archangel*, and Bayning thus shared in the rich spoils of Newport's last privateering cruise.[2]

Bayning played a particularly important part in the foundation of the East India Company. He was elected treasurer as soon as the company got down to the serious business of organising a voyage, and the small working committee of seven which was set up in October 1600 was appointed to meet in his house. One of the four ships on the first voyage was called the *Susan*.[3] He died in the same year as Watts, in 1616, and appears by his will to have been an even richer man. To his wife Susanna he left £300 a year to be paid as a rent charge out of his lands in Essex. To his brother Robert he left certain lands in Suffolk, the remainder of the real property going to his son Sir Paul, later Viscount Bayning.

---

[1] Willan, *Studies*, pp. 26, 32; H.C.A. 13/26, 3–7 March 1586/7, 30 June 1586; Lansdowne MS 135, f. 33; *Principal Navigations*, v, 192–202; S.P. Dom. Eliz., ccxxxix, f. 80.

[2] H.C.A. 25/2 (5) 13 March 1586/7; above, p. 67; H.C.A. 25/3 (9), 21 Sept. 1592; H.C.A. 24/62, no. 41; H.C.A. 13/33, 28 March 1598; above, p. 77; and below, pp. 178, 180–1.

[3] Stevens, *Dawn*, pp. 40, 100.

The charitable bequests were generous. A characteristic clause bequeathed £10 to Mr John Simpson, minister of St Olave's parish in Hart Street, five pounds of which were to be 'for the instructing of Anthony my negro in the principles of the Christian faith and religion when he shall be fit to be baptised'.[1]

Thomas Cordell, another alderman and a member of the Mercers' Company, had the same sort of interests as Watts and Bayning. He and his partner William Garraway claimed losses in Spain in 1585 to the value of £9,058, and Cordell had also been trading in Morocco in the sixties. Along with Bayning he played a leading part in the Venice Company and was admitted to the Levant Company on its formation. He was a sugar dealer and ran a refining business. He was the chief owner of some of the biggest ships trading to the Mediterranean—the *Merchant Royal* (350 tons), the *Edward Bonaventure* (250 tons), the *George Bonaventure* (200 tons), the *Centurion* (250 tons) and the *Royal Exchange*. During the war these ships were employed frequently in privateering, particularly the first two mentioned, which were sent with Raymond and Lancaster to the East Indies in 1591. Like Bayning and Watts, Cordell had a large interest in Drake's Cadiz expedition and in Cumberland's Puerto Rico voyage. He became a 'committy' of the East India Company at its foundation.[2] Alderman John More of the Skinners' Company, a factor in Bilbao in 1582, a great promoter of West Indies ventures and a 'committy' of the East India Company in 1600, was a similar figure.[3]

These and other Levant Company men pursued their trade and privateering operations separately. When they sent their ships into the Mediterranean it was not for prizes, though the ships would often carry letters of reprisal. If a prize were taken, this would be an incidental windfall, whereas on the Morocco run privateering was a normal concomitant of trade. The Levant Company merchants, however, and especially the Venice traders and others who joined

[1] P.C.C. 99 Cope.

[2] A. B. Beaven, *The Aldermen of the City of London*, II, 45; Lansdowne MS 135, f. 33; Willan, *Studies*, pp. 131, 161, 218, 318; *Principal Navigations*, V, 192–202; S.P. Dom. Eliz., ccxxxix, f. 80; Cordell's activities are described more fully in ch. 10. For his interest in Cumberland's ventures, see pp. 76–7 above. He died in 1612 leaving very little property considering his eminence as a merchant pioneer (P.C.C. 32 Fenner).

[3] A. B. Beaven, II, 46; H.C.A. 13/27, 18 Oct. 1588; *E.P.V.*, pp. 98–9, 185, 209–10, 226, 298, 326. More was also interested in the expeditions to Pernambuco and Puerto Rico.

the Turkey men in 1592, took a more active part than the Barbary traders in unadulterated plunder ventures. Thus a Levant merchantman might often be found making a trading venture one year and a privateering cruise the next—anywhere but in the Mediterranean. But the Barbary and Levant merchants had much in common. The members of the two companies overlapped, and many of them had business in Spain and Portugal. Both companies were, in different senses, developments of the Iberian trade, and in either case the new development grew out of an interest in valuable imports such as Spain, Portugal and their colonies could provide. The Barbary and Levant men who took to privateering did so in the first place to redress wrongs and recoup losses incurred in Spain. But because of the nature of their trade, they not only had the powerful ships most suitable for privateering, but could also find in privateering an appropriate substitute for and supplement to their normal dealings. Inevitably their appetite grew with what it fed on, and privateering reinforced both their power and their ambition to penetrate the enemy's colonial trade. It is not suggested that all merchants with a considerable interest in privateering had been trading to Spain and Portugal before the war, nor even that all the members of the Spanish Company went in for privateering. It is very clear, however, that the Iberian traders formed the weightiest element in the mass of merchant privateering promoters.

Another instance of this is Sir Thomas Pullison. He was Lord Mayor when reprisals began, had been a leading member of the Spanish Company and claimed losses of £10,000. Together with Robert Cobb and Thomas Starkey, likewise sufferers from the confiscations, Pullison was very active in reprisals in the early years of the war. William Holliday, also associated with Cobb, was an equally busy promoter. These four do not seem to have constituted a company on the Colthurst model, for they often acted independently of each other, but all of them seem to have withdrawn from privateering in 1594 when Starkey died.[1] Henry

[1] For their Iberian interests and their losses in 1585, see Shillington and Chapman, *The Commercial Relations of England and Portugal*, pp. 141, 153 and appendix; Lansdowne MS 115, f. 196; Lansdowne MS 144, ff. 353–61; H.C.A. 13/25, 1 Dec. 1584; H.C.A. 13/26, 27 May 1586. On Starkey as a Barbary trader, see Willan, *Studies*, pp. 288–92. In 1586 Pullison, Starkey and Cobb set forth the *Samaritan* and the *Post* [25/1 (4) 19 Jan. 1585/6; 3 Feb. 1585/6]; in 1585 Cobb, Holliday and George Collimore set forth the *Prudence*, the *Golden Dragon*, the *Brave* and the *Seraphim* [25/1 (4), 23 June 1585, 15, 20, 27 July 1585]. Backed by Pulli-

Seckford was another member of the Spanish Company. His ships—the *Discharge*, the *Supply* and the *Return*—were on reprisal during the first seven years of the war, and he was one of the chief investors in Cavendish's ventures. He was also a groom of the royal chamber and keeper of the privy purse, but there is no evidence that he was acting on the queen's behalf in his capacity as a privateering promoter.[1] The list could be extended considerably: William Towerson, George Barnes and Richard Goddard were all powerful men in Iberian trade, in oceanic projects and in privateering. Robert Flick, Samuel Foxcroft and James Lancaster were factors and merchants in Spain and Portugal up to the outbreak of the war and after 1585 took command of merchantmen to raid enemy commerce; all three played a significant part in projects of colonial trade.[2]

The case of Sir Thomas Myddelton offers an interesting variation on the main theme.[3] He was the fourth son of Richard Myddelton, governor of Denbigh Castle, who had sixteen

son, Starkey and Cobb, the *Post* continued active until 1591 [H.C.A. 13/26, 13 May 1586; Harleian MS 598, f. 2; H.C.A. 25/2 (5), 22 Sept. 1586; H.C.A. 13/28, 28 Jan. 1590/1; H.C.A. 13/29, 14 Jan. 1591/2]. After 1591 the *Golden Dragon* sailed under Newport in expeditions financed by Cobb and a different group of partners—the West Indies expeditions of 1592 and 1593 (*E.P.V.*, pp. 184–208, 225–35). The *Margaret* and the *Prudence*, in which Cobb had the major interest, were in the West Indies together in 1591 and 1592 (*E.P.V.*, pp. 98–9, 184–208); the *Prudence* went again in 1593 (*E.P.V.*, pp. 225–35) and the *Margaret* was taking prizes in 1589 (Lansdowne MSS 144, f. 36, 133 f. 23; H.C.A. 14/26, no. 69; H.C.A. 24/57, nos. 58, 107). Holliday was owner or part-owner of the *Seadragon*, the *Salamander*, the *Tiger* and the *Galleon Holliday*, all of them privateering in the four years after the Armada.

[1] He was frequently involved in spoil cases in the seventies and early eighties—see, for example, *A.P.C.*, IX, 307; X, 129; XI, 44, 99, 173, 243, 334, 423; Lansdowne MS 144, ff. 406–7; S.P. Dom. Eliz., clxv, no. 71; H.C.A. 1/43, 21 Oct. 1583, 19 May 1584. For the *Discharge*, the *Supply* and the *Return*, see appendix.

[2] See pp. 203–6, 209–12 below.

[3] The following details are based chiefly on Cokayne, *Lord Mayors and Sheriffs*, pp. 60–5; the *D.N.B.*; W. M. Myddelton, *Pedigree of the Family of Myddelton*; the H.C.A. records; and the MS book of Myddelton's entitled 'A jurnal of all owtlandishe accomptes begyninge this 14th May 1583' now in the National Library of Wales (hereafter referred to as 'Journal'). Since writing this brief summary of Myddelton's privateering activities I have had the pleasure of reading the general account of his affairs given by Professor A. H. Dodd in *Elizabethan Government and Society* (*Essays presented to Sir John Neale*, ed. Bindoff, Hurstfield and Williams), pp. 249–81. This gives a fuller picture of the man's varied interests, but does not seriously modify my view of the place of privateering in his commercial dealings.

children—nine sons and seven daughters. Thomas also had six
uncles on his father's side. The ramifications of this enormous
Welsh tribe were of some significance in Thomas' dealings, for
he frequently lent his relatives money and made use of them in
business. Not a few of them became London merchants themselves: his younger brother Sir Hugh, of the Goldsmiths' Company and a banker, was responsible for the New River project;
another younger brother, Robert, became Thomas' partner and
an important merchant in his own right, a 'committy' of the East
India Company and later an M.P. for Weymouth; Thomas'
youngest brother Peter was also a London merchant, as were
several of his nephews. Thomas entered the commercial world as
apprentice to Ferdinand Poyntz in 1571. Poyntz traded with the
Netherlands, and in 1578, at the age of twenty-three, Myddelton
was his factor in Flushing.[1] A few years later he married Hester,
daughter of Sir Richard Saltonstall, the governor of the Merchants
Adventurers. After this he frequently acted in partnership with
his father-in-law, and the alliance was further cemented by the
marriage of his brother Robert to another of Saltonstall's daughters.

Myddelton's commercial interests, like those of the other great
merchants of his day, were wide-ranging. By 1583 he was a freeman of the Grocers' Company and was conducting trade at
Antwerp on a large scale. The exports were of course chiefly
cloths, but among the imports the main item was sugar. For
Myddelton was now a partner of Nicholas Farrar and Erasmus
Harby in one of the two leading London sugar refineries.[2] Saltonstall was a leading member of the Spanish Company and Myddelton's own connection with Antwerp probably gave him an
interest in Iberian trade. At any rate his continental ties enabled
him during the war to edge into this trade that was now dominated largely by the Hollanders. In 1590 he and Saltonstall, John
More and his own brothers-in-law, John Harby and Richard
Weych, freighted three Hamburg ships with cloths and wax for
Seville, receiving by return Seville oils. The operation was repeated
in 1591.[3] Again in 1591 Myddelton and others sent three vessels
with corn and cloths to Madeira and the Azores, but this voyage

[1] H.C.A. 13/23, 16 April 1578.
[2] Journal, pp. 2–9, *passim*. Poyntz himself had been a sugar-refiner (Willan,
Studies, p. 317).
[3] Journal, pp. 84, 85, 92. The trade was resumed in 1595, but soon abandoned
(Dodd, *Elizabethan Government and Society*, p. 260).

was less fortunate. The goods were arrested by the Spanish and many of the English were imprisoned, including Myddelton's brother, Peter.[1] Myddelton was also prominent in the Venice trade and joined the Levant Company in 1592. The Merchants Adventurers trade to Stade and Middleburg occupied much of his attention, but equally important was the sugar business, and it was chiefly this that gave him an interest in privateering. He frequently bought the Lord Admiral's tenths of prizes and purchased whole cargoes of prize sugar. He was also interested in pepper, cochineal and brazilwood and played a big part in handling the sale of the *Madre de Dios* cargo.

But his part in privateering was not merely passive. In 1589 he set forth his ship the *Elizabeth and Mary* on reprisal under William Myddelton and it returned with a prize of sugar and cotton wool to the value of £2,700.[2] In 1590 his *Riall* of Weymouth (160 tons), also commanded by William Myddelton, shared in the spoil of two very rich prizes carrying pepper, cloves, mace, sugar, ivory, brazilwood and many precious stones and other goods, with a total value of some £25,000. Myddelton's chief partner in this venture was Erasmus Harby, and Harby's servant Thomas Lother was the captain of another ship, the *Bark Randall*, which played a great part in this incident. The prize-goods did not all come to Myddelton and Harby because there were five privateers present at the capture. In any case some of the goods were probably restored in the end to certain Italians who claimed them. For in fact the prizes had been freighted by Italian merchants resident in Lisbon and had only just left that port for Florence when they were captured. Sir George Carey, who was an adventurer in the *Bark Randall*, referred to the claimants as 'Spaniardised Italians' and Myddelton himself wrote to Sir Robert Cecil indignantly about the favourable hearing the Italians were getting. However, it seems unlikely that the original owners recovered much of their property.[3]

[1] H.C.A. 13/32, 6 Nov. 1596, 3 Dec. 1596. An attempt was made to disguise the English vessels as Scottish.

[2] Lansdowne MS 133, f. 22; Lansdowne MS 142, f. 115; Journal, pp. 45, 54, 55.

[3] Lansdowne MS 144, f. 368; Lansdowne MS 140, ff. 14, 18, 20, 22, 24, 26, 34, 36, 38, 39, 43, 85, 91–3; H.C.A. 13/28, 26, 29, 30 Dec. 1590; 9 Jan. 1590/1; 17, 18, 19, 22 Feb. 1590/1; H.C.A. 13/29, 2–12, 17 March 1590/1; 1, 8, 21, 22 July 1591; 19, 20 Nov. 1591; H.C.A. 13/101, 20 Oct. 1591; H.C.A. 14/27, nos. 16, 27, 77, 78, 85, 95, 118–20; H.C.A. 14/28, nos. 157, 175–83; S.P. Dom. Eliz.,

In the same year Myddelton joined with James Bagg, Nicholas Glanville and William Finch to set forth the pinnace *Conclude* of Plymouth, which consorted with Sir William Sanderson's *Moon-light* and Watts' ships in the West Indian and Virginia voyage of 1590.[1] In 1591 the *Riall* and the *Hare* of Myddelton's were out on reprisal, and the *Riall* went out again in 1592, possibly with another Myddelton privateer, the *Harte* (40 tons). In 1594 the *Rose Lion* (170 tons), a powerful Londoner employed in the Levant trade, began her privateering career with a voyage to the West Indies under Captain Thomas West. Myddelton had an eighth share in the venture, the other shareholders being Nicholas Farrar, Thomas Cordell, William Garraway, Christopher Baker (of the famous Elizabethan shipbuilding family) and one Richard Allett. She brought home a substantial prize of ginger, sugar and other goods. Further prizes resulted from her voyages in 1597, 1598 and 1599.[2] Probably all the voyages we have mentioned, with the exception of the *Conclude*'s, were profitable—some, indeed, very profitable. However, a note in Myddelton's account book in 1602 shows that he was not uniformly successful. The entry reads: 'Per inventory unto adventure in reprisal, £147. 3. od, and is for so much by me adventured in the victualling of divers ships gone forth upon reprisal and returned without taking any prizes, so that all was lost.'[3] We may assume that he also lost the £200 he contributed to Richard Hawkins' South Sea venture in 1593.[4] Nevertheless, there is no doubt that he had been largely successful up to about 1602, and the fact that he was still putting money into privateering at this time is an indication of the attractiveness of this form of investment.

But from 1600 the commercial climate was changing. In that year the East India Company launched its first voyage, to which the Myddelton group contributed, both in money and in sea-service. Richard Weych was one of the 'committies', Thomas and

---

ccxxxviii, nos. 32, 44, 114; ccxxiv, no. 5; ccxl, no. 70/71; ccxli, no. 129; ccxlii, nos. 129, 130; ccxliii, nos. 87, 89; ccxliv, nos. 30, 34, 87, 135–6; ccxlv, no. 10; ccliii, no. 106; *A.P.C.*, xx, 223, 77, 282; xxi, 39, 50, 73, 82, 118, 169, 230–1, 259, 320, 347, 381, 433; xxii, 125, 204, 251, 396, 405, 411, 460, 461, 465; *Cal. Salis. MSS*, iv, 93, 244. See also p. 25 above.

[1] *Roanoke Voyages*, pp. 579–716.

[2] For the 1591 ventures, see below, p. 254. 1592 ventures: H.C.A. 13/30, 18 May 1592, 3 Aug. 1592; H.C.A. 25/3 (9), 8, 13 Sept. 1591. For the *Rose Lion's* ventures: *E.P.V.*, pp. 338–76.

[3] Journal, p. 165.   [4] Journal, p. 114.

Robert together with various of their relatives and close business associates subscribed money, and John and Henry Middleton, their cousins, commanded two of the ships.[1] There were now opportunities for trade in the West Indies too, and Myddelton fitted out the *Rose Lion* and the *Vineyard* for the purpose. The captain of the *Rose Lion*, Sir Richard Cowper, made her venture into a 'warfare voyage', and the merchants promptly disclaimed any interest in her;[2] but the *Vineyard* made a successful trip. Myddelton himself adventured £1,569, John More £900 and Samuel Saltonstall and Richard Hawkins £300 each, on which they realised a thirty per cent profit.[3] Soon afterwards the war ended and Myddelton's prize business with it. He had been much concerned with the great official and semi-official expeditions since 1590, acting as treasurer for Drake's last voyage, for example; now that peace was restored Myddelton was able to apply himself wholly to a great range of normal commercial business, which included money-lending and banking as well as overseas trade and the colonising activities of the Londonderry and Virginia Companies.

He was knighted in 1603, having already been M.P. for Merionethshire in 1597–8 and Lord-Lieutenant of the County in 1599. He was Lord Mayor in 1613 and M.P. for the City in 1624, 1625 and 1626. He lived on to the age of about eighty at his manor of Stansted Mountfichet in Essex, where he died in 1631. By this time he had already advanced his two sons and other dependants in the world, but his estate was still very large. It included lands in Essex, Somerset, Worcestershire and Yorkshire, the Chirk Castle estate in Denbighshire and houses and lands in Thames Street, London, which he left to the Grocers' Company. There were sizeable charity bequests.[4] Sir Thomas Myddelton was a religious man. It is recorded that he made 'a very religious speech and exhortation to the whole assembly of the mystery of the grocery of London' in 1621,[5] and there are many entries in his account book which read like the following: 'Per grey squirrels' skins, unto gains and loss £7, and for so much that is gained by the sale of them above the price they cost, for the which and all other blessings I thank god.'[6] To the devout merchant God meant various things,

---

[1] Stevens, *Dawn*, pp. 1–4, 6; Foster, *Lancaster's Voyages*, p. 100.
[2] H.C.A. 13/37, 25, 27 June 1604; 14 Sept. 1604; 1, 6 Oct. 1604.
[3] Journal, entries 1693 and 1739. See also below, pp. 184–5.
[4] P.C.C. 94 St John.   [5] Brown, *Genesis*, p. 949.   [6] Journal, p. 29.

according to the context. 'Ce Dieu que l'on remercie c'est la raison des marchands, la prudence du calcul.'[1] When Myddelton sent the *Vineyard* to the West Indies he wrote in his account book, 'beseeching almighty god to bless and preserve the said ship with her pinnace and all the company in them and send them safely to return into England with all their lading, to god's glory and our comfort—I say my part is £1568. 19s. 9d.'.[2]

Merchants' privateering ventures varied a great deal in profitability, even leaving aside the voyages that combined trade and plunder. But by and large the merchant had important advantages over the amateur promoters and even over the professionals. In the first place they had at their disposal substantial ships, especially if they were interested in the southward trades—ships which either normally earned their keep in trade or at least were employed in trade when the moment was opportune. A middleweight privateer of the *Golden Dragon* (130 tons) class was a burdensome expense for anyone but a merchant, but with the right management it could earn the highest dividends. This particular vessel would have been worth some £570 with her main armament, and the provisions for a voyage would have brought the total investment up to about £1,000. To make a saving voyage for her owners she would have to take prizes to the value of at least £800. This would mean capturing several smaller prizes or one fairly valuable one. Such a task was not difficult for a substantial privateer armed as the *Dragon* was, with two demi-culverins, six sakers, seven minions, and four falcons, thirty-one muskets and three harquebuses, apart from swords and pistols, and manned, as she was, with seventy or eighty men. She could man home two or three handsome prizes and bring further plunder in her own hold, and she was strong enough to tackle any merchantman afloat except a carrack. In fact she made a considerable man-of-war. This was the kind of vessel Watts himself used most. His *Centaur*, *Hopewell*, *Little John*, *Margaret and John*, *Pegasus*, *Affection* and *Jewel* were all of this class. As for the largest class of privateer, when the *Merchant Royal* went out for prizes she represented an investment of about £10 per ton burden—about £2,200 for the ship and guns and another £1,300 for expendable provisions. To make a profit of two or three hundred she would have to return prizes to the value of £3,000. It

[1] J. Gentil de Silva, *Stratégie des Affaires à Lisbonne entre 1595 et 1607*, p. 10.
[2] Journal, entry 1693.

would almost be a waste of time to hunt after little Portuguese caravels—a good-sized Brazilman at least or a West-Indiaman would be required even to cover expenses. The cost was in fact almost prohibitive for the non-merchant. A group of merchants who already owned such a ship might not grudge the thousand or more she would need for a cruise, but the financial strain experienced by Chidley, Cavendish or Sherley, who bought such ships to make a venture, was something very few men would contemplate. If the number of such ships employed in privateering increased during the war, as it certainly did, this was because the great merchants could make them pay their way by combining or alternating voyages of trade and plunder.

The merchants' ventures were not without their special difficulties, of course, most of which arose from their comparatively remote control over their seamen, but these difficulties were more than offset by advantages over other promoters in the disposal of prize goods. They would either have the facilities for storing, transporting and marketing the goods or else the contacts, knowledge and credit to obtain the facilities at reasonable rates. Alternatively, they might sell their cargo to other merchants, but in this event they would probably make a better bargain than a sailor or an amateur would. In any case great gains would fall to the wholesalers who dealt in the types of goods most frequently captured—sugar, hides, wines and so forth. What they acquired by way of prize would be considerably cheaper than ordinary stocks, and if the promoter was himself a wholesaler he would have the chance to sell at a very high rate of profit. Here indeed was probably the chief incentive for many of the great merchant promoters like Myddelton. Some, no doubt, were chiefly interested in the other end of the business—John Bird, the great shipowner, and Henry Cletherow, the rope merchant and naval contractor, for example.[1] But the Barbary and Guinea traders clearly had an appetite for the sugar, pepper and similar West African products they so frequently captured. The Glanvilles, as goldsmiths, were probably drawn in originally by dealings in prize bullion and jewels, and the same is perhaps true of William Shute.[2] Above all, those interested in the

---

[1] Corbett, *Spanish War*, pp. 222, 249; John Nicholl, *Some Account of the Worshipful Company of Ironmongers* (1851), p. 552; *E.P.V.*, pp. 50-1, 59-60, 72, 98, 112, 185, 195-6, 204, 206, 226, 229-30, 298-9, 302-3.

[2] H.C.A. 24/62, no. 107 (purchase of embezzled gold and jewels by Glanville). Shute owned the *Galleon Shute* (H.C.A. 13/30, 21 June 1593), the *Prosperous*,

southward trades combined an appetite for prize-goods with the means to satisfy it—the powerful ships commonly employed in those trades.

Hence these Londoners, with a few of like substance in the outports, did not merely set forth their own vessels. They dominated the whole business of sea-plunder, collaborating with each other, financing amateurs like Cumberland, working hand-in-glove with the professional seamen, buying up prize cargoes. In all its ramifications and diversity privateering was largely knit together by their ubiquitous activities. For they were active in the provincial ports as well as in London and obtained a large measure of control over privateering from Southampton, Weymouth and Plymouth. There was nothing exclusive about their influence —it merely pervaded the large and fluctuating penumbra of more casual promoters. Thus there developed what might be called a 'privateering interest'. It was not an interest in the eighteenth-century sense of a compact and organised pressure-group with precise economic aims, but a loose agglomeration of persons connected by their common pursuit. Nearly all privateering ventures were joint stock enterprises formed for one voyage only. Hence every expedition was a rather *ad hoc* affair and the membership of the promoting syndicates was continually changing. The resulting flux and contact among promoters was of course typical of the shipping business of any port in peace or war, but what gave greater cohesion to the privateering world, apart from the frequency of consortships and joint expeditions, was the far-reaching influence of men like Myddelton, Bayning, Cletherow, Cordell and Watts.

There is no mistaking the wealth and eminence of these London promoters. They were among the élite of late-Elizabethan and Jacobean merchants. Myddelton already during the war was reaching out from ordinary commercial business to take a hand in finance, public as well as private; twice in James' reign, when the City under-subscribed government loans, he stepped in with a large personal contribution to help make up the amount required. Meanwhile in Wales he had established a large estate, and from Chirk Castle the family 'continued to dominate the politics and

which served with Essex in 1597 and Cumberland in 1598, and the *Report* (H.C.A. 13/33, 23 March 1597/8; H.C.A. 24/65, nos. 29, 31; H.C.A. 24/66, no. 7). Shute was an adventurer in Lancaster's Pernambuco enterprise (see below, pp. 209–12).

society of East Denbighsire until the eighteenth century'.[1] Bayning's son, Sir Paul, ancestor of Lord Melbourne, began lending to the Crown immediately on his father's death in 1616. He contributed more than £40,000 in the first three years of Charles I's reign and was rewarded with the title of Viscount Sudbury in 1628.[2] Henry Cletherow's son, Sir Christopher, became in his time governor of the East India Company, Lord Mayor and M.P. for the City. Cordell's son, Sir John, followed his father as a City magnate and a great figure in the Mercers' Company, being elected master in 1632, 1643 and 1648.[3] Watts' son, Sir John, was not only a merchant and sea-captain, knighted for service in the 1625 Cadiz expedition, but also a landed gentleman and author of 'A discourse upon trade'.[4] Each of these five was an outstanding figure in the privateering business. In fact among the London merchants there was only one other—Alderman John More— with an interest comparable in scale and consistency. Of them all Myddelton had the most diversified investments, yet even in his case it has been sufficiently demonstrated that adventures in reprisals helped substantially to make his fortune. Bayning became an alderman in 1593, Watts in 1594, Cordell in 1595, More in 1597, and the dates of these awards of civic dignity seem to indicate success made good in the war period itself. Losses in Spain manifestly did not halt their rise, but presented the opportunity to reach the top rank of their class. It cannot be proved in pounds, shillings and pence, but every approach points to the conclusion that the riches of these very rich men were built in large measure on the spoil of Spanish and Portuguese shipping. Not far behind these magnates of reprisal came a numerous company of London and outport merchants whose interest was more than casual. Each was a leading promoter of several expeditions. The Londoners included Henry Colthurst, Bartholomew Matthewson, John Newton, John Bird, Henry Seckford, Robert Sadler, Robert Cobb, Oliver and Nicholas Stile, George Bassett, John Stokes, James Lancaster, William Holliday, Thomas Bramley, Roger Ofield, William Garraway, John Davies, William Shute, Simon Boreman, William Towerson, Roger Howe, John and Arthur

---

[1] A. H. Dodd in *Elizabethan Government and Society*; R. Ashton, *The Crown and the Money Market, 1603–40*, pp. 118, 123.

[2] R. Ashton, *op. cit.*, pp. 73–4.

[3] V. Pearl, *London and the Outbreak of the Puritan Revolution*, pp. 296–8.

[4] *Historical MSS Commission, Third Report*, appendix, p. 66.

Jackson, the Glanvilles, William Bygate, Robert Bragg, Anthony Dassell, Robert Flick, Edward Leckland, Thomas Pullison, George Southwick and Thomas Starkey.

The generation of Watts, Bayning, Cordell and Myddelton spanned a vital phase in the development of the London merchant class. As young men they would have known a vigorous and influential company of traders, with a few magnates of the stature of Gresham, Hawes and Ducket, but in their old age they stood among a great community of magnates, dominating the economic life of the nation to an extent that early Elizabethan merchants could scarcely have contemplated. The wealth of Jacobean London provided a prop to royal finance that Elizabeth would have envied in the days of Gresham; it made possible colonial projects that seemed idle dreams in the sixties; it overflowed into land purchases, mortgages and organised benefaction on an unprecedented scale. Yet what had intervened to bring about this great inflation of fluid capital? A period of war; a period, we are often assured, of economic depression, marked by bad harvests and unemployment in the cloth trade. Cloth exports, it is true, saw no significant expansion during the reign of Elizabeth. The new wealth, then, did not come from England's traditional trades. But just as war brought dearth and depression to the old and solid trunk of the economy, so it created opportunities for a relatively new and to some extent parasitic growth. The wealth of the Jacobean merchant capitalists was seen by some as gotten at the expense of depressed outports, needy landowners and hard-pressed clothiers—a concentration rather than a real expansion of resources. But if war in many ways thus strengthened the hold of London on the provinces, it also brought to Londoners more than to others windfalls that were of great importance in an age of very slow capital growth. This was for England the longest war since the Hundred Years War, the longest until the end of the seventeenth century, and it is hardly surprising that it marks the entry of the merchants into the sphere of state finance for the first time on any considerable scale.[1] But what is peculiar to this war is that the merchants did not merely finance the state to wage it, but themselves undertook the waging of its maritime phase for their own profit. The gains they made thereby are comparable to the gains of the French bourgeoisie from investment in Valois and early

[1] See, for example, E. P. Cheyney, *History of England from the Defeat of the Armada to the Death of Queen Elizabeth*, II, 217.

Bourbon wars; only in the English case the gains were harvested directly and at no cost of political dependence. We cannot measure the quantity of capital accumulated from privateering nor have we any way of calculating its proportionate contribution to the general fund of fluid wealth. The next chapter, however, will attempt some more precise qualitative statements about the process and its results.

Chapter 7

PRIZES AND PROFITS

In eighteen years of unremitting commercial war hundreds upon hundreds of Spanish and Portuguese merchantmen surrendered to English privateers. There is no way of counting accurately how many were taken, nor can we calculate exactly their value. Nevertheless we have enough detailed information to make a reasonable assessment. These details are provided in the Appendix to this volume, which lists individually the prizes taken in the three years 1589–91 and in the year 1598, giving the nature of the cargo and its approximate value where these are known.[1]

As Table 5 shows,[2] there is record of 299 prizes captured in the three years following the defeat of the Armada. For 145 of these we can make a fair estimate of value, obtaining a total of £280,000. The prizes of unknown value must have been worth considerably less in aggregate, because they probably included few worth as much as £5,000 and not many worth more than £1,000. The sum of the 299 may thus be put very roughly at £400,000. The figures for 1598 (Table 6) show[3] 76 prizes, of which 40 were worth about £39,000. For this year there is no reason to suppose any marked disparity between the known and unknown values, since neither group included any of great worth. We may therefore put the total at a round figure of £75,000. There is a striking difference between the figures for 1589–91 and those for 1598, the annual total and the average value being reduced to nearly half in the later year. The reason for this is the complete absence in 1598 of prizes worth £5,000 or more, which in 1589–91 contributed more than half the 'known values' total.

[1] The character of the source material is also examined. It should be explained here that the documentary evidence available is heterogeneous and fragmentary and can give nothing like a complete index of prizes. The estimates of value, moreover, are necessarily rough. The quantitative problems essayed in this section of the chapter cannot be answered to the satisfaction of a statistician; the rough answers provided, however, should give some measure of the economic scale of privateering.

[2] P. 125.   [3] P. 126.

Table 5. Number and Value of Prizes, 1589–91

port of origin of privateers	total no. of prizes	no. of unknown value	prizes worth £1–£999		prizes worth £1,000–4,999		prizes worth £5,000 and over		prizes of known value (totals)	
			no.	total value (£)	no.	total value (£)	no.	total value (£)	no.	total value (£)
London	71	30	15	5,470	19	39,813	7	52,000	41	97,283
Southampton	34	13	12	3,458	9	19,113	0	—	21	22,571
Dorset	35	15	8	2,026	8	16,200	4	53,000	20	71,226
Devon and Cornwall	41	29	6	1,135	4	7,195	2	26,000	12	34,330
Bristol and Bridgewater	41	11	25	7,103	4	12,045	1	12,000	30	31,148
Other ports	4	1	2	770	1	4,070	0	—	3	4,840
Port unknown	47	36	4	980	7	14,740	0	—	11	15,720
Other prizes	26	19	7	2,595	0	—	0	—	7	2,595
Total	299	154	79	23,537	52	113,176	14	143,000	145	279,713
Average value (£)				298		2,176		10,214		1,929

Table 6. Number and Value of Prizes, 1598

port of origin of privateers	total no. of prizes	no. of unknown value	prizes worth £1–£999		prizes worth £1,000–4,999		prizes worth £5,000 and over		prizes of known value	
			no.	total value (£)	no.	total value (£)	no.	total value (£)	no.	total value (£)
London	44	23	8	2,500	13	22,555	0	—	21	25,055
Southampton	9	1	6	1,288	2	3,180	0	—	8	4,468
Dorset	11	3	4	274	4	8,660	0	—	8	8,934
Devon and Cornwall	7	7	0	—	0	—	0	—	0	—
Bristol and Bridgewater	3	0	3	354	0	—	0	—	3	354
Other ports	0	0	0	—	0	—	0	—	0	—
Port unknown	2	2	0	—	0	—	0	—	0	—
Other prizes	3	3	0	—	0	—	0	—	0	—
Total	79	39	21	4,416	19	34,395	0	—	40	38,811
Average value (£)				210		1,710				970

Are we to assume that the privateers of the immediately post-Armada period were exceptionally fortunate, or that those of 1598 were unlucky, or are both these hypotheses reasonable? In the absence of a complete list of prizes for the whole war period, this question cannot be answered categorically, but a general survey of the materials leaves the impression that there was no great variation in the number of small and medium prizes taken from year to year. On the other hand the total returns for particular years were dramatically affected by the appearance or non-appearance of the richest sort of prize. The *Madre de Dios* alone provided privateers with half a normal year's takings. Prizes captured by ships of John Watts in 1591 were worth at least £40,000. Lancaster's raid on Pernambuco in 1595 yielded at least £50,000. In 1594 some £30,000 worth of treasure and other goods were captured in a succession of assaults on Puerto de Caballos in Honduras. William Parker probably brought back more than this from his triumphant cruise in 1601. In fact 1598 was an exceptionally poor year for the privateers, and this was largely due to the absorption of the energies of the great promoters in Cumberland's unprofitable Puerto Rico expedition.

Can we, on the basis of these rough figures, make an estimate of the rate of influx of prize-goods throughout the war? Such an undertaking is only dangerous if we are not forewarned of the hazards, and with this in mind we stress that any figures we eventually reach are to be taken only as pointers to the scale of the returns. Let us first, then, try to fix a reasonable minimum. 1598, a poor year, saw returns of about £75,000 for the known voyages. There is good reason to believe that various unrecorded prizes were taken in these voyages, and that unrecorded voyages occurred. At a modest estimate these would raise the total to £100,000. For the maximum figure the year 1591 gives a fair indication. In that year there is mention of fifty-one prizes with a total value of £93,169, with a further fifty-two of unknown value. Even assuming that the fifty-two make up only half the value of the fifty-one, we still reach a total of £140,000 for the 103 prizes. Again we should add to this figure to account for unrecorded prizes and voyages. For example, it is likely that Newport took several prizes at La Yaguana in Hispaniola this year, though we have not mentioned them in the list because this is not certain; and there were more privateers with Howard at the Azores than those indicated in our list. As for Watts' prizes, we have priced them at the official valuation—£31,000, whereas in fact they were probably worth all of £40,000. Fortunately, for the year 1591 we have a check on our calculations, since Lord Burghley made a note to the effect that goods brought into the realm by way of reprisal during the six months preceding Lady Day 1591 paid customs amounting to £3,651 7s. 11d.[1] At the rate of five per cent duty this would suggest some £73,000 worth of prize-goods for the half-year, or £146,000 for a complete year. As it was notorious that privateers frequently evaded the customs, Burghley's evidence confirms an estimate of prize-goods rising towards £200,000 for the year 1591. We may therefore reasonably conclude that the value of prize-goods ranged from about £100,000 to about £200,000 a year.

If we bear in mind that our figures do not take into account the returns of official and semi-official ventures, this total annual haul is impressive. No reliable trade statistics exist for this period, so that only the roughest estimate of England's total imports is possible. Misselden gave a figure of just over £2,000,000 for 1613,[2] but a great increase took place in the ten years after the war. Such material as we have for the early years of Elizabeth's reign suggests a figure of about £1,000,000, and there was no remarkable expansion in the volume of trade during the reign.[3] Imports in the eighteen years of the war were therefore in the region of £1,000,000 to £1,500,000. Prize goods, by this reckoning, would account for some ten to fifteen per cent of England's total imports. Another yardstick, and one of particular relevance for us, is the value of English imports from the Iberian peninsula before the war, which amounted to about £100,000 to £120,000 a year.[4] Thus the returns of privateering were worth at least as much as those of the Iberian trade.

Fourteen years after the end of the war a Venetian ambassador reported: 'Nothing is thought to have enriched the English more

[1] Lansdowne MS 67, f. 146.

[2] Misselden, *The Circle of Commerce* (1623), pp. 121–2.

[3] L. Stone, 'Elizabethan Overseas Trade', *Economic History Review*, 2nd Ser., II (1949), 31–58.

[4] V. M. Shillington and A. B. W. Chapman, *The Commercial Relations of England and Portugal*, put imports from Portugal to London, Bristol and Southampton at £14,000 in 1584, and the total for England would presumably be somewhat higher, though not much. They also estimate that England's trade with Portugal made up about one-sixth of her trade with the peninsula as a whole.

or done so much to allow many individuals to amass the wealth
they are known to possess as the wars with the Spaniards in the
time of Queen Elizabeth. All were permitted to go privateering
and they plundered not only Spaniards but all others indifferently,
so that they enriched themselves by a constant stream of booty.'[1]
The composition of this stream is at least as interesting as its size.
Was it similar to the stream of imports formerly acquired by trade
with the Iberian countries? To some extent it was—and inevitably,
since most of the cargoes that were legitimate prey consisted chiefly
of the products of Spain, Portugal and their empires.[2] Thus the
most common sort of prize had a lading of the characteristic
Iberian products: wines, oils, olives, oranges, raisins, figs, walnuts,
almonds—sometimes a mixed cargo, sometimes of one item alone,
especially of wine. This was of course one of the great staples of
European trade, not least of Iberian trade. Wine is mentioned
among prize-goods more frequently than anything else except
sugar; and the wines of the peninsula itself more frequently than
other sorts. Spanish wine was popular in Falstaff's England, and
though during the war that 'intolerable deal of sack' came mainly
through French ports, the privateers made an appreciable contribution. Sometimes along with wines, oils, fruits and nuts would
be found various manufactures—woollen cloth, for example, and
ironware such as horseshoes—but very seldom do manufactures
make up the bulk of a prize cargo; more common are the chief
Iberian minerals—iron and salt—more often than not single-item
cargoes, indicating a specialised trade. All these Iberian exports
were the stock-in-trade of the lesser privateer. The caravels and the
barks which carried them were the typical vessels of local west
European trade, with a capacity more often under than over fifty
tons and perhaps a dozen crew. As for the cargo, it was hardly
ever worth more than a thousand pounds and usually less than
five hundred.

Corn—another staple of European trade—was captured occasionally. The Spaniards and Portuguese imported corn in large
quantities and most of it came in the hulks of the North from
Danzig, Lübeck, Hamburg, Denmark and the Netherlands.
Early in the war the English government declared food supplies
for Spain contraband and so these cargoes were legitimate prize

[1] *Cal. S.P. Venetian, 1617–19*, p. 146.
[2] The following description is based on Table 7, p. 130, an analysis of the prize
cargoes listed in the appendix.

K   A.E.P.

Table 7. Prize Cargoes, 1589–91 and 1598

port of origin of privateer	European				fish	Extra-European				total	wines	hides	sugar	gold, etc.	brazilmen
	N	S	M	G		A.A.	AM	E	G						
London	4	16	7	4	5	3	27	1	0	67	15	21	19	7	6
Southampton	2	11	4	2	2	2	10	0	0	33	5	5	11	1	6
Dorset	3	3	2	2	2	0	10	1	3	26	2	4	15	2	9
Devon and Cornwall	1	8	3	0	1	4	9	0	0	26	3	7	4	2	2
Bristol and Bridgewater	3	14	2	0	7	2	6	0	0	36	6	4	4	2	4
Other ports	0	2	0	0	0	1	0	0	1	4	1	0	0	1	0
Port unknown	5	14	2	2	6	1	10	1	0	41	8	4	12	0	7
Other prizes	4	7	0	0	4	1	5	0	0	21	5	1	4	1	0
Total (1589–91)	22	75	20	12	27	16	75	3	4	254	45	46	69	16	34
1598	11	20	1	8	2	7	19	1	0	69	9	8	22	4	4

[1] The first nine columns classify the cargoes according to the general nature and origin of the goods in each case. N = North European, S = South European, M = manufactures, G = general, i.e. cargoes of mixed European products, not predominantly N, S or M; $A.A.$ = African and Atlantic (Canaries, Azores, Madeira), AM = American, E = Eastern, G = general, i.e. cargoes of mixed extra-European products, not predominantly $A.A.$ AM or E. The columns headed Wines, Hides, Sugar, Gold, etc., indicate the number of occasions on which these products appear as main items of cargo. There are often two and occasionally three main items in one cargo. The column Gold, etc., includes references to silver, money and precious stones.

and were often brought in by the queen's ships. For the ordinary privateer, however, they were too large a prey, and one could never be sure that the cargo would turn out to be contraband, as poor Sherley found with his Lübeckers in 1598.[1] In fact the corn ships taken by privateers were usually of the smaller sort—hoys, canters, or caravels with a lading worth less than five hundred pounds.

Cargoes of fish were brought in quite often (27 known, 1589–1591) and the majority were condemned as Leaguers—ships from French ports under the control of the Catholic League. Fish prizes were worth up to five hundred pounds as a rule, and of these the most valuable were the Biscayans—sizeable vessels of two or three hundred tons, many of which were taken on their return voyage from the Newfoundland banks. These were formidable opponents, as Monson testified, and the men in them were as tough and aggressive as the English.[2]

Such were the main types of European goods captured by the privateers. When to the Iberian exports we add corn and other North European products such as timber and the very few manufactures and the fish prizes, we have accounted for well over half the number of prize cargoes. In value, however, these made up but a small proportion of the returns of privateering—some ten per cent. The remainder consisted of extra-European products—some from Africa and the Atlantic islands, some from the East, some from the Americas.

The trade with the Azores, the Canaries and the Madeiras yielded chiefly prizes of wines, sugar and woad, the sugar and woad ladings being rather more valuable than the typical European cargoes. More valuable still were the occasional captures of sugar ships sailing to Portugal from São Thomé island off the Guinea coast—two, three or four thousand pounds worth of sugar at a haul. The Portuguese West African trade offered even richer prizes, of gold, ivory and slaves, which might be worth ten or twenty thousand pounds, though rarely taken. Much less attractive, but still worth having, were the prizes of the Barbary trade—caravels laden with sugar and often carrying some molasses, goatskins or succades as well. But altogether prize-goods from Africa and the Eastern Atlantic comprised only a small fraction of the total—about a tenth of the number of cargoes and of the total value.

[1] See above, p. 66.   [2] See above, p. 95.

As for the products of the East, they were very seldom captured by ordinary privateers. Spices, drugs and perfumes, calicoes, carpets and silks, rubies, emeralds, diamonds—these came in the carracks, giants of a thousand, even two thousand tons, which could fend off a whole fleet of privateers. When the *Madre de Dios* was taken in 1592 it took the combined strength of the semi-official fleet under Sir John Burgh, Cumberland's squadron and other privateers to subdue her. Two years later a powerful force of Cumberland's failed to capture the *Cinco Chagas*. The carrack cargo brought back by James Lancaster in 1595 was not captured at sea but in the warehouses of Recife, and Lancaster's company of ships and men was exceptionally strong for a purely private expedition. In fact such few eastern goods as fell to ordinary privateers were taken after their trans-shipment, when the prize cargo would include other goods. The two prizes of the *Bark Randall* and her consorts in 1590, for example, were on their way from Lisbon to Florence, carrying pepper, mace, musk, cinnamon, rubies, cloves, civet, ambergris, diamonds, oriental pearls, ivory—all from the East—but also sugar, brazilwood, wheat, conserves and drinking-pots. Valuable but rare, the returns of the eastern trade probably contributed less than ten per cent to the total value of prize-goods.

It remains to consider the American products. From Spanish America came the 'West-Indiamen', with hides and sugar chiefly, but often with ginger, sarsaparilla, indigo, cochineal, campeche wood (or logwood), gold, silver and pearls. The typical prize of hides and sugar was worth two or three thousand pounds and cochineal in any quantity would raise the value markedly. Sizeable prizes of this sort were to be had anywhere between Havana and Seville, but the majority of them were probably taken in the West Indian waters, where a raiding force would also normally obtain various other pickings—small caravels or frigates of the coastal trade and plunder from outlying settlements. West India prizes often carried considerable sums in rials of plate or pearls, but English privateers rarely obtained their heart's desire, a cargo consisting primarily of treasure. Most of the treasure, whether belonging to the king or to private citizens, was carried in powerful silver galleons or fast-sailing gallizabras, and the ordinary privateer stood little chance of capturing either. The occasional lucky windfall did occur, of course, as for the *Julian* of Lyme in 1589 and Watts' fleet in 1591, and such a prize might well be worth twenty or thirty thousand.

But the commonest prize of all was the Brazilman, with its stereotyped cargo of sugar and brazilwood, worth usually two or three thousand pounds. These ships came regularly from Pernambuco and frequently fell into English hands. Sometimes they carried hides or cotton instead of brazilwood, but the major item was invariably sugar. Thirty-four Brazilmen were taken in the three years following the Armada, with a total value of some seventy or eighty thousand pounds. Unquestionably among all these American prize-goods sugar was the most important. It made up the greater part of the Brazil cargoes in terms of value and was frequently a major item in West-Indian cargoes. It is impossible to calculate exactly how much sugar was captured, but when we take into account the Barbary, Canary and São Thomé prizes as well it is safe to say that at least £100,000 worth of sugar was taken in the years 1589–91.[1] Hides were almost as common as sugar in American prizes, and likewise occurred in other cargoes. The resulting influx of this vital raw material into England may help to explain why the price of leather did not rise appreciably during the last quarter of the sixteenth century, when prices generally were rising fast.[2]

In sum these American cargoes accounted for about seventy per cent of the total value of prize-goods, though only for about thirty per cent of the number of prize cargoes. Taking the non-European products together—Eastern, African, Atlantic and American— they make up nine-tenths of the value of the English plunder. Before the war the greater part of our imports from the Iberian peninsula had consisted of Iberian produce, though the proportion of non-European goods was rising. Clearly, therefore, prize-goods did not simply replace Iberian imports. Such a shift of emphasis in the country's imports over nearly two decades was bound to have a considerable effect upon home consumption.

Looking at the stream of booty as a whole, one can hardly fail to notice the great differences in value between the main types of cargo. The 'European' columns of Table 7 correspond almost exactly to the '£1–999' columns of Tables 5 and 6, and the average value of these cargoes was a mere two or three hundred pounds. The typical American, African and Atlantic ladings made up

---

[1] For the repercussions of this, see ch. 10 below.
[2] See L. A. Clarkson, 'The Organization of the English leather industry in the Late Sixteenth and Seventeenth Centuries', *Economic History Review*, 2nd Ser., XIII (1960), 245.

the middle range, with an average value of about £2,000, and the most valuable group comprised West African gold, American silver and eastern goods, with an average value of about £10,000. These are arithmetical averages, but the mean for each of the three groups would be much the same. This conclusion must be borne in mind when we come to consider the gainfulness of various kinds of privateering.

This stream of booty we have assessed and analysed was by no means all profit. How much of it was profit? Was there, indeed, any profit? Sir William Monson, in his *Naval Tracts*, would have us believe that there was none, though he offers no evidence to support his contention. However, as the editor of the *Tracts* observes, 'there is various evidence—the tenths paid to the Admiral, the steady increase in the number of ships employed in privateering, the fact that the same owners are often found engaged in it year after year, and the ruinous effects on Spanish commerce—to show that when carried on in a business fashion it was profitable enough. Of course the great expeditions, the Queen's and Cumberland's, were failures, but the small men made it pay'.[1] Those who are acquainted with Oppenheim's work will appreciate that this opinion cannot be brushed aside lightly, and yet it is Monson's view that has prevailed among historians.

We might attempt to settle the argument by calculating from our table of costs the approximate expense of the 271 known voyages for 1589–91 and balancing this against the shares likely to have accrued to the promoters from the £400,000 worth of prize-goods returned in those three years, checking the result against the figures for 1598. The calculation would indicate an average profit of about sixty per cent on the fixed capital (ships and guns), but unknown quantities, variables and imponderables play such a large part at every stage that this figure cannot be regarded as even roughly accurate. At most it may be taken as an indication that privateering was not unprofitable. However, a quantitative statement about total or average profits is really less significant than the qualitative distinctions we can make between more and less profitable forms of enterprise. A review of these, together with some comments on forms we have not yet considered, will help us to reach an impression of the general trend.

The chief factors affecting profits were the cost of the venture,

[1] *Monson's Tracts*, II, 246.

the value of the goods captured, the extent of pillage and embezzlement, the size of the official share, in the form of the queen's custom (five per cent) and the Lord Admiral's tenth, and the size of the crew's 'thirds', apart from their pillage and embezzlement. On most of these counts the voyage which combined trade with plunder was highly rewarding. The cost of the privateering would be nil or negligible, since the owners would have arranged for expenses to be met out of freight charges. What is more, since these vessels were well-armed and fairly strongly manned, the prizes they took were often valuable. The crews employed in trading voyages were better disciplined than those in plain privateering; they would receive their wages as well as a third of the prize-goods and in consequence could be trusted, at least more than most reprisal sailors, to bring home the booty more or less intact. The promoters probably paid their customs and tenths more regularly and fully in this sort of venture than in any other, but the advantage would fall to them again in the disposal of the prize-goods. For these often consisted of the very commodities in which they dealt, commodities, moreover, of a kind that the crew could not easily market, so that they would be obliged to take what the owners thought reasonable for their 'thirds'. This was undoubtedly the most profitable form of privateering enterprise and it became more common during the course of the war, being adopted in the new trades to the East and West Indies which were emerging at the turn of the century.

In their more normal privateering ventures the great merchants still had some advantage in the matter of costs, partly for reasons we have observed and partly because their syndicates would often include not merely shipowners but shipping magnates like Bird and dealers in ships' stores like Cletherow. Their ships stood a better chance than most of a reasonable haul of prizes, and their success was due not only to their size and power, but to the practice of sending out two, three or more ships together. There were seven partners, for example, in Watts' 1591 expedition of four substantial ships and a pinnace; eleven shareholders set forth Newport's four ships in 1592. In both cases expenses would have been fairly high, but high returns in prizes more than compensated for this. Watts' squadron represented a total investment of about £5,000, of which some £2,000 would have been spent in fitting out; it brought in prizes worth about £40,000, though some of this had to be shared with consorts. Newport's ships probably cost about £1,500 to fit out and had a total value of about £3,000. He took nineteen prizes and shared in the spoil of the *Madre de Dios*; we do not know the value of his haul, but it may well have been over £10,000. These of course were exceptionally fortunate voyages. More moderate was the return of a Brazilman worth £2,680 by William Holliday's 50-ton *Seadragon* in 1589, a privateer which would have cost perhaps £200 to fit out, the ship and guns representing another £200. But merchants were apt to lose heavily by pillage and embezzlement, as were all promoters who stayed on dry land. They usually gave detailed instructions to their captains and masters, but their only real hope of preventing the worst excesses lay in having loyal agents. Hence some syndicates would give command to one of themselves, like James Lancaster, or to a trusted factor like Robert Flick. Often the family tie was brought into play. Watts made a 'general' of his eldest son and Myddelton employed some of his numerous relatives. But the loyal man was not necessarily the best commander. Thomas Watts, for example, John Watts' brother, proved a rather ineffective commander in the 1588 expedition, in the course of which he was violently assaulted by the master. The latter 'disliked that Thomas Watts took upon him to be captain, and openly said that he was no captain there or had to do with the men or the victuals, and that John Watts his brother requested him to suffer the said Thomas Watts to go with him in the said ship'.[1] Family relationship to the owner would not endear a captain to his crew unless he were thought to be worth his salt. Even so, it was a worse case when there was no effective bond between the captain and the promoters. John Watts himself had great trouble with the captains and masters of his 1591 squadron. His general, William Lane, was loyal, but the other captains, Michael Geare, Stephen Michell and William Craston, proved their powers of leadership by leading their men in an orgy of illicit appropriation. Against such professional plunderers the merchant or gentleman promoter stood little chance. The poacher, to be useful to the man of property, must become a gamekeeper, the unruly captain must be made a partner. A man like Christopher Newport, a professional privateer captain with an interest in his ship, was probably the best guarantee the owners could have against embezzlement or excessive pillage. Nevertheless adventurers could not always find such reliable agents, and might have to resign themselves to losing a

[1] *E.P.V.*, p. 45.

considerable part of their due. Nor did the merchants themselves gain when the queen and the Lord Admiral were cheated, for when this happened the seamen were intent on theft as well as smuggling. Hence the numerous court actions in which merchants were associated with the Lord Admiral against their own seamen, actions which, however, rarely achieved the desired effect of recovering the lost goods. Watts had sufficient influence to win his case over the 1591 booty against so exalted a personage as Sir George Carey, whose own methods with the judge we have observed, but no amount of influence could make a man like Michael Geare yield up the gold and jewels he had won by fighting. Merchants would be able to offset these losses to some extent by purchasing the crew's thirds at a favourable rate, but their two-thirds share of the cargo, after pillage, embezzlement and taxation, probably amounted in most cases to less than half the value of what was actually captured. Even still, William Holliday and his partners would have made a clear profit of £1,000 on a fixed capital of £200. This was a good voyage, but not an exceptional one.

In many respects the professional owner-captain would do better than the merchant. He would be able to keep down costs by personal supervision of the details of fitting out, keep a strict eye on his crew at sea and in port and above all provide effective leadership. Professionals did not often have trouble with their men. Naval men like Raymond and Preston knew their sailors, selected those they trusted from the port, harbour, creeks in which they themselves had learned their sea-craft. They took out a privateer with full knowledge of what they could expect from those strange birds of seamen, swayed by custom and superstition, childish in their naïve deceits, respectful and insolent by turns; and with full knowledge of what was expected of them, the captains. Sir Thomas Sherley was an owner-captain, and his men did as they pleased. Cavendish and Chidley fared little better. It was not enough to be on the spot—what mattered in the last resort was the personal authority of the commander, and here the professionals had the edge on the amateurs.

The professional owner-captain was also best placed to cheat the queen and the Lord Admiral. All privateers were legally bound to declare their prizes and any prize-goods they might have shipped in their own holds. The local admiralty officers had instructions to make inventories of all prizes and to find six honest men of the port to assess the value of the goods. In practice, of course, they neglected their duties; inventories and appraisements were sometimes so belated that a large part of the cargo escaped taxation, and often goods were under-valued, presumably by agreement with the captors. Now there is no reason to suppose that the merchant or gentleman promoter was any less able or willing than the professional to oil the palm of a deputy vice-admiral or a collector of customs. In this respect all men were equal, provided they had the money or goods to satisfy the official conscience. Where the professional owner-captain scored was not in the art of compromise, but in the craft of evasion. Bribery might reduce the taxation to, say, five or ten per cent, but why pay anything at all if ways and means of thwarting the government could be found? In fact smuggling was easy and for an owner who could personally supervise the operation it was profitable. Embezzling and smuggling clearly went together, and a promoter who wished to smuggle without losing by embezzlement had to know his crew. Further, he had to have the contacts ashore to manage the disposal with speed and discretion. In effect, he had to be a professional seaman, unless he happened to be a customs officer or an admiralty man. For the amateur owner-captain or the shore-bound promoter this sort of crime did not pay. It was only when it came to selling his cargo that the professional was at a disadvantage. Altogether a professional owner-captain who took his proper share of the pillage and was not scrupulous about paying his dues to officialdom could reckon on having well over half the original prize to sell for himself and those who had subscribed to his venture. We have seen the fantastic profits this meant for Robert White of Weymouth. Perhaps more typical were the Prowses of Southampton.

They evidently came from London, but their voyages were conducted from Southampton. Laurence Prowse was captain of the *Eleanour*, financed by Thomas Heaton and Henry Rogers in 1586 and 1587. Although he was in trouble for spoiling a French ship at this time, he brought home two Portuguese prizes together worth at least £1,822. In 1589 he and William Dudson set forth the *Minion*, of sixty tons, under Captain Thomas Prowse, who captured a prize of iron. The *Minion* sailed again in 1590, with William Prowse as master, achieving only, so far as we know, two small wine prizes; in the following year she consorted with Howard's fleet in the Azores. Meanwhile Prowse had had some share in prize-goods returned by the *Laurence* of Weymouth and in 1590 had collaborated with Heaton and Henry Cletherow of London in a rewarding venture of the *Eleanour*. She brought back some £5,000 worth of Brazil goods and in the following year, under Laurence's personal command, took a West-Indiaman and a Brazilman together worth at least £4,000. In 1592 William, as master of the *Desire*, was responsible for a São Thomé man to the value of £1,584. In 1593 the *Minion*, still owned by Dudson and Prowse, made another voyage, with Edward Crandell captain and William Prowse master.

The same year the *Angel* (eighty tons) owned by Laurence Prowse and Richard Goddard, made the first of a series of voyages under William Prowse, returning with a Brazilman worth £3,890. Her 1594 voyage evidently yielded only £155 worth of ivory, and in 1595 she sailed with Preston and Somers to the Spanish Main, where the captain died 'by the water side' near the town of Coro. Laurence, however, pursued his private war. In 1596 he commanded the 30-ton *Elizabeth* of Southampton in the Cadiz expedition. In 1597 and 1598 his *Welcome* brought in three small prizes and in the latter year another was returned by the *Angel*, which he now shared with Sir Oliver Lambert as well as Goddard. These were all fairly small privateers, and Prowse, though his returns may have declined in the later years, made large gains over the period as a whole. The family evidently had good standing in Southampton, for a certain Laurence Prowse became mayor in 1618–19.[1]

In comparison with the professional and great merchant ventures—indeed by any standard—those of the amateurs were uneconomic. Some of them lost large sums, ruining themselves and causing serious loss to fellow-adventurers. These losses must be set off against the profits of the great merchants and professionals. It is

[1] J. L. Wiggs, 'The Seaborne Trade of Southampton in the Second Half of the Sixteenth Century', M.A. thesis (unpublished), Southampton University, 1955. I am indebted to the author for permission to use the results of her research; R. C. Anderson (ed.), *Letters of the Fifteenth and Sixteenth Centuries*, p. 115; H. J. Moule (ed.), *Catalogue of Weymouth Records*, pp. 163–4; Harleian MS 598, ff. 2, 4, 10, 13, 17, 26, 31, 43, 45; H.C.A. 14/26, no. 133; H.C.A. 13/28, 19, 20 March 1589/90; H.C.A. 24/57, nos. 11, 18; Lansdowne MS 133, f. 23; A.P.C., XVIII, 370; Lansdowne MSS 67, f. 177; 144, f. 27; H.C.A. 25/3 (9), 8 March 1592/3; R. C. Anderson (ed.), *The Book of Examinations 1601–2*, pp. 61, 63, 64, 68, 71; *Principal Navigations*, X, 213–26; J. Rutherford (ed.), *The Miscellaneous Papers of Captain Thomas Stockwell, 1590–1611*, I, xi, 7.

worth noting, however, that the amateurs formed only a small minority of promoters and that few of them could afford to persist with their gambling for long.

Many of the ships of reprisal operating in the early years of the war were owned and equipped by provincial merchants. One or two of these—substantial men like the Auldworths of Bristol or Richard Dodderidge of Barnstaple—combined and alternated privateering with trade after the manner of the great Londoners, and a few notable shipowners, like William Walton of Bristol and Weymouth or Thomas Heaton of Southampton, were privateering magnates of no mean stature. But plunder seems to have been a somewhat disappointing investment for some of the outport merchants. Some twenty or more Bristol merchantmen, mostly ranging from thirty to seventy tons in burden, such as had formerly plied to La Rochelle, Bordeaux, Vianna, Aveiro, Lisbon, Seville and Cadiz, were bringing home modest prizes for several years after 1585. The prize-goods were the typical small beer of the privateering business—European and especially Iberian produce captured from caravels and barks in the Bay of Biscay and off the western shores of Portugal and Spain. These were not powerful privateers; compared with the merchantmen of the Barbary trade—let alone the Levant trade—they were weak; rarely are they found in the Azores or the West Indies or off the African coast.

The *Diamond* of Bridgewater, for example, a 60-ton vessel, was set forth by Robert, John and William Puddy, Thomas Holcomb, Humphrey Dorrington, John Sly, George Watkins, George Parsons, Richard Godbeare, John Morgan and Thomas Neathway. These were local men; Watkins and Neathway were sailors; Holcomb, Sly and Godbeare were merchants. This sort of parcellation of the enterprise was fairly common in petty ventures, and the sums invested were quite small. A vessel of sixty tons could be fitted out for about £200, the fixed capital in ship and armament costing about the same. In 1589 the *Diamond*, in company with a flyboat of Bristol, took a Flemish prize off the coast of Spain. The value in this case is not known. If the *Diamond*'s share had been worth £500, pillage, crews' thirds and customs and admiralty dues would have reduced the promoters' share to £250 —a profit of £50 on their initial outlay of £400. Few of these European cargoes were worth as much: their average value, after pillage, was some £300. The *Diamond* went out again in 1590.

This time she brought in a prize of earthen pots and salt valued at £75, a prize of tar, which had to be returned to its Swedish owners, and a cargo of wines, kettles and other goods, the value of which we do not know. Again, however, there cannot have been much profit on the venture. The next voyage in 1591 resulted in a Portuguese prize of corrupt wines, iron and pitch to the value of £140. Of course there may have been more prizes; but several such cargoes would be required each year to make this kind of venturing worth while.[1]

It would seem that the game was hardly worth the candle, and in fact this kind of privateering dwindled remarkably after 1591. Bristol, where the small merchantman privateer predominated, had twenty-nine ships on reprisal in 1589–91, and a mere three in 1598. In the former period seventy-five per cent of the vessels of known tonnage were under 100 tons in burden, but in 1598 two of the three were 150-ton ships. One of these belonged to John Hopkins, the other to William Walton, both consistent and important promoters, the latter probably treating prize-mongering as his main business interest. It may be that the smaller merchantmen had paid their way in the earlier years of the war by combining prize-hunting with trade to French ports or even with illicit traffic in Portugal and Spain. Whether this was widespread, and whether it became more difficult as the war went on, is hard to say. Certainly there was a pronounced decline not only in Bristol privateering but in Bristol shipping and trade generally during the war.[2]

The same tendency can be discerned at Southampton, though here, as we have seen from the example of the Prowses, the professional element was also strong. The merchants of the town, however, were for the most part men of rather limited resources, and their interest in privateering, save in a few cases, did not survive the first few years of the war. The men who led and increasingly monopolised Southampton privateering were Londoners, professionals and one or two outstanding Southampton merchants. John Crooke was one of those who came to grief. Before the war he conducted trade to France, Spain, the Atlantic islands and the Netherlands, had a considerable interest in Newfoundland fishing, owned or partly owned several ships and was

---

[1] H.C.A. 13/29, 1 Feb. 1591/2; H.C.A. 13/28, 2, 6 Nov. 1590; H.C.A. 14/27, nos. 5, 45, 68/9; Lansdowne MS 142, f. 115; Harleian MS 598, ff. 7, 11, 12.
[2] E. Lipson, *Economic History of England*, II, 252.

concerned in the Southampton brewing industry. His ships the *Marigold*, the *John Evangelist* and the *Primrose* were out on reprisal in the first eighteen months of the war, and in 1590 he shared in the *Bark Young*'s West Indies venture. But in 1591 he was referred to as having been 'a merchant of good wealth and trade and now decayed by losses at the seas and other ways'.[1]

On the other hand in Weymouth the local merchants seem to have gone into partnership with the professionals with great success, and to have organised their own equally successful ventures. Here the outstanding local seamen, apart from Robert White, were Henry Rogers, who had a major interest in the 100-ton *Eleanour* of Southampton before 1588 and in the nineties set forth the *Seadragon*, the *Endeavour* and the *Amity* (later known as the *Tobacco-Pipe*); and John Reynolds, who was also interested in the *Endeavour* and the *Amity*, had been a promoter of the *Anne Huddy* in 1590 and was still privateering in 1600 with the *Diamond*.[2] Nicholas Jones, the captain of Portland Castle, was another regular Weymouth promoter.[3] The most important local figure, however, was John Randall, gentleman-merchant, owner of the highly successful *Bark Randall*, the *Grace* of Weymouth and a Portsmouth bark. Randall was connected with Raleigh, who had a share in the *Bark Randall*, the two men being co-owners of the *Heart's Desire* of Weymouth in 1596.[4]

Such was the vigour of the professional element here that local merchants were drawn in and the port became a major privateering base. Syndicated enterprises were common, and in these the Weymouth promoters were joined by London and Southampton men and even by one—William Walton—from Bristol. Thus the

[1] H.C.A. 25/1 (4), 2, 16 July 1585; H.C.A. 13/23, 7 June 1578, H.C.A. 13/25, 1 April 1586; H.C.A. 13/26, 6, 9 Aug. 1586; *E.P.V.*, pp. 86–94; J. L. Wiggs, *Seaborne Trade*.

[2] Lansdowne MS 144, f. 25; Harleian MS 598, ff. 2, 4, 9, 22, 24, 25, 43; H.C.A. 25/3 (9), 7 Feb. 1591/2; H.C.A. 13/30, 24 May 1592; H.C.A. 13/31, 13 May 1594; H.C.A. 13/34, 16–21 July 1600, 28–9 Aug. 1600, 9 Sept. 1600; H.C.A. 24/62, no. 55; R. C. Anderson (ed.), *Letters of the Fifteenth and Sixteenth Centuries*, p. 115.

[3] Lansdowne MS 142, f. 109; H.C.A. 25/3 (9), 19 June 1591, 20 Feb. 1592/3; Harleian MS 598, f. 35.

[4] Son of Hugh Randall, an active promoter of piracy in the seventies; interested in goods brought in by the *Anne Huddy* before 1590 (Lansdowne MS 144, f. 27). For the *Bark Randall* in 1590, see above, pp. 115–16. For other ventures, see Harleian MS 598, ff. 20, 38; H.C.A. 14/33, nos. 173/4, 263; H.C.A. 25/3 (9), 19 Aug. 1590, 24 March 1591/2, 30 Nov. 1592, 13 Dec. 1592.

ships of Weymouth, though small, often took substantial prizes and would cruise as far as the Azores and the Caribbean in search of them. The conditions for success were present: there was a sufficient supply of able captains and masters who would usually, as partners in the enterprise, do their best for the promoters; the local officers of the queen and the Lord Admiral were deeply involved in the spoil business and could be relied upon to make a suitable arrangement with their friends and business associates; the machinery of prize-disposal, of the market, was ready to hand, with London buyers supplementing the purchasing power of local merchants.

One Weymouth merchant syndicate which prospered was that of John Bond, William and Richard Pitt and William Holman, who set forth the 56-ton *Bark Bond* in 1589. That year she brought in a Brazilman worth about £5,000 and in 1590 a leaguer worth about £700. The following year Bond and the captain, Roger Geyer, combined with Robert Sadler and Edward Leckland, owners of the *Globe* of London, to fit out the two privateers, which shared a £3,000 prize with the *Swallow* of London. In 1592 Captain Nicholas Ayers sailed the *Bark Bond* into Weymouth with a rich haul of jewels. These he had illegally and forcibly obtained from the *Grace* of Dover, which had been entrusted with putting the *Madre de Dios* passengers ashore in the Azores. The jewels were impounded, but Ayers had probably taken another prize this voyage. In 1595 the *Bark Bond* went with the *Scorpion* and the *Violet* to the West Indies in a venture promoted by John Bond and a group of Londoners. Prizes to the value of £1,500 resulted.[1] Such returns seem profitable enough. Bond, who had been a factor for Richard Pitt before the war, had the *Jesus* and the *Bark Bond* on reprisal before 1590; Richard, William and Henry Pitt had acquired commissions for the *Matthew* and the *Lion* at the beginning of the war; William Pitt collaborated with Nicholas Jones in a 1590 venture and had some share in an early voyage of the *Riall*; Henry Pitt set forth the *Aid* of Lyme in 1590; and John Pitt had an interest in the *Carouse* as well as the *Eleanour* of Southampton in the late eighties, owned the *Mayflower* in 1593 and joined with Bond to send out the *Seraphim* in 1595. All these

[1] Harleian MS 598, ff. 3, 5, 13, 19, 21, 32, 34; H.C.A. 25/3 (9), 19 May 1591; H.C.A. 14/28, no. 83; H.C.A. 13/29, 15 Nov. 1591; Lansdowne MS 67, f. 190; *E.P.V.*, pp. 326–9. She took a small prize in 1593 (Harleian MS 598, f. 21).

except the *Aid* and the *Eleanour* were Weymouth privateers, and the *Eleanour* was sometimes called the *Ellyn* of Weymouth. So much we know of the activities of this group, but it is more than likely that in reality they contributed to each other's ventures to a much greater extent, working together and keeping a ship or two at sea most of the time. It is therefore perhaps significant that Bond now disappears from the record and that the name of Pitt occurs only once after 1595—in connection with Henry Pitt's privateer, the *Greyhound*, which took a prize in 1597.[1]

The Bond-Pitt syndicate may have been dropping out of privateering after 1595, but it seems to have done well up to that date. Nor were they the only outport merchants to make a success of the business. The evidence seems to suggest that those who went in for it seriously could thrive on it. It may be that the lesser Bristol promoters, regarding privateering merely as a temporary substitute for trade and lacking resources in money or suitable ships, made but half-hearted efforts. Certainly there is a remarkable contrast between their failure and the experience of William Walton, himself a Bristol man. He set forth the *Salamander* (120 tons), the *Looking-glass* (100 tons), the *Flying Dragon* (150 tons) the *William* (80 tons) and the *Phoenix* (60 tons), all Bristol ships. He also owned several Weymouth ships of reprisal—the *Jane Bonaventure* (20 tons) and the *Pearl*, the *Prudence* and the *Francis*, whose tonnage we do not know. In the list of the Lord Admiral's tenths of prizes Walton's privateers are mentioned seventeen times in the years 1588 to 1598, and the tenths rendered amount to £2,219, apart from certain unassessed quantities of bullion and jewels. A number of Walton's prizes are not listed—we know, for example, that one of his ships shared in Randall's rich plunder in 1590, and that he received more prizes after 1598. Incomplete though they are, these figures of tenths sufficiently explain why Walton persisted. He was elected mayor of Weymouth in 1597.[2]

Walton was evidently a specialist in reprisals. Shipping mag-

[1] H.C.A. 13/24, 9 June 1580; Lansdowne MS 144, f. 25; H.C.A. 25/1 (4), 21, 24 July 1585; Lansdowne MS 142, f. 109; H.C.A. 14/26, no. 53; H.C.A. 13/96, 26 Aug. 1591; *Cal. Southampton MSS*, p. 122; R. C. Anderson (ed.), *Letters of the Fifteenth and Sixteenth Centuries*, p. 115; H.C.A. 25/3 (9), 20 Feb. 1592/3; Harleian MS 598, ff. 22, 43; H.C.A. 13/32, 23 Dec. 1595.

[2] Harleian MS 598, ff. 4, 10, 21, 24, 26, 29, 30, 31, 32, 33, 39, 40, 43, 46, 69; H.C.A. 25/3 (9), 15 Aug. 1590, 17 June 1591, 26 Feb. 1592/3; H.C.A. 13/32, 23 Dec. 1595; H.C.A. 13/33, 29 July 1598, 10 Nov. 1598, 18 Jan. 1598/9; H.C.A. 14/33, nos. 122, 131; H.C.A. 13/148; *A.P.C.*, XXIX, 246; H.C.A.

nates like him had an interest in a variety of vessels, great and small, and were in a sense professionals. Not all of them were successful. Thomas Heaton, customer of imports at Southampton, was a promoter on a still greater scale, and in the first ten years of the war he appears to have prospered, steadily increasing his privateering force and engaging heavily in the business of prize-disposal. In 1595 he sent three ships under Moses Willis to the West Indies. The expedition was a failure, and this may explain why he sold a great part of his shipping to Sherley at the end of the year. He must have suffered further loss from his investment in Sherley's venture. In any case this was his last fling in privateering. In 1599 he fell into debt with the Crown and was imprisoned, though soon released, possibly on the intervention of Essex. In the same year, however, he made a contribution to the East India Company.[1] In the scale of his enterprise Heaton was typical of the merchant privateering magnates; but his failure was not typical. On the whole those who made a business of privateering—men like Walton, Watts, Cletherow and John Davies— were successful.

John Hopkins, fishmonger of Bristol, master of the Bristol merchants adventurers and mayor of the city in 1600, was a rather different kind of promoter. In the twelve years following 1588 he had, at various times, seven ships on reprisal: the *John*, the *Maryflower*, the *Elizabeth Bonaventure* (80 tons), the *Moonshine*, the *Daisy* (40 tons), the *Ferret* and the *Mary Fortune* (150 tons). The list of tenths mentions sixteen prizes with a total value of £18,276. This would have meant a consistently respectable profit, even if the ships averaged 100 tons in burden. Hopkins represented Bristol in parliament in 1601 and was a founder of the Virginia Company. How much of his wealth and influence he owed to privateering we cannot say, but our evidence suggests that it was at least an important and gainful side-line for him.[2] The Auldworths

24/66, nos. 163, 164; H.C.A. 13/34, 30 May 1600, 15–21 July 1600, 28, 29 Aug. 1600, 9 Sept. 1600, 2 Dec. 1600; H.C.A. 24/67, no. 99; H.C.A. 24/62, nos. 31, 32, 47, 48.

[1] Wiggs, *Seaborne Trade*, pp. 152–3. Heaton was interested in the *Eleanour*, the *Jack Sauce*, the *Blessing*, the *William Bonaventure*, the *Bevis*, the *Hare*, the *Grace of God*, the *Prudence*, the *Hopewell*, the *Mermaid*, the *St George*, the *Archangel*, the *Wolf*, the *Galleon Constance*, the *Swan* and the *Little John*. See Harleian MS 598 *passim*; E.P.V., p. 383; R. C. Anderson (ed.), *Book of Examinations, 1601–2*, pp. 63–74.

[2] Harleian MS 598, ff. 4, 12, 15, 16, 18, 19, 22, 23, 27, 29, 30, 35, 38, 45; H.C.A. 25/3 (9), 7 Sept. 1591, 28 Dec. 1592, 31 Jan. 1592/3; H.C.A. 14/28,

(Thomas, Robert and Richard) were equally eminent Bristolians, with an interest in sugar-refining, in the Levant and East India Companies and in western planting. Privateering for them was simply one of a number of commercial activities. They set forth the *John*, the *Green Dragon* (60 tons), the *Gabriel* (80 tons), and the *Sugar* in the early nineties, and in the five years 1591–5 six of their prizes occur in the list of tenths, having a total value of £7,000. In the same period they frequently bought prize-goods and on one occasion collaborated with Henry Cletherow of London in a reprisal venture. As late as 1603 Robert Auldworth (evidently the most active of the family in this field) had an interest in a Bristol privateer called the *Consolation*.[1] Richard Goddard of Southampton was a similar figure. Mayor of the city in 1583–4, M.P. in 1588, a trader to France, Spain and the Azores, he was interested in privateering throughout the war period and evidently made a success of it.[2] Goddard, Hopkins and the Auldworths were hardly professionals in the prize business. Like most of the Londoners interested in privateering, they were merchants whose interest in Iberian trade and oceanic enterprise gave them the means and the incentive to add sea plunder to their already varied commercial activities.

The conclusion is fairly evident. Resounding failures like Sherley's and Chidley's and Cumberland's attracted so much attention at the time that anyone without specialised knowledge might pardonably write off privateering as a snare for fools.[3] The casual observer, too, will note complaints in the state papers uttered

nos. 43, 81; H.C.A. 24/58, no. 17; Lansdowne MS 133, f. 23; H.C.A. 24/62, nos. 33, 34; H.C.A. 13/34, 30 Jan. 1599/1600, 30 April 1600; D. Powell, *Bristol Privateers*, p. 24; A. B. Beaven, *Bristol Lists*, pp. 122, 166, 184, 195, 222; Corbett, *Spanish War*, p. 293.

[1] Harleian MS 598, ff. 15, 22, 27, 29, 30, 35; H.C.A. 14/28, nos. 82, 166; H.C.A. 25/3 (9), 4 Dec. 1592, 23 Jan. 1592/3; H.C.A. 13/36, 8 March 1603/4; D. Powell, *Bristol Privateers*, p. 48; P. V. McGrath, 'The Merchant Venturers and Bristol Shipping in the Early Seventeenth Century', *Mariner's Mirror*, XXXVI (1950), 69–80.

[2] Wiggs, *Seaborne Trade*, pp. 151–2. Harleian MS 598, ff. 26, 31; R. C. Anderson (ed.), *Book of Examinations, 1601–2*, p. 63; Lansdowne MS 142, f. 109; H.C.A. 25/3 (9), 23 Sept. 1591; H.C.A. 14/27, no. 96; J. Rutherford (ed.), *The Miscellaneous Papers of Captain Thomas Stockwell*, I, xi; *E.P.V.*, p. 153; H.C.A. 24/58, nos. 52, 53. Is to be distinguished from the London alderman of the same name.

[3] Hooker had the impression at the time that after Drake's 1585–6 voyage there

by individuals and corporations about their 'losses had at sea' and naturally he will not find people or towns boasting to the government of their wealth 'had at sea'. But on closer examination there is nothing to be said for the view that privateering was generally unprofitable. Admittedly some promoters were unlucky, incompetent, or both (and it is remarkable how often these misfortunes went together). But these were a minority and probably many of them gave up before their losses reached the same proportions as the gains of their successful contemporaries. It would not take many John Crookes to warn off the rank and file of casual outport investors. Everything points in fact to the corroboration of Oppenheim's diagnosis: 'that when carried on in business fashion it was profitable enough'.

The result of the superiority of the professional and great-merchant forms of privateering was that they tended to supersede the other forms. This usually meant the big men in the business taking over as the lesser fry left the field, and as they did so the profits flowed with increasing steadiness in one direction—to London, and especially to those sections of the London merchant community interested in shipping and imports. The proportion of London ships among the privateers increased greatly during the war, and there was an even greater rise in London's share of the total privateering tonnage.[1] The outports, with their limited resources and hinterland, could not handle much of the exotic produce now pouring in: at Southampton, the Dorset ports and Plymouth imports by way of reprisal outweighed the ordinary trade in value; London's wholesalers, sugar-refiners, tanners, goldsmiths and so forth had to assist, and were not slow to enter the market. Big merchants of the capital would often have a connection with outport merchants, and large quantities of prize-goods were shipped coastwise from the ports of Hampshire, Dorset and Devon to London.[2] But the London interest was not limited to dealing in the booty; in practice much of the privateering activity of these ports was financed either by Londoners or jointly by local men and Londoners. Thus Myddelton and his

---

was a spate of adventuring, by which 'many were undone and themselves in the end never the better', but he was presumably judging from the experiences of his friends at court. See above, p. 4.

[1] See Tables 1 and 2, pp. 32 and 33.

[2] Willan, *Studies*, pp. 78–82. Of the London buyers Thomas Myddelton, Henry Beecher and Richard Burrell were among the leaders.

partners had a great interest in Weymouth shipping, while Cletherow, Davies and other London men managed a great part of Southampton's reprisal venturing. Conversely the important local promoters—Walton, Randall, Heaton and Auldworth, for example—had strong ties with London.[1] It might be thought that by such means the commercial strength of London would invigorate the privateering outports, helping to develop their facilities and resources. And it is true that Southampton experienced during the war a transitory prosperity based upon privateering, as Weymouth and Plymouth did. It has been shown for Southampton, however, that the privateering industry was a specialised and largely a closed trade, from which the major profits went to the Londoners and the few local men who managed it.[2] The same is probably true of Weymouth and Plymouth.

In effect a comparatively small group of wealthy men exercised increasing influence over a great part of the privateering business. These were chiefly London merchants, and as they dominated the field so they took a lion's share of the profits. Moneyed men in the position of John Bird and John More could exploit not only the abilities of professional captains but the difficulties of gentlemen. Myddelton lent money to Cavendish; Cordell and others battened upon the earl of Cumberland. Of course too close an association with amateurs might be embarrassing: Watts, Walton, Cletherow and perhaps Bayning lost money in Chidley's venture, but the loss of the few hundred they each invested made no apparent difference to their fortunes. They could afford such reverses.

The most significant feature of the profits of privateering is that the greatest gains were made by these magnates of mercantile

---

[1] John and Richard Walton, presumably relatives of William, shared his venture in the *Looking-glass* in 1591, and are described as Londoners. Randall is sometimes called a London merchant. Heaton was probably originally a Londoner and as customer kept close contact with the capital. Richard Auldworth joined the Levant Company and collaborated with Henry Cletherow in setting forth a London privateer, the *Harry*.

[2] Wiggs, *Seaborne Trade*, pp. 113, 145, 156–60. Sir John Oglander, writing about the Isle of Wight, testified to the transitoriness of the wartime prosperity, but also gave the impression that it was widespread: 'The Isle of Wight . . . is infinitely decayed by reason of so many attorneys. . . . Or else it is for want of the good bargains they were wont to buy from men-of-war, who also bought all our commodities at very high prices, and ready money was easy to be had for all things. Now Peace and Law have beggared us all, so that within living memory many of the gentlemen and almost all the yeomanry are undone.' [Francis Bamford (ed.), *A Royalist's Notebook*, pp. 13–14.]

capital. They were not the only gainers—some professional seamen made their fortunes, some sea-faring gentry did very well, and a good deal of the surplus was dissipated among the whores and tavern-keepers of Elizabethan England. But even in such an inevitably disorderly business there was still scope for a steady concentration of profit by men in whose hands it would become capital.

TAIL-PIECE

William Grafton 1592[1]

OUR LADYS RETORNE to England, accompanied with saint Frances and the good Jesus of Viana in Portugall, who comming from Brasell, arived at Clavelly in Devonshire, the third of June, 1592. *A wonder of the Lorde most admirable, to note how many Spanish saintes are enforced to come one pilgrimage for Englande.* With the most happie fortune of that brave gentillman William Graftone[2] Cittizen of London, Captaine and oner of our Ladies. Written by H.R. Imprinted at London by A.I. and are to be sold by William Parlye at his Shop in gratious streete, over against Leaden Hall. 1592

H.R. In Captaine Graftons worthie deserved commendations.

Brave noble brutes, ye trojan youthfull wightes,
Whose laud doth reach the sentaure of the sunne :
Your brave attempts by land, one seaes your fightes,
Your forward hearts, imortall fame hath wonne.
The world reportes, what Londoners hath done,
Freemen I meane, and prentices of worth :
For countrie service, that are called forth.

Amongst which of name let grafton have his due,
Valiant brave man whose courage none could quaile :

---

[1] This pamphlet (H.M. 82178) is reproduced by permission of the Huntington Library, California. The copy appears to be unique. It has unfortunately been cropped in such a way that some of the text is lost—most seriously in the dedication. The numerous misprints are as characteristic of the original as the punctuation, the doggerel and the nonsensicalities of the narrative, and have therefore been reproduced without alteration here. The author was Henry Roberts, whose writings are significant for their emphasis on the patriotic deeds of the common people. The enterprises he celebrated in verse and prose were nearly all privateering ventures, and those who won his loudest praises were the London merchants. See L. B. Wright, *Middle-Class Culture in Elizabethan England*, pp. 515–24.

[2] Later in the same year, Grafton set forth the *Grace of God* of London under Captain Derivall. Earlier in the year Grafton had been at sea in the *Grace of God* (H.C.A. 13/30, 23 August 1592) and had, as the pamphlet relates, taken two prizes, one of which he converted into the privateer *Our Lady*, whose activities are described here.

His actes at larg heere after shall insue,
And how in fight he often did prevaile,
When three to one one seaes did him assaile,
Seekinge by force his ruine to have wrought:
Which he surpraised and them to england brought.

Read Graftones deedes, you cavelires of worth,
Surevay his life, and learne by him to live:
Whose bountie kindnes, and valoure showed forth,
If I shoulld write the dastard hart might greeve,
Casting great doubtes how they might me beleeve,
Yet Ile maintaine, this captaines actes are such:
As fewe I knowe will hassard halfe so much.

. . .[1] *at his lodging in London.*

Syr knowing your kind nature to be such, as joyed that your freinds welfare, especially those that for there countries good deserve honourably to be spoken, of as your selfe in younger yeares have many waies jeperied [jeopardised?] your bodie, in your countries service whose scars yet remaine as badges of your forewardnes, and desire to gaine that your ancesters of fame, long time to there great commendations maintained, the consideration of which moved me here to fore, from dungarvan, to advertize you of the arivall of our good freind, & your especiall favouret maister *William Grafton*, at Kinsall, whose succes I wrot you at large, for that my last lettres (and joy of your freindes good) was so gracious with you, as one that loves you both well, I make bold to signifie unto you the saide captaines safe landing at Clavelly in the west partes, where my selfe being commanded on some busines of my captaines from my place, bownd for england, crossed by north windes, whereunto travelers are subject being destressed we wear enforced to put in for the said port of Clavelly, where happely I met & well met, this brave gentleman Captain *Grafton*, who as here to fore I sertified you, having prepared hir small carvell called our Ladie fitte for the seas, embarqued himselfe at youholl in Ireland well furnished with brave and resoluit men, & vittailes store, betaking himselfe to the fortune of the seas, where oprest with extreame weather, doing what men might do by the parmission of God, they endured as long as possible they might, til for releef they bare for england, et at Clavelly againe replenished there decaied victuals,

---

[1] Probably 'To the worshipful George . . . esquire'.

& other necessaries & on sonday the 28. of Maye being the sonday
next after trinitie sonday, they set saile from the said port, having
all that day and night a faire bearing gall, on twesday they espied
two saile as much to windward as in the top they might descry
whom they gave chace unto, and by tenne of the clock in the
morning, came up with them, which shipes were both of Bristow,
the one the Unicorn and the other a small barke of the same place.
The companie of these two shippes they kept untill the next
morning, when captaine *Grafton* espying som other sailes, standing
upon the sailing of his carvell, which is very good, he parted with
the said Unicorne & here consort, & bare with there late descried
huls in hope of good hap which according to his worth he doth
deservedly merit as time finisheth many things, so time and short
time hath brought him within the plaine vewe of those two last
descried sailes, whom they fownd to be two mightie great flyboats
who serving the King of spaine, straied from the fleet, the sight of
those made divers of his companie appaled, whom the good captaine with wordes of great courage so comforted, that if his discretion had not been more for his safitie and thers, then there
wilfull hardines, they would have attempted to have taken the one
of them, but the captaine having perswaded them they neverthe-
lesse bare up with them, & thorowly vewed them, and so departed,
shooting ahead the biger of them, when captaine *Graftonnes* men
that lay close shewed themselves, & were of the other perceived,
there came presently two shot from them which mist the carvill the
lesser flieboat being good of saile gave them chace, that day till
three a clock, whom the Captaine perceived and by little & little
slacked there saile, to see what they durst doo, being from her
consart, which she had overshot at least two leages.

The flyboat feching uppon the Captaine who made no hast to
runne away, but determined to change a shot or two with them,
provided themselves for the same fight, knowing well they might
at their pleasures leave or take, having but one cast Peece aboord,
and that the mouth broken, the guner a stout & proper man made
readie, by that time all things was fited to the Captaines mind, the
fly boat with fourteene or fifteene men in armour wanned them to
leeward, railing and reviling them, with speeches most odious, to
whom the guner sent such a token by his Minion, that with the
crossebarre, he was charged, he split the missen mast in the step, &
did much other harme as well in the Captaines Cabin through
which it went, as slaiing some men which was seene to be cast over

boord. Thus for three houres they continued a sore fight, the Captaine being ever foreward to[1] . . . there ordinanc otherwise should have done them most harme, yet of such height was this foule cart from the Carvill sides, that their talest man migh hardly reach their channell holes, so that there was no entering but with great danger, and therefore for safegarde of their men, the Captaine gave over the fight, and not of feare for his men were resolute, and doubted not the good successe, and happie conquest of their enemies.

Thus neere six a clock in the evening the carvill parting, the fight bareing rome from them, whose consart was now come up with them, continuing his course towardes the Ilandes,[2] with faire and good weather where they had many chaces, which because their actions were little worth to rehearse, I omit to tell you of the blessing of the Almighty, on this worthy deserving Captaine, whose godly mind and good dealinges with all men the Lord doth reward. Sailing stil towards the Ilandes the seventh day after they lost the sight of our owne land, (silly)[3] they espied in the height of fortie two leages, two sailes the one of them, being of burthen an hundreth and twenty tuns or there abouts, having in her of men forty six, furnished with ten cast Peeces, the other of some three score tunne or there abouts, with sixteene men in her, well sir after the captaine had hailed them, and bad them strike, they bearing Spaniards proud mindes, seeing so smale a Carvill as this our Ladie of the Captaines, scorned to yeeld, but made reddie to fight, and both began with all their force to assaile him most hotly, the gunner, from the great ship, shot the Carvilles meane missen from the yardes shered many ropes and did them great mischeefe, so that with splicing and repairing, the same company was greatly pusseled, in this time the Captaine calling for a canne of Wine and drinking hartely to them, desired them all as they loved him to follow him, and at the next comming up they would boord her where to they were al very willing, and comming up with them againe, the Gunner with his broken mouth Minion, racked him fore and oft [*sic*], the barre entring at the starre, went thoroughout: then comming up in her quarter, the Captaine leapt in at their cheane holes, and one other with him who was hardly . . . other hand weapons, yet kept[4] . . . place, when the shippes faling

---

[1] A line of print illegible owing to cropping.
[2] The Azores.   [3] The Scillies.
[4] A few words illegible owing to cropping.

off, he had no remedy, but abide that chance God had alotted them, the company aboord loth to let their Captaine rest in so great danger came aboord againe, when valiantly they entered, his boy being with the first aboord had taken downe their Flag, to the great greefe of the enemie, who now repenting their hardinesse craved mercie, the other smale Shippe seeing all the men of Warre almost aboord, their Prise layed the Carvel aboord, but to their great cost. For there beeing courageous men, entered but six of them with their swordes and dagers, swordes and targates and such as they had, and stowed the fifteene Portingauls so that they were possessed of both sooner then they exspected, the Captaine seeing the other was taken gave God thankes for his goodnes, then demanded the Captaine of whence they were, they answered (of *Viana* in Portugale, and came from Parmabucca)[1] loden with fine white Sugars, and dyvers Negros, when the companie had made through sarch for pillage, the Captaine determined to bare for England, which his company willingly agreed unto, praising him that giveth all victories for their good successe, first in delivering them without perill from the flie-bootes, next for their prises, who was able being furnished with English-men, to have beaten foure such Carviles, with ten peeces and fortie and six men, the other sixteene men besides Negros, the Carvill in all had but thirtie seven men one cast peece, wherefore having named [*sic*] their prises, they had men fewe inough to carry home the Carvil, which compelled them to leave one other Carvil loden with Sugar behind them, a good pleasure to the poore Portugalles, which loked with their neighbours to goe for England, thus in five weekes retorned the Captaine to Clavelly from whence they went & sooner might if God had favored them with faire windes. At the same port the said Captaine discharged his goods royally, paied each man as the best had no cause to complaine, the Portugalls his prisoners he kept a shore at boord wages, so long as they remained with him, and after his busines ended, causing the good Jesus his smale prise to be rigged and vitled for three monethes, he gave her the prisoners to bring them home with their Negroos and mony largly, by which his bountie and charitie to these poore men no doubt he gaineth as well love of God, as favour and the loving kind hartes of men.

Thus farre with favour I beseech you exscept my simple writing and joy with mee as I know you doo for your freind whom God

---

[1] Pernambuco—these were Brazilmen.

by his grace hath sufficiently blessed with welth, as heere tofore I certified you, his owne ship was the grace of God, who took our Lady and saint Anthonie, our Lady she made a man of warre, who hath taken now those two prises loaden with sugar the one called saint Fraunces, the other the good Jesus, both of *Viana*, a wonder of the Lorde, to appoint this Spanish saints to make rich his english sailours, as by this valiant Captaine is shewed, for how many Captaines hath had such blessinges as this gentleman, or who more fortunate, whom Jesus our Lady S. Fraunces & S. Anthony, hath brought their blessinges there news, ther is none worthy to write, but for your hawkes, I hope by saint James tide to bring you, till then with my heartiest commendationes, I leave you to his protection whom I daily pray to blesse us all from Barnstable in the north of Devonshire this 6 of July 1592. yours ever redie to use H.R.

Part III

PRIVATEERING AND
OVERSEAS EXPANSION

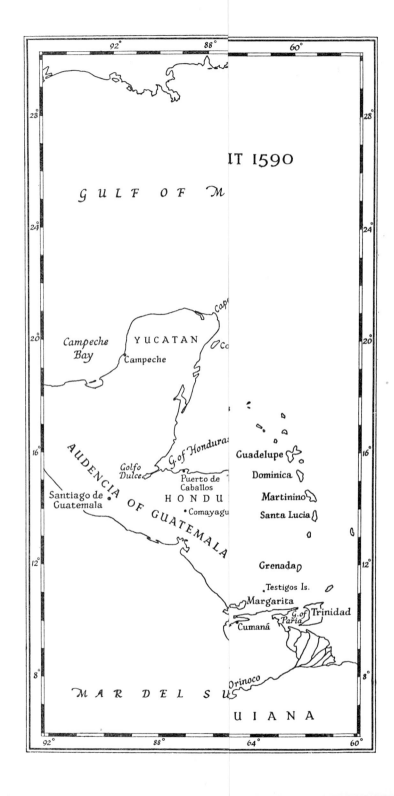

Chapter 8

THE WEST INDIES

The West Indies became one of the main hunting grounds of the privateers. Already before the war the wealth that passed through the region had attracted the attention of English corsairs, and at the very beginning of hostilities Drake's destructive raid had exposed the inadequacy of the Spanish defences. What did the privateers make of their opportunities? The usual view is that Drake's success awakened the Spanish to their own vulnerability, and that while the English failed to press home their attack the Spanish took such effective measures for their defence that they were able to repel the next big assault when it came ten years later. In sum, it is maintained, the record of the English in the Caribbean during the Spanish war was one of unfulfilled promise.[1] The main substance of this argument is sound, but it needs some modification now in the light of the fresh material from English and Spanish sources that has been steadily accumulating for some years past. The English, it is true, failed to make any dramatic break-through in the West Indies, but in some respects the Spanish hold on the region was weakening, and the privateers, accompanied increasingly by traders, made no small contribution to this trend.

The West Indies, though distant, were not difficult to reach. Running south to the Canaries or as far as the Cape Verde Islands, a ship could cross the Atlantic with the northeast trades and strike the great convex chain of the Lesser Antilles within a few weeks of setting sail. Here there would be no danger from Spaniards while the crew bartered with the Caribs for water and fruits and refitted or careened the ship. Beyond these islands the Caribbean Sea stretched away for fifteen hundred miles, bounded on the south by the Spanish Main or Tierra Firme, the mainland of South America, and on the west by the coasts of Honduras and Yucatan, while to the north lay the larger islands of Puerto Rico,

[1] See, for example, A. P. Newton, *The European Nations in the West Indies, 1493–1688*, pp. 108–20.

Hispaniola, Jamaica and Cuba, the last reaching almost to the northern tip of Yucatan. Strong easterlies prevailed throughout this region, so that a sailing ship could approach almost any part of it with ease and speed from, say, Dominica or Martinique. On the northern side the Mona Passage, between Puerto Rico and Hispaniola, and the Windward Passage, between Hispaniola and Cuba, provided possible exits from the Caribbean, but most vessels, whether by way of the Greater Antilles or the Main, held their course westward with the wind to debouch through the Yucatan Channel. Further west still lay the Campeche coast and Mexico, but the normal course now was to double the western tip of Cuba, Cape San Antonio, creeping up towards Havana and the Florida Channel, the highway to Europe.

Along the thousands of miles of coastline at infrequent intervals were Spanish settlements ranging in size from single farms or plantations to sizeable cities. Of the latter there were very few, Havana, Santo Domingo, Cartagena, Nombre de Dios (or later Porto Belo), Vera Cruz and San Juan de Puerto Rico being the most important. Apart from these major centres, whose *raison d'être* we shall examine, there were perhaps a score of ports which amounted to something more than coastal villages: places like Cumaná, Rio de la Hacha and Santa Marta on the Main, Trujillo in Honduras, Campeche and Tabasco in the Gulf, La Yaguana in Hispaniola. Such minor ports handled most of the local trade, collecting the produce of their respective areas for eventual transmission to Spain. Much of this trade in sugar, hides, pearls, indigo, sarsaparilla, ginger, dyewoods, cassia fistula and cochineal was conducted by small vessels—boats, barks or caravels—which did not leave the Indies, but larger merchantmen would sometimes sail from these ports to join the homeward convoys or even attempt the crossing alone.

What mattered to the Spanish government, however, was the shipment of treasure; and the rhythm of West Indies trade and the scope of West Indies defence depended largely upon this fact. The other important factor in the regulation of trade and defence was the highly monopolistic colonial policy of Spain, which confined transatlantic commerce to the Andalusian cities of Seville and Cadiz. It was to enforce this monopoly and to protect shipping against the repeated attacks of the French corsairs that an elaborate system of Indies navigation was developed during the middle third of the sixteenth century, reaching in the years 1564–6 the more or less definite organisation it was to retain throughout the Hapsburg era. Each year two fleets were to sail for the Indies. One of these was the Mexican fleet, or *flota*, which made its way to Vera Cruz via the Greater Antilles; this would include some vessels for Honduras and the Islands, which would be dropped on the way through the Caribbean. The chief part of the *flota*, with the two warships (*armadas*) convoying it, would proceed to San Juan de Ulua, the roadstead of Vera Cruz, and winter there, taking aboard the rich produce of New Spain—chiefly treasure, cochineal, indigo and dyewoods. The following spring the *flota* was supposed to sail for Havana, where it would be re-joined by the Santo Domingo, Honduras and other ships for homeward convoy. The other fleet was destined for Cartagena and Nombre de Dios (or later Porto Belo). This, the Tierra Firme fleet, came to be known as the *galeones* because it was customarily accompanied by a number of men-of-war which not only convoyed the merchantmen but took aboard at the Isthmus the silver bullion from Peru. The *galeones* took their course from the Lesser Antilles along the Main, dropping ships at some of the Tierra Firme ports and pressing on to the Isthmus. In the spring they would return with the bullion to Cartagena to load the pearls, gold, hides, cochineal and other produce of the Main which had been concentrated there by local shipping. Thence they would make for Havana. In practice the composition and the timing of these fleets varied a good deal from year to year, particularly in the period of the war with England. The assembly of the homeward convoys at Havana was delayed again and again by weather and by enemy movements, so that, for example, in 1590 the departure of the merchantmen of both fleets from Havana had to be postponed until the following year, and the same thing happened in 1592. The cost of this convoy system, which was organised by the *Casa de Contratación* in Seville, was met by a general tax on all Indies merchandise, known as the *avería*. In addition to the great official fleets a certain number of 'loose ships', sailing to and from Europe, were permitted.

The system was not without its advantages. The treasure was of great importance to Spain, and nearly all of it arrived safely. Perhaps, too, the merchantmen would have fared worse had individual sailings been the rule, at least after 1585, when all the seas from the Yucatan Channel to the coast of Spain were infested with foreign marauders. On the other hand, the successful transshipment of the treasure after 1588 cannot, as we shall see, be at-

M   A.E.P.

tributed to the general convoy arrangements. Again, once West Indies raiding became prevalent and not merely occasional (i.e. after 1585), there was considerable danger in the practice of concentrating all shipping at Havana, since this presented the enemy with an obvious target area in the approaches to that focal point of American wealth. Above all, while much attention was paid to the safety of the fleets and some to the defence of the few major ports, the rest of region went largely unprotected, and even places on the main fleet routes could be attacked when the *armadas* were not in the neighbourhood.

At the outset of the war, in fact, large areas of the Caribbean were open to all forms of infiltration and attack. In the fifteen-seventies intermittent French and English raids had largely devoted their attention to the Isthmus and the mainland east and west of it. Here Drake and others had taken considerable booty and caused no little anxiety, but it is not surprising that their depredations failed to rouse the Spaniards to improve the defences of the remoter parts. At Santo Domingo, it is true, two galleys arrived in 1582 to patrol the coast and prevent illicit trade, but by 1586 they had ceased to operate. At Cartagena there were two galleys at the beginning of the war, their task being to patrol the Main. Such was the extent of the naval forces defending the Caribbean in 1585, when Drake arrived with a formidable array of men-of-war, royal and private. The ease with which he captured Santo Domingo and Cartagena and demolished San Agustín gave a salutory shock to the Spanish authorities. Already indeed they had been contemplating, even to the verge of action, measures to strengthen the puny naval forces in the area and the defences of the main cities. Now at last active steps were taken. Extra galleys were sent out almost immediately, and the garrisons were increased and provided with more artillery. In 1589, after a careful inspection, work was begun upon an extensive programme of fortifications for Puerto Rico, Cartagena, the Isthmus of Panamá, San Juan de Ulloa and Havana. What is more, the emergency naval needs of 1588 gave rise to the beginnings of a new practice for the conveyance of the plate. This was now increasingly entrusted to small, swift frigates, or *gallizabras*, especially constructed for the purpose. Soon these were bringing home a large part of the treasure of the Indies, sailing independently of the slow-moving convoys and at times overtaking them.[1]

---

[1] *Further English Voyages*, pp. lxvi–lxvii, lxxi–lxxv; R. D. Hussey, 'Spanish

To what extent did these measures solve the problem of West Indian defence? We can perhaps best approach this question by examining the activities of the English privateers in the decade following Drake's raid.

In the period up to 1590 nearly all the English privateering visits to the Caribbean were connected with the Virginia enterprise. One of the most important objects of the Roanoke voyages was to establish a base from which continuous attack on the Spanish Indies could be maintained, and in the meantime the colonial projectors endeavoured to pay their expenses, at least in part, out of prizes.[1] The failure of the Roanoke experiments did not, however, mark the end of Caribbean ventures. These went on in a more or less continuous crescendo from the year of the Armada until 1595. Throughout the period ships and men were occasionally lost, and a few of the raiders gained little or nothing for their pains, but the majority made a saving voyage at least and some took rich hauls. What is significant is that their success varied markedly from one area of the Caribbean to another.

There was one obvious place where the dreams of every captain and cabin-boy might become reality—the waters from Cape San Antonio to Havana on the northwestern shore of Cuba. This lay moreover on the normal route homeward from the Caribbean, and it was almost difficult to avoid once a ship had threaded the lesser Antilles. Again, it was not only treasure that converged on Havana. There were ships from Santo Domingo and Honduras and other parts sailing singly or in small groups, all sizeable and fully laden, bound for the assembly port. Even in the two great fleets there were, apart from heavily armed silver galleons and swift-sailing silver frigates, numbers of lumbering and un-weatherly craft which might stray into the hands of those who lurked in the harbours and shoals of that difficult stretch of water. Most of the privateers, therefore, contrived to reach the Havana coast in the spring or summer, at which time the homeward shipping was generally finding its way thither. In July the hurricane season was already beginning, but the Spaniards were often late and the English, torn between their cupidity and their anxiety,

Reactions to Foreign Aggression in the Caribbean to about 1680', *H.A.H.R.*, ix (1929), 286–302; Diego Angulo Iñiguez, *Bautista Antoneli: Las Fortificaciones Americanas del Siglo* xvi (Madrid, 1942), *passim*.
[1] These voyages are dealt with in ch. 9 below.

simply waited as long as they dared. The weather and the movements of Spanish shipping thus largely determined the timing of English venturing. It was usual to set forth in the later winter or early spring (very often in March, but sometimes as early as November or December), and to spend some time haunting the capes and ports of the Caribbean for minor prizes, making shore raids with pinnaces or boats, ransoming, trading or log-wood cutting before joining the irregular patrol at the approaches to Havana. Cape San Antonio could of course be reached by way of the islands or by way of the Main—the choice lay open to the privateers.

Precisely because this was the focal point of Spanish-American trade, the Havana coast had its dangers, especially for the singleton privateer, but the sporadic patrols of the two galleys which had been stationed there since 1586 did not deter the marauders. Captain William Michelson of the *Black Dog*, for example, went off with ten men in a captured frigate to reconnoitre this coast in 1589. He was reported to have taken two prizes, but this is the last that was ever heard of him.[1] The following year Watts' ships under Abraham Cocke, in consortship with the *Moonlight* and the *Conclude*, kept the Spaniards in a state of irritated anxiety throughout most of July and August. 'The shamelessness of these English ships,' wrote Rodrigo de Rada, general in command of the New Spain fleet, 'has reached such a point that they have come very close to this harbour, even pursuing the barges which bring water from a league away.' The English took no notable prizes here, but Newport with his two of Watts' fleet sank one rich Mexican and caused the loss of another, which ran aground and broke up. Meanwhile numerous small fish fell into the English net. As Juan de Texeda, campmaster of Havana, reported, 'this coast has been so overrun with corsairs, sailing in pairs and in quartets, that not a vessel left this port that was not immediately captured'.[2]

1591 saw the convergence of several expeditions upon the western end of Cuba. It is worth digressing a little to give a fuller account of this year's cruises because they illustrate well the character of Caribbean privateering and the degree of collaboration between different ventures. There were three main expedi-

---

[1] *Principal Navigations*, x (1904), 156–7. Related documents are printed in *E.P.V.*, pp. 50–8.

[2] *Roanoke Voyages*, pp. 579, 716; *Further English Voyages*, pp. 245–62.

tions: the fleet of John Watts and partners; two ships sent out by
another London syndicate; and three ships of Sir George Carey's.[1]
Watts' fleet consisted of the *Centaur*, commanded by William
Lane, the *Pegasus* under Stephen Michell, the *Hopewell* under
William Craston, the *John* under Michael Geare and a pinnace
called the *Fifth Part*. Lane, a member of the London Clothworkers' Company and thus an old associate of Watts, had been
on reprisal regularly since 1585. Michell, who was only twenty-
one, had lived in the Watts household for five years and described
himself as 'famulus Johannis Wattes', and Craston, now aged
thirty-one, had probably held the same dependent status in his
youth. Geare, a turbulent spirit, had already made two voyages to
the Indies and was to make at least four more after this. Watts was
the major shareholder in this 500-ton expedition, but the most
eminent was Sir Walter Raleigh. What exactly was Raleigh's
interest, financial or other, in this venture is not clear. It is just possible that there was some intention of visiting Virginia, but the
evidence for this is slender. The other venturers were Henry
Cletherow, John and Roland Stokes, Randall Symes and John
Coken—all London merchants and all, except the last, shareholders in other privateering ventures.

, A second London syndicate was responsible for the voyage of
the *Margaret* (60 tons) under Christopher Newport and the
Prudence (50 tons) under John Brough. The merchants setting
forth these ships—Robert Cobb, John More, John Newton and
William Jones, all of whom played an important part in the promotion of privateering—arranged that the first leg of the voyage
should be to Barbary (Morocco) for trade. Carey's expedition
comprised the *Bark Burr* (130 tons) under William Irish, the
Swallow (35 tons) under Ralph Lee and the *Content* (30 tons)
under Nicholas Lisle. Irish and Lee were both gentlemen adventurers of the lesser sort, wearing the livery of Sir George, and both
had sailed regularly in Carey's ships since 1585. The master of the
Content was William King of Ratcliffe, who was to lead an
Indies expedition in 1592 and was possibly the author of the
Hakluyt account of the fight of the *Content*.

Carey's three ships sailed late in March or early in April and are
next heard of between Dominica and Puerto Rico towards the
end of May. Meanwhile Lane and his men left Plymouth on 5
April in the company of Lord Thomas Howard, having agreed

[1] These voyages are dealt with in *E.P.V.*, pp. 95–172.

to serve under his command for that month. The *Hopewell*, however, almost immediately dropped out and late in May joined
Carey's ships as they approached Puerto Rico. Watts' other three
ships also managed to give Howard the slip and a few days later
took a rich prize westward of Cadiz. In the ensuing squabble
over pillage Geare and Michell made as if to board the admiral,
but the quarrel luckily subsided and course was set for the West
Indies. Here they probably met with the *Margaret* and the *Prudence*
and joined with them in the capture of four prizes in the harbour
of La Yaguana in Hispaniola. The *Margaret* now seems to have
returned home with one of the prizes.

Meanwhile the *Hopewell* and Carey's ships were making their
way to Cape Corrientes, at the western extremity of Cuba, which
they reached on 13 June. Here they were intercepted by a Spanish
patrol from Havana consisting of four substantial men-of-war, two
frigates and two galleys, which, under Diego de la Ribera, had
been assigned to sweep the coast clear for the New Spain *flota* and
escort it to Havana. A fierce engagement followed; the *Bark Burr*
was blown up by the explosion of her own powder and only Irish
and sixteen others were saved. The *Content*, armed only with a
minion, a saker, a falcon and two port-bases, fought desperately
against the greater part of the enemy force for twenty-four hours
and eventually escaped, mauled, but not seriously damaged. She
then stood north and waited for her consorts at a pre-arranged
rendezvous, which may have been on the coast of Florida. Failing
their arrival, however, she came on home, for the *Swallow* and the
Hopewell had returned to Cape Corrientes, there to find the
Centaur, the *Pegasus* and the *John* together with the *Prudence* and
another privateer, the *Lion* of Southampton.

Now at last prizes fell thick and fast. Three Santo Domingo
men bound for Havana with hides, sugar and ginger were taken
at Cape Corrientes before the company of corsairs together doubled
Cape San Antonio and escorted the prizes past Havana to send
them home with the *Lion* and the *Prudence*. The rest—Watts' four
ships and the *Swallow*—returned to lie off Havana, awaiting the
New Spain *flota*, which had still not arrived. Meanwhile they
baited the fretful Juan de Texeda, sending him love-messages and
compliments; then, while with cavalry and infantry he looked on
helpless, they took in rapid succession a rich prize of hides and
cochineal, four more Santo Domingo men, and lastly one of the
biggest privateering hauls of the war—the *Trinity* of Seville, laden

with silver, cochineal and hides to the value of £20,000. Apart from the Santo Domingo men, these were stragglers from the New Spain fleet, which entered Havana on 6 July. With so much in hand and the hurricane season coming on, the privateers loitered no longer and were back in England by the middle of September. For the Londoners, if not for Carey, this had been a highly successful venture, and it no doubt played a significant part in stimulating investment in West Indies privateering in the next few years. Watts' men alone brought or sent home prize-goods worth some £40,000. Pillage, embezzlement, the crews' thirds, customs duties and the Lord Admiral's tenths probably took away half of this return, but there was still left a huge margin of profit.

In 1592 Texeda's worries were greater still. No less than thirteen English ships foregathered off Havana: four of Lord Thomas Howard's, led by Benjamin Wood; three of Watts' men, under William Lane; William King with two ships financed by a group of London merchants and Sir Henry Palmer; George Kennell in the *Bark Randall*, Henry Roberts in the *Exchange* of Bristol, and possibly William Parker in the *Richard* and John Myddelton in the *Moonshine*; there may have been others, not to mention prizes already taken.[1] Texeda reported that there were fourteen on watch at the entrance to the port, three ships and two pinnaces haunting Cape San Antonio and three ships and a pinnace patrolling back and forth every three days from this cape to the Sonda de las Tortugas, which is situated towards the entrance of the Florida Channel. There was probably less organisation in the English movements than Texeda imagined, but they were certainly hoping for the arrival of the New Spain fleet. Unfortunately Texeda had sent word to Mexico to delay departure until the Havana coast should be clear of privateers. In fact the fleet did not reach Havana until December, nor the Cartagena ships until October; the English left about the end of August to avoid the hurricanes, having fought one or two inconclusive duels with the galleys and taken a few minor prizes. Nevertheless they had seriously delayed the Spanish fleets, which did not sail for home until March 1593.[2] In the summer of that year Texeda was due to be relieved by Don Juan Maldonado y Barnuevo, but the latter was obliged by the presence of privateers around Santo Domingo to approach Havana by the north coasts of Hispaniola and Cuba.

[1] The 1592 voyages are dealt with in *E.P.V.*, pp. 173–223.
[2] *Further English Voyages*, p. xcii.

As if this were not humiliation enough, Maldonado had to put in at Matanzas and march thence to Havana because the latter port was bottled up, in spite of the efforts of the galleys, by five English ships.[1] In 1594 Watts' men were again on the Havana coast in June and July. The *Centaur* under William Lane, the *Affection* under John Myddelton and the *Jewel* under Richard Best all took prizes, but Myddelton, who had already been captured once in 1592, was now taken prisoner again, with seven of his men, by two pinnaces sent out from Havana by Maldonado.[2] At last it looked as if the tide was turning, for now, as I. A. Wright has observed, 'the formidable English squadrons which had been blockading Havana disappeared'.[3] The following year Michael Geare, with the *Michael and John* and the *Handmaid*, was assaulted by a galleon and three shallops, which captured his pinnace and twenty-five of his men and killed many more.[4] The focal point of Spanish-American commerce was becoming a dangerous place for privateers.

The Tierra Firme coast presented serious difficulties throughout the period. The stakes were high—pearls and gold were to be had —but there were not many easily accessible small settlements. Consequently it was generally the more powerful privateering forces which chose the Main, and even they often reaped a poor harvest. Wood, for example, had little success in 1592 and Myddelton, with whom he joined forces near Cartagena, lost his consort, a converted prize, while thirteen men were captured in an attempted landing. James Langton, with Cumberland's ships, plundered the more or less defenceless pearl fishery at La Margarita, but failed to effect a landing at Cumaná and retired with some loss. Again at Rio de la Hacha Langton found the port on guard and had to content himself with exchanging a few musket shots and chivalrous letters. In the same year, 1593, Sir John Burgh was heavily repulsed in an attempt to march on the capital of La Margarita, and was obliged to leave several of his men dead and wounded ashore. The following year Benjamin Wood, detached from Dudley's force with two caravels, tried to conduct trade at Rio de la Hacha, but received a sharp rebuff and departed.[5]

---

[1] A. de I., Santo Domingo 128, 24 April 1594; A. de I., Santo Domingo 127, 9 Aug. 1593 and 8 Aug. 1593.

[2] *E.P.V.*, pp. 298–307.

[3] I. A. Wright, 'Rescates with Special Reference to Cuba, 1599–1610', *H.A.H.R.*, III (1920), 333.

[4] *E.P.V.*, pp. 330–7.   [5] *E.P.V.*, pp. 173–83, 225–83, 310.

In fact the only notable successes on the Main were achieved by Amyas Preston, who was in command of something more than an ordinary privateering force. In a pinnace and four ships—the *Ascension*, the *Gift*, the *Darling* and the *Angel*—he carried a landing force three hundred strong, and for the greater part of the cruise he had the consortship of three Southampton ships under Moses Willis. He was evidently expected to co-operate with Raleigh's Guiana expedition, and a Spanish source suggests that a part of Raleigh's plan was to destroy all the ports along the Main from Trinidad, presumably with the object of isolating Guiana. Raleigh makes it clear that he was expecting Preston to join him in Trinidad, whence they would have invaded Guiana together. In fact, however, Preston left Plymouth five weeks after Raleigh and wasted further time attacking the island of Puerto Santo. Consequently when he arrived in American waters, Preston made no attempt to join Raleigh, but made straight for La Margarita, though his subsequent movements, when compared to those of Raleigh, seem to suggest that he was doing his best to follow the general lines of an agreed plan of action. About the middle of May he reconnoitred La Margarita and withdrew. A few days later Raleigh did the same thing. In both cases the Spanish alleged that a landing was intended and only averted by the defenders' show of force. Preston meanwhile passed on by way of Coche Island to Cumaná, where he again refrained from landing, because, according to a Spanish account, he decided to leave the capture of Cumaná to Raleigh. Whatever truth there may be in this, there can be no doubt of the fierceness of the opposition met by Raleigh when he attempted to take the town towards the middle of June. His own statement that he captured the place was in fact an idle boast, or at best an attempt to conceal the bitter beating he received. The Spaniards put the English dead at as many as seventy-two, including John Gilbert, John Grenville and Captain Calfield. Moreover, it would appear that whereas Raleigh, before leaving Trinidad, had every intention of sacking all the Tierra Firme ports at least as far as Caracas, he now decided to sail directly for England.

Already, however, the city of Santiago de León de Caracas had been conquered by Preston and his men, whose boldness and resolution in this enterprise were only matched by the complacency and ineptitude of their opponents. The place yielded little in the way of loot, but this evidently was not Preston's main object; he set fire to the town and left believing it destroyed, but in fact only a part of the principal church and some houses were burnt. The next important town to the west was Coro, which he treated in the same fashion. Lastly he attempted to reach Laguna on Maracaibo Lagoon, the next worthwhile objective. Failing in this, he made his way out of the Caribbean by way of Cape San Antonio, where, ironically, he at last met Raleigh.[1]

In spite of Preston's performance, it is clear that the Main was no place for a minor privateering venture. What is more, there is no evidence of corsairs at all westward of Cartagena as far as the Isthmus: the coast from the capital of the Main to Nombre de Dios was well protected, and the corsairs knew it.

On the other hand the Spaniards in Hispaniola were by 1595 completely demoralised. Newport in 1592 held to ransom the settlement of Ocoa, west of Santo Domingo, and then went on to capture La Yaguana, which, in default of ransom, he burned. But the difference between conditions on the Main and those in the islands could not be better illustrated than by the contrast between Langton's reception at Cumaná and Rio de la Hacha and his easy success on the Santo Domingo coast. Here he raided sugar mills and cattle farms with impunity and dominated the approaches to Santo Domingo, loitering for two or three months, plundering and trading. For the English were now beginning to join in the trade which the French had been conducting for years in the north and west of the island, for which they used the curious name 'Perou',[2] though both were soon to be outstripped, here as elsewhere, by the Dutch. La Yaguana, a fairly important centre with 150 house-holds, and further north Guanahibes both carried on a thriving trade with the foreigners. Nor was the south coast, in spite of its proximity to the capital, much better off. Ocoa Bay, less than a hundred miles by sea from Santo Domingo, was raided again and again, and the old capital of the Indies was itself humiliatingly besieged for months in 1594. In May of that year there were reported to be twenty-three corsairs and contrabandists on the coasts of Hispaniola.[3]

The situation was summed up towards the end of 1595 by the

---

[1] *E.P.V.*, pp. 377–98.
[2] This term had been applied by Frenchmen to the Main and the West Indian Islands generally, and was probably at this very juncture acquiring the more localised reference, which was soon to exclude the older meaning.
[3] A. de I., Santo Domingo 127, 13 May 1594.

treasurer of Santo Domingo: 'But for the last four years, as I have said, corsairs are as numerous and assiduous as though these were ports of their own countries. They lie in wait on all the sailing routes to the Indies, particularly the courses converging on this city of Santo Domingo. Coming or going, we always have a corsair in sight. Not a ship coming up from the outside escapes them; nor does any which leaves the harbour get past them. If this continues, either this island will be depopulated or they will compel us to do business with them rather than with Spain. The special judge, sent by Your Majesty to deal with vessels departing from their lawful course and with contrabandists, is unable to prevent this trade from continuing, though he proceeds uprightly and with clemency. They make their incursions safely and find persons with whom to barter, for the land is sparsely settled and full of horned cattle, so that anywhere that they put in they find opportunity awaiting in the presence of negroes and other wretched delinquents who live outside the law in the bush, certain that neither the special judge nor any other representatives of justice can lay hands on them. Therefore the way to avoid the damage done by these thieves and culprits is to drive the corsairs from these seas, and this can only be accomplished by the galleys Your Majesty is entreated to send promptly in order to forestall the serious consequences which must otherwise ensue.'[1]

Long had they been pleading for galleys, and long miserably contrasting their lot with that of favoured Cartagena and Havana. But they were not alone in their plight. At about this same time the governor of La Margarita complained: 'Winter and summer enemies hang off this island all the time, which is why the canoe owners do not dare to fish. The bad part of it is that the fishery is fifteen leagues from here. To protect the canoes I have built many trenches and other defensive works there. It is necessary to keep half my men stationed there all the time. It is quite the usual thing for a three hundred ton ship to appear with a safe-conduct from the Queen of England, claiming to be Flemish; which, finding no entrance possible in any port here, then proceeds to Cumaná and lies there two or three months quite as though in its home port, trading and treating with the inhabitants while here we are continuously arms in hand. Among such vessels there was one in particular [*sic*], Captain Anton Martín, who in years past raided this pearl fishery and now makes threats against us. I assure Your

[1] A. de I., Santo Domingo 81, 14 Oct. 1595.

Majesty that he has been at Cumaná three months now, enjoying the good reception extended to him. It drives me wild to have to look on. From where he lay at anchor in the port of Cumaná he sent out and took and looted a canoe belonging to Nicholas de Aguiar, a resident of La Margarita, which was bringing food supplies from Puerto Rico. The very men who looted it are airing themselves in Cumaná today. Since Your Majesty cannot prevent this, because Your Majesty is far away, then may Jesus Christ remedy the situation.'[1]

His Majesty was even farther away from the Gulf of Honduras. Here the main port was Trujillo, a well-defended stronghold, but further west into the Gulf lay Puerto de Caballos, a smaller port, unprotected and exposed to attack from any point along miles of beaches. Newport was the first to raid it, in 1592. He approached flying a Spanish flag, but this ruse failed to deceive the local commander, who promptly warned the inhabitants to remove their valuables into the bush and at the same time took steps to do likewise with a quantity of plate from a frigate lying at anchor. Newport's men therefore made no great haul, but they took six tons of quicksilver, some money and a variety of other goods. According to his usual practice, Newport also removed the church bells and destroyed the images.

In 1594 the town was raided three times. Langton came first and found seven substantial ships lying in the harbour ready to receive the treasure collected from Guatemala and Honduras. In three days of fighting six of these were taken, including the flagship, into which the captors laded the best of the prize-goods and came away, as was reported from Trujillo, 'very triumphant indeed with this haul'. 'This affair,' it was added, 'has been very deeply felt through the country, as is natural, both because of the damage to the province in general and also because of the individual loss suffered by the owners of the ships and their cargoes and by the inhabitants of Puerto de Caballos.' No treasure was taken, nor was the town occupied, but Langton returned richly laden.

Caballos had no time to recover; a fortnight after Langton's departure Newport arrived with the *Golden Dragon* and the *Prudence* and took the town, but finding nothing there and suspecting an ambuscade, beat a hasty retreat. Two ships were captured in the harbour and two more burnt. Meanwhile the

[1] A. de I., Santo Domingo 184, 8 Oct. 1595.

governor, with twenty unarmed men, five harquebuses and neither powder nor shot, refused him refereshment and defied him to come and burn the town. Newport sailed away and with much relief the governor and the residents came back into the town, bringing with them from the bush their merchandise and money. Three weeks later fifty-five English and French corsairs landed silently from pinnaces two or three hours after midnight, seized the sentinel and marched rapidly with muffled drum to surround the governor's house. From his sick-bed the governor, Gerónimo Sánchez de Carranza, rose unperturbed and, spurning the back door, strode sword in hand through the huddle of armed men crowding the main entrance to the house. Then, wounded but ignoring the musket-fire that pursued him, he made his cool and dignified way to the bush, where he found 'all the householders of Puerto de Caballos and merchants clad only in their shirts, without shoes, uncombed and without swords, among them Captain Diego Ramírez, commander of the Honduras ships'. Such at least was his own story, duly corroborated by a government notary. The raiders this time were William Parker, in the *Richard*, and a French Captain, Jeremy Raymond. A day or two before they had caught off Trujillo Point an advice-boat from Caballos, and had thus obtained the services of a mulatto oarsman from that port, whose knowledge contributed largely to the victory. For fourteen days they remained in possession, lading great quantities of hides, sarsaparilla, anil, money and bullion into the privateers and the prizes previously taken, dividing the spoil equally between English and French. One of Parker's frigates foundered at sea and another ran into difficulties with customs and admiralty officials at Kinsale; but the most valuable part of the booty came home safely. Spanish losses in the second and third raids on Caballos were estimated at over 100,000 ducats (roughly £30,000 in English money at that time), and most of the loss occurred in the third raid. Parker came again in 1595, nor was this to be the end of the sufferings of Caballos. No wonder the governor advised the removal of the town to a safer place.[1]

Eastern Cuba was as exposed as Hispaniola and the Honduras coast; Jamaica and much of Puerto Rico were in much the same position; as for the Lesser Antilles and the Guiana coast, they were open to all and sundry. In fact the harassing pressure at Havana and the constant danger of an assault in strength on

[1] *E.P.V.*, pp. 323, 184–208, 236–83, 298–325.

Cartagena, Nombre de Dios, Vera Cruz or Puerto Rico caused the Spanish to neglect the defence of the West Indies as a whole in favour of the treasure route itself. Perhaps it would have been impossible to provide adequate defence for the whole enormous area; certainly no attempt was even made. For the inhabitants of a great part of the Caribbean there was no choice but flight when raiders arrived, no choice but to remove what valuables they could and hope to ransom the rest. As for the traders, they offered, in exchange for hides, sugar and other local produce, the manufactures needed by the settlers. Moreover in direct trade they could afford to make their wares cheaper than those that came, taxed and belated, through official channels.

Such was the situation when at the end of October 1595, after ten years' absence from these waters, Drake arrived at Guadelupe. He and Sir John Hawkins shared the command of six of the queen's ships and some twenty others, carrying about 2,500 men —a force appreciably but not greatly superior to that of 1585. The expedition, as everyone knows, was a failure. There is no space here, nor is it relevant to our purpose, to examine in any detail the sorry sequence of reverses, but some explanation of them is necessary. Those who have considered the subject appear to agree in pointing to three main factors in the failure: mismanagement in the preparation and conduct of the voyage; Spanish foreknowledge of the approaching attack; and the strengthening of Spanish forces by land and sea in the years since the defeat of the Armada. The protagonists of Drake on the one hand and of Hawkins on the other have said enough to convey the importance of the first factor and above all the folly of dividing the command. It was the weakness in these respects that was chiefly responsible for the fact that the Indies were warned in time from Spain and from Las Palmas of the English intentions. Puerto Rico, already reinforced and on guard, received further and exact information of the impending attack a week before it occurred, and this again was partly the fault of the English leaders. The other factor has perhaps been overstressed. Corbett writes: 'In the failure to grasp that Spain had become a great sea power with a fleet in a constant state of mobilisation and admirals well practised in handling and protecting large numbers of ships, lay the fatal misconception that overhung the whole expedition.' In fact Spain's naval forces did not come into action against the English in the Indies until after

Drake's death, when the fleet was already returning dispirited by repeated reverses and decimated by disease. Even then the engagement was indecisive and both sides claimed the victory. Probably the main strongholds of the area were now somewhat better fortified and manned to defend themselves against attack from the sea, but it is doubtful whether this was really the decisive factor. The very same fortress which repulsed Drake in 1595 was captured by the earl of Cumberland with a smaller force three years later, and Spanish evidence on the 1595 episode suggests that the successful resistance here and at the Isthmus of Panamá was due far less to progress with long-term fortification (which had been very slow up to this date) than to the timely reinforcements of men and guns received at both places a very short time before the English attack. It was the effectiveness of Spanish intelligence and communications, and the conjunction of this with the leisureliness of the English fleet, that fundamentally decided the issue.[1]

Thus Drake's failure cannot be regarded as a positive triumph for Spain's forces, nor does it mark the recovery by Spain of general control in the Caribbean. In fact Drake's last raid made little difference to the situation there.[2]

There does not appear to have been any significant decline in the numbers of English ships frequenting the West Indies after 1595. If we leave aside Drake's force, we have seventy-eight voyages of ships identifiable by name in the period 1588 to 1595, and seventy-three in the remaining eight years of the war. Of course these figures are incomplete, and there may well have been twice as many; but as our sources of information are of much the same nature for both periods, it is unlikely that the proportion of known to unknown voyages changed to any considerable extent.

[1] No thorough study of this voyage has yet been published, and in particular the voluminous Spanish materials have been neglected. A list of the printed and MS authorities would be far too long to include here, but the present writer hopes to produce in due course a detailed study together with documentary materials from both sides. Modern commentaries on the events occur in J. S. Corbett, *Drake and the Tudor Navy*, II, 402–37; *Monson's Tracts*, I, 312–40; J. A. Williamson, *Hawkins of Plymouth*, pp. 332–43.

[2] Contrast the conventional view as expressed by R. D. Hussey, ['Spanish Reactions to Foreign Aggression in the Caribbean to about 1860', *H.A.H.R.*, IX (1929), 286–302], 'The débacle of Drake and Hawkins in 1595 . . . illustrates the growing power of Spanish forces in the region, and it is doubtful if the foreign raiders shortly thereafter usually gained expenses, whatever be true of the contraband trade.'

Nor were the expeditions of the later years any less successful than those we have examined. Sherley's voyage of 1596–7, as we have seen, was a dismal failure, but at least he achieved more, with the capture of Jamaica, Santa Marta and Puerto de Caballos, than had the luckless John Chidley. William Parker's venture, which coincided with Sherley's, was costly in men, for he not only suffered losses at Campeche, having held it only for a few hours, but shortly afterwards lost his pinnace and its crew to two frigates of war manned out from Campeche. Nevertheless, the prize of 'a frigat which rode ready fraught with the kings tribute in silver and other good commodities', together with the booty from Campeche, must surely have 'made' the voyage.[1] In 1596 the *Scorpion*, under Anthony Hippon, made a short trip which was probably moderately rewarding,[2] and the following year found Newport, Geare and Ridlesden joint captains of the *Neptune* and her pinnace in the Indies. The chief promoters of this last venture were Newport himself and Richard and Francis Glanville, London goldsmiths, and this partnership in what was a formidable fighting ship was to continue until the end of the war. On this occasion Michael Geare appears to have made off with the pinnace to pursue his own devices, which were highly lucrative. After taking a prize off southeast Cuba he joined up with Sherley at Jamaica and accompanied him and Parker to Honduras. Gaining more prizegoods here, he then (perhaps in company with Parker) made for Campeche and took a further haul—all this with fifteen men and a pinnace. Meanwhile Newport cruised back and forth along the Havana coast, waiting in vain for the pinnace which was indispensable for privateering operations in the Caribbean.[3] In the same year a squadron of four of Watts' ships, led by his son John, captured and held to ransom a pearl-fishing village near Rio de la Hacha. A squabble ensued with the Lord Admiral's men in the *Lion's Whelp*, but the venture was in any case a success for John Watts, since the *Centaur* returned to Bristol with another prize worth nearly £6,000.[4]

[1] *Principal Navigations*, x, 277–80.

[2] H.C.A. 13/32, 11 Aug. 1596; H.C.A. 24/64, nos. 67/8 (*bis*).

[3] H.C.A. 13/32, 23–24 June 1597, 15 July 1597, 25 Aug. 1597; H.C.A. 13/33, 1 Feb. 1598–9; H.C.A. 13/34, 27 April 1599; H.C.A. 24/65, nos. 137, 138; H.C.A. 24/66, no. 49; H.C.A. 24/67, no. 116. Robert Bragg had a share in this venture.

[4] H.C.A. 13/32, 29 Oct., 24 Nov., 2, 24, 30 Dec. 1597; H.C.A. 13/102, 12 Dec. 1597; Harleian MS 598, ff. 42, 44; Additional MS 12505, ff. 467–9.

The main enterprise of 1598 was of course Cumberland's capture of Puerto Rico, which we have already examined. This must be classed as a private venture, for although it far outstripped all other such in its scale and its achievement, and had as its object much more than immediate plunder, it consisted only of privately owned ships and was financed entirely by private individuals. It was not indeed a saving voyage, but in more important respects its success was striking: both the East and the West Indian trades were seriously dislocated and Spanish prestige suffered a heavy blow.

Henceforth until the end of the war the privateers continued to thrive. We hear of three ships lost—the *John* of Henry White's in 1599,[1] the *Desire* of London, captain George Deane, which was cast away in the Indies in March 1600,[2] and the ship and pinnace under Simon Boreman, captured by the enemy in 1601.[3] But there were many successful ventures. The *Neptune*, under Newport, came home with two valuable prizes in June 1598,[4] and before the year was out departed again for the Caribbean with her pinnace the *Triton* to make another rewarding cruise under Captain John Paul.[5] In 1599 Newport resumed the command for another expedition, taking the *Neptune*, the *Blessing* and the *Triton* into the Bay of Mexico. Here he captured the town of Tabasco and brought away 888 ounces of plate, £200 in money, 14 ounces of gold and pearls, 41 hides and the bells of the town.[6] Early in 1601 he was again in the Indies, but this time we only catch a glimpse of him off the south coast of Hispaniola, where he took a prize.[7] Then towards the end of December 1601 he set forth once more in the *Neptune*, accompanied by the *Diana* under Edward Glanville. Prizes were taken on the Havana coast, and it is some measure of the financial returns of this venture, that the *Neptune*'s men were said to have received £3 2s. 6d. for each single share of the crew's third. The men of the *Diana*, who were given a paltry

[1] H.C.A. 13/34, 11 June 1599.
[2] H.C.A. 13/34, 26 July 1600; H.C.A. 14/34, no. 152; H.C.A. 24/68, no. 210/211.
[3] A. de I., Santa Fe 38, Cartagena de Indias, 30 January 1603. I am indebted for this information to Professor Sluiter of the University of California.
[4] H.C.A. 14/33, No. 263; Harleian MS 598, f. 46.
[5] H.C.A. 13/34, 11 June 1599, 21 July 1599, 4, 20 Dec. 1599, 8 Jan. 1599/1600; H.C.A. 24/67, nos. 3, 11.
[6] H.C.A. 13/34, 13 Sept. 1600; H.C.A. 24/68, no. 174.
[7] H.C.A. 13/35, 14 Sept. 1601.

A.E.P.

27s. per share, sued Newport and Glanville and eventually won their case. One of the witnesses stated that the *Neptune's* men were themselves disappointed, having expected to obtain £7 a share.[1]

Successful cruises were also made in 1599–1600 by Paul Bayning's *Golden Phoenix*, under Captain John Adey, in company with the *Flying Hope* (alias the *Handmaid*) under Captain William Cabreth;[2] by the *Trial*, under Captain Thomas Cowper, who made his voyage by a carefully planned and coolly executed piece of kidnapping at Mochima on the Pearl Coast;[3] by Thomas Burward in the *Antelope*, who, before seeking prizes, cut enough logwood at Nevis and other places to give him a worthwhile return cargo;[4] and by Sir Thomas Gerrard's *Scorn* under Captain Richard Kingston.[5] In 1601 Michael Geare in the *Archangel* of London and David Middleton in the *James* of Plymouth coasted the Tierra Firme as far as Cape de la Vela, though apparently without luck. January found them off Cape San Antonio, and they took a prize which Middleton brought home. It must have been shortly after this that a very valuable prize —the *St Anthony of Good Fortune* of Seville, laden with 2,500 kintalls of Campeche wood, 190 hides and some money—fell into their hands on the Havana coast.[6]

Meanwhile William Parker accomplished one of the most remarkable feats of the whole maritime war—the capture of Porto Belo. He left Plymouth in November 1601 with the *Prudence* (100 tons), the *Pearl* (60 tons), a pinnace and two shallops, and a total complement of 208 men. En route he took St Vincent in the Cape Verdes, held the Cubagua pearl-boats to ransom for £500 and captured a Portuguese slave ship off Cape de la Vela. As he approached the Isthmus Parker had six vessels—two ships, two pinnaces (described by the Spanish as large launches) and two

[1] H.C.A. 13/35, 2, 15 Sept. 1602; H.C.A. 13/36, 9 March 1603/4; H.C.A. 13/37, 15, 18, 21 May 1604; H.C.A. 24/70, nos. 188 (*Law and Custom*, I, 345) and 222; H.C.A. 24/69, no. 6; H.C.A. 14/36, no. 69.

[2] H.C.A. 13/34, 3, 5 Sept. 1599, 25, 26 Aug. 1600; H.C.A. 24/67, no. 106; H.C.A. 24/68, nos. 201 and 208; H.C.A. 14/35, no. 63.

[3] H.C.A. 24/68, nos. 182, 188, 189.

[4] H.C.A. 13/34, 1 Aug. 1600; H.C.A. 24/68, no. 173.

[5] H.C.A. 13/34, 1, 3 Nov. 1600. Richard Fishbourne sailed in this voyage.

[6] *Purchas*, XVI, 298–301; H.C.A. 13/35, 19 April 1602, 7 May 1602; H.C.A. 24/69, nos. 7, 136, 174, 201; H.C.A. 14/35, no. 160; H.C.A. 13/104, 8 July 1602.

small shallops. Leaving his ships at an island east of the now deserted Nombre de Dios, he took the pinnaces and shallops on to the Bastimentos Islands, which lay within a few miles of his quarry. Here he caught negro guides, and on the night of 15–16 February 1602 (5–6 February 1601 English style) approached the harbour of Porto Belo. The entrance was supposed to be guarded by a new fort—the Castle of San Felipe—which had been built at great cost in recent years, while on the other side of the harbour and closer to the town stood the fort of Santiago. Challenged by the sentry on watch at the Castle of San Felipe, the English replied, through a Portuguese, that they were from Cartagena, bringing tiles and planks for the fort. They were instructed to haul off and anchor by the entrance and accordingly did so. No suspicion had been aroused, and about an hour later the two shallops, carrying forty musketeers rowed stealthily along the shore without being seen from the castle.

They were again challenged as they passed the other fort, but managed again to allay suspicion and so were able to land un-hampered. Firing their muskets and giving an impression of over-whelming force to the completely bewildered citizens, they made straight for the government buildings and the barracks. A brave attempt by the Spanish commander, Captain Pedro Meléndez, to rally his men was of little avail. The two pinnaces had meanwhile entered the harbour and after capturing two frigates at anchor, went on to land the main body of the attacking force to support the spearhead; but the battle was already over. It was won by good use of intelligence, a fair amount of luck and the shattering effect of surprise action carried out with an *élan* worthy of Drake himself. On the Spanish side there were the usual recriminations. The Castle was said to be useless for purposes of defence or offence, badly planned, rickety; of the two companies that made up the garrison of the town, 200 men in all, some 150 were in Panamá; and reasons were given for all this that did no credit to the president of the Audiencia and governor of the province, Don Alonso de Sotomayor. He it was, of course, who, having arrived after the event, investigated the catastrophe and punished those who were thought responsible: i.e. soldiers up to the rank of ensign. The sentry who failed to give the alarm was hanged; others received sentences varying from fines to floggings. The president then sent off a report of the whole affair with sufficient adjustment of the facts and circumstances to make it seem a matter of bad luck rather than mismanagement—a very different impression from that given by the earlier and extremely critical account sent by Francisco Suárez de Amaya to his brother Diego, governor of Cumaná. Parker held the place for twenty-four hours, and though he missed by a week a large consignment of bullion, took substantial booty. He refrained from burning the town on the curious grounds that 'the good that I should have done my selfe, and mine thereby should have beene very small in comparison of their damage'. As he at length retired from the harbour with his two pinnaces and two shallops and the two frigates and a bark which he had taken there, Parker remained on deck near the mainmast and joked that he would catch the shot from the forts as they vainly tried to hit him. The last the Spanish heard was the sound of his laughter and of trumpets, as Parker went to rejoin his ships 'under the rock where Sir Francis Drake his coffin was thrown overboard'.[1]

In the early months of 1603 a large joint force of English and French corsairs was operating in the Caribbean. The leader of the English was Christopher Newport in the *Neptune*, and with him were Michael Geare in the *Archangel* and Anthony Hippon in Paul Bayning's *Phoenix*. The French were led by a captain the Spaniards called 'Buxar', who had been with Jeremy Raymond at Utila Island in the Gulf of Honduras in 1595, when Raymond had been killed. The Spanish reported a landing by 500 men at Jamaica on 24 January, which they claimed to have driven off. Another Spanish source, however, suggests that the Anglo-French force was not interested in acquiring more than victuals here, and that, having obtained them, it pressed on to its main objective.[2] On 16 February eight ships and six lesser vessels appeared off Puerto de Caballos, carrying, as the Spanish avowed, more than 800 men. Anchored at the port lay two Spanish war-

---

[1] *Purchas*, XVI, 292–7; A. de I., Santo Domingo 187, Francisco Suárez de Amaya to Diego Suárez de Amaya, 1 June 1601; A. de I., Panamá 45, Alonso de Sotomayor to the Crown, 20 July 1601. The Spanish material has been transcribed and translated by Miss I. A. Wright, to whom I am most grateful for permission to use this evidence.

[2] A. de I., Santo Domingo 129, Don Pedro de Valdés to the Crown, Havana, 6 June 1603, quoted in I. A. Wright, 'Rescates with Special Reference to Cuba, 1599–1610', *H.A.H.R.*, III (1920), 333; A. de I., Guatemala 39, Don Jorge de Albarado to Crown, Trujillo, 20 March 1603 (Wright transcript); and documents quoted in F. Cundall and J. L. Pietersz, *Jamaica under the Spaniards* (Kingston, 1919), pp. 26–7.

ships—the *capitana* and the *almiranta* of the *armada*. After a hard fight lasting about eight hours these were subdued and the port itself occupied. The booty amounted to 200 kintalls of anil, 3,000 hides and the artillery of the two prizes, together with miscellaneous goods from the town and from the Golfo Dulce. The *capitana*, which had borne the brunt of the fighting and had inflicted considerable casualties on the enemy, was too badly damaged to bring away, and so the prize goods were all laded into the other prize. Leaving Caballos once more devastated and the flow of treasure once more interrupted, the English and French now seem to have parted company, the former making directly for home.[1] Already a month after the action at Caballos rumour had reached England 'of one Newport a seaman that with two shippes hath taken five fregats laden with treasure comming from Cartagena and Nombre de Dios towards the Havana: yf all be true that is reported yt will prove the greatest prize that ever I heard of, for they that are most modest talke of two millions at least: the king of Spaine hath sent out eight men of warre to way-lay and intercept him . . .'.[2] Further rumours followed and it was finally reported by the Venetian secretary in England that the prize, consisting of two ships bringing gold from Havana to the value of a million, had been brought to Ireland.[3] After this there is silence. It can hardly be doubted that this was, after all, mere rumour, based on a wild exaggeration of what had really happened. It is inconceivable that if Newport had taken treasure of any great value there would have been no official notice of it, no spate of letters, inventories, claims and counter-claims such as featured every really large haul of the war. Nevertheless this was no mean achievement of Newport's, and though there is no evidence that he took any considerable quantity of treasure, he probably made a handsome profit on his venture. One more highly successful cruise that is worth mention was the voyage of Captain Fisher in the *John and Francis*, who in February 1603 took a ransom of 585 ounces of pearl for nine pearl boats captured near Rio de la Hacha and off the Havana coast took a prize of campeche wood and another of hides.[4]

---

[1] The Caballos episode is described in A. de I., Guatemala 39, Don Jorge de Albarado to Crown, Trujillo, 20 March 1603 (Wright transcript).

[2] N. E. McClure (ed.), *The Letters of John Chamberlain*, American Philosophical Society, Memoirs, XII (1939), I, 187–8.

[3] *Cal. S.P. Venetian, 1592–1603* (1897), p. 555.

[4] H.C.A. 13/36, 2 July 1603.

It is clear that whatever improvements the Spanish made in their defence of the West Indies, they did not diminish the onslaught of the privateers. The strengthening of Puerto Rico did not save it from Cumberland, nor could the Castle of San Felipe prevent the capture of Porto Belo. Though frigates of war were kept in the Caribbean now, and occasionally pursued and took a privateer, the English could reply in kind with crushing effect. Moreover prizes were still taken off the Havana coast. As for the remoter parts, their position had evidently deteriorated during the war.

From Honduras in 1603 came the oft-repeated complaint of the defenceless state of all the coast except Trujillo—'and if your majesty does not provide some order or remedy, he will lose the trade and commerce of these provinces, because each year they come at the same time as this with the forces they see to be necessary to do their work, and your majesty will lose much of his royal revenue and the enemy will gather more strength'.[1]

From 1598 the Dutch were trading in Guiana and in 1602 they were joined by Captain Charles Leigh who reconnoitred the coast for the settlement he was to start two years later. At Punta de Araya from 1595 increasing numbers of Dutchmen arrived to lade salt and smuggle European goods to Cumaná. Englishmen played but a small part in these commercial activities, but La Margarita, Cubagua and all the pearl settlements as far as Rio de la Hacha were repeatedly attacked and ransom extorted. The eastern end of the pearl coast seems to have borne the brunt of these raids, and this does no doubt partly explain the shift in the centre of pearling activity to the vicinity of Rio de la Hacha in the later sixteenth century.[2]

As for Hispaniola and the greater part of Cuba, they were so weak that practically all semblance of resistance had gone. In 1600 the archbishop wrote from Santo Domingo to the King: 'I understand that the defence of this city now consists in its poverty, because force for resisting there is not. The *vecinos* do not exceed two hundred, and at most have twenty or thirty men among them who can, with the *Presidente*, make front to the enemy. The others have neither arms nor desire except to go to the forests as they have

---

[1] A. de I., Guatemala 39, Don Jorge de Albarado to Crown, Trujillo, 20 March 1603 (Wright transcript).

[2] For discussion of this point see S. A. Mosk, 'Spanish pearl-fishing operations on the pearl coast in the sixteenth century', *H.A.H.R.*, XVIII (1938), 398.

done at other times.'[1] If the capital was in this state, what can be expected of the minor ports? In fact they were given over almost entirely to what the Spanish called 'rescates'—illicit dealing with the enemy or other unlawful contrabandists. Of the latter many were Dutch and French, who for the most part confined their activity to trade, selling European goods of all kinds to the eager inhabitants in exchange chiefly for hides, but also for sugar and various other local produce. Fernando Melgarejo de Córdoba, governor of Jamaica, reported in June 1604 that there were nine contraband ships at Manzanilla in Cuba and another five at Guanahibes in Hispaniola, while the mouth of the Cauto River at Bayamo was so firmly occupied by enemies that no ship could leave without a safe-conduct from the foreigners. At Manzanilla they had brought artillery ashore and were constructing a *corps-de-garde*. Shops had been set up and the people of the country about frequented the place if only for medical treatment and for games of bowls.[2] In this trading, which was directly conducted to a large extent by the numerous Portuguese and other foreigners who had emigrated to the two islands, almost everyone was involved, and the attempts of the Spanish to stamp it out in the early years of the seventeenth century were in the long run unavailing. For a short time, however, they met with some apparent success. Don Pedro de Valdés organised locally built *armadillas*, or small squadrons of armed frigates, when he arrived as governor of Cuba in June 1602. At the same time he took strong measures against the *rescatadores*, the chief offenders among the local population. A similar campaign was mounted in Hispaniola. These measures did not achieve much, however, because the contrabandists and their allies ashore were so numerous. Consequently a drastic step, which had been adumbrated as long ago as 1587, was at last taken. In 1604 an edict was received ordering the evacuation of the north and west coasts of Hispaniola and the removal of the towns of Puerto Plata, Bayaha and La Yaguana to the south. In the following year, in the face of revolt and social chaos, the ruthless order was carried out. Numbers of the inhabitants fled to the hills or aboard foreign ships. A few months later Don Luis Fajardo, who had already inflicted heavy losses on the Dutch

[1] A. de I., 54-1-9, no. 491/2, quoted in R. D. Hussey, 'Spanish Reactions to Foreign Aggression in the Caribbean to about 1680', *H.A.H.R.*, IX (1929), 286-302.
[2] Quoted in F. Cundall and J. L. Pietersz, *Jamaica under the Spaniards*, pp. 29-30

shipping at Araya, dispersed a large fleet of smugglers—twenty-four Dutch, six French and one English—near Cuba. Further stringent measures followed, and the Spanish thus temporarily checked the rising tide of foreign commercial penetration of the Indies, but at great cost to themselves and in such a way as to present to the corsairs of the future a magnificent base of operations. Thus the age of the privateers gave place to that of the buccaneers.[1]

What part did the English play in this contraband trade? Privateers did of course often trade with the local people, but their opportunities for doing so were rather limited. For the inhabitants were not inclined to trust them far, and in any case the men-of-war could only barter such goods as they had captured at sea, which were usually not of the kind desired or needed by those ashore. Thus in the matter of trade the English privateer could not compete with the Dutchmen and Frenchmen who came mainly for this purpose, well supplied with European wares. It is in 1602 that we find the first evidence of attempts by the English to imitate the Dutch and French. In this year the *Prosperous* of London, owned by William Shute, went out in what was by all appearances primarily a trading venture, though this ship was a very powerful merchantman which had been employed in privateering before this. In November she was at Guanahibes (Port Gonaïves) in western Hispaniola, and her factors freighted a ship called the *Angel Gabriel* to bring goods to Europe.[2] In the same year Nicholas Farrar and Thomas Myddelton, partners in sugar-refining and other business, made ready their ship the *Rose Lion* for a West Indies trading voyage, and when they heard that the captain was intending a 'warfare voyage', they did all they could to stop the venture and have the ship arrested.[3] In December 1602 the London merchants John Eldred and Richard Hall sent out the *Mayflower*, the *Neptune*, the *Richard* and the *Dispatch* in trade, the chief factor being William Resould, an experienced merchant. From Guanahibes during 1603 these ships conducted a thriving trade in company with the *Dorothy*, set forth by Robert and William Bragg, and the *Vineyard*, another of Thomas Myddelton's

[1] This account is based on I. A. Wright, 'Rescates with Special Reference to Cuba, 1599–1610', *H.A.H.R.*, III (1920), 333, and E. Sluiter, 'Dutch-Spanish Rivalry in the Caribbean, 1594–1609', *H.A.H.R.*, XXVIII (1948), 165–96.
[2] H.C.A. 13/37, 19 Nov. 1604.
[3] H.C.A. 13/37, 25, 27 June, 14 Sept., 1, 6 Oct. 1604.

ships. It happens that we know of the presence of these vessels in the great bay from Cape Tiburon to Cape St Nicholas because they all laded goods, chiefly hides, aboard two ships, the *Andrew* and the *Christopher*, which were Spanish prizes taken by one Captain Cleeve after the end of the war. There is no reason to assume, therefore, that these were the only English merchantmen in the area in 1603.

The experience of these traders in the West Indies was symptomatic of the situation. Their trading apparently went well until August 1603. In that month Captain Christopher Cleeve in his privateer, the *Elizabeth and Cleeve*, took the two prizes we have mentioned in the Old Channel north of Cuba. With him at the time were the *Neptune*, under Captain Andrew Miller, with sundry men from the *Mayflower* aboard, and two pinnaces. Cleeve had already made rewarding raids on Santiago in the Cape Verdes and on Jamaica. Miller had of course served in privateers before this, and his ship, the *Neptune*, was probably Newport's man-of-war. Whatever may have been the intentions of Eldred and Hall, or the fine distinctions drawn by Thomas Myddelton and Nicholas Farrar, trade and plunder were not easily to be kept apart in the circumstances. Moreover, the Spanish authorities, just at this moment trying desperately to end the contraband trade, made no such distinctions between merchants and robbers. In the same month the *Richard*, trading at Montecristi on the north coast of Hispaniola, was set upon and captured, two of her men being killed and the rest imprisoned. After this the Spanish inhabitants, it was said, were afraid to deal with the English for fear the latter would entrap them and take revenge. Cleeve, who must have been on perfectly good terms with the English factors at Guanahibes, now laded some of their goods and brought them to England, where they were promptly arrested. Cleeve's own prize-goods and what he had acquired in exchange for prize-goods were adjudged unlawful spoil; as for the English merchants, they were obliged to go to law to secure the restoration of the goods they had, rather foolishly, freighted with Cleeve.[1]

Nevertheless, the trade did not immediately cease. In May 1604 Newport was reported to have left for the Indies 'in the Peter of

[1] H.C.A. 13/37, 24–25 May 1604, 9, 18, 19, 21 June 1604, 13, 14, 18, 21 July 1604, 4, 22, 30 Aug. 1604, 25 Jan. 1604/5, 19 March 1604/5, 4 April 1605; H.C.A. 24/70, nos. 20, 31, 164, 169, 193, 194, 210; H.C.A. 13/104, 30 June 1604, 20 July 1604, 25 Oct. 1606.

London in trade' and was not expected to return that year. In September 1605 he was received at Court and 'brought two young Crocodiles and a wild Bore from Hispaniola, and were presented alive unto his Maiestie'.[1] In the Spring of 1605 the *Great Phoenix* of London was in the Indies, and a pinnace of hers under George King fell out with the Spaniards at Jamaica. It was alleged that King, hearing of plots against his pinnace, seized two Spaniards, hanging one and cutting off the ears of the other, and that the Spanish thereupon attacked him in a frigate and killed some of his men.[2] This kind of incident was not encouraging; nor was the comment of Henry Challons on the failure of his own attempted Virginia voyage in 1606 and on the capture of Captain Legat's crew in the Indies in the same year: 'This I had the rather noted to the end that it may the better be considered what numbers of ships and men have gone out of England, since the conclusion of peace betwene England and Spaine, in the way of honest Trade and Traffique, and how many of them have miserably miscarried. Having beene slaine, drowned, hanged or pittifully captived, and thrust out of their ships and all their goods.'[3]

It would appear, then, that towards the end of the war and during the first year or so of the peace the English, as well as the Dutch and French, made a considerable effort to exploit the gains of the privateers and the weakness of Spanish control in the West Indies in order to establish trade. This drive, however, was not supported by James I in his negotiations with Spain, for insistence upon Spain's acknowledgement of free trade would have meant the continuation of the war. At the very same time Spain made strenuous efforts to mend her fences in the Caribbean. The result of this complex of circumstances was that for a time at least the traders turned their attentions to areas of less vital concern to Spain—to Virginia and Guiana—leaving the Caribbean to the sporadic depredations of the buccaneers.

---

[1] H.C.A. 13/37, 15, 18, 21 May 1604; John Stow, *Annales* (ed. Hawes, 1631), p. 871.
[2] H.C.A. 24/71, no. 119.   [3] *Purchas*, XIX, 296.

Chapter 9

WESTERN PLANTING

The reign of Elizabeth saw the beginnings of English colonial enterprise in the New World. The influence of privateering on such momentous developments would clearly merit attention even if it were but slight; in fact, however, privateering and American planting were so closely related that no satisfactory history of either could be written without some account of the other. Englishmen first became interested in the colonisation of America at the time of Jean Ribault's Florida settlement, but it was not until the seventies that they took up American projects seriously, and not until the eighties that their schemes materialised in the form of colonial expeditions. The movement thus marched more or less in step with the growth of Anglo-Spanish hostility and reached its first climax in the earliest and most critical phase of the war, from 1585 to 1588.

No one would maintain that this was pure coincidence. A movement which entailed some breach in Spain's monopoly of the western hemisphere was bound to be caught up in the swirl of religious and political antagonism that finally brought the two nations to war. The Spaniards, for their part, showed their determination to prevent foreign intervention by their ruthless destruction of the French Florida colony in 1565. The safety of their western empire was a matter of vital concern to them, and any development which might endanger the flow of treasure had to be frustrated. Hence the acute anxiety they displayed at any prospect or rumour of foreign settlement on the north American coast. A colony here, they feared, might well provide an effective base for operations against the treasure fleets as they emerged from the Florida Channel, or even against the Indies themselves. This concern largely explains the establishment of the Spanish garrison at San Agustín in Florida in 1565 and of more northerly posts as far as Santa Elena in latitude 32° 20′ N. A mission station, which might have become a military outpost, was even maintained on Chesapeake Bay for a short time in the early seventies. Until 1580 it was chiefly the French who provoked these Spanish security measures, but Spain was equally on guard against the English, and her ambassadors were quick to report any signs of English interest, whether in Florida, as in the early sixties, or in 'Norumbega' (New England), as in the early eighties.[1]

What justification was there for Spanish suspicion of English colonial enterprise? What were the real intentions of the English projectors? These questions are difficult to answer with any precision for the period up to 1584, partly because until then the motives and intentions were undoubtedly mixed, and partly because until then aggressive intentions could not be publicly avowed. On the other hand there is enough evidence to show that this was by no means a purely peaceful movement. Even its commercial motives were not entirely pacific. Much emphasis was laid on the arguments of economic nationalism. An American settlement would provide a market for English cloth and other goods and thus help to alleviate unemployment at home. It would also serve to absorb some of the surplus poor. It would strengthen England by producing timber and naval stores, for which sinews of defence the nation should not have to depend on foreign sources. It would stimulate fishing, and thus develop the reserve of ships and seamen. Many other commodities for which we paid dearly abroad might likewise be obtained, so that we could save treasure and gain independence in commerce. All this sounds peaceful enough, and such arguments were most frequently used by those interested in a settlement in New England or further north—by Edward Hayes, for example, whose patron, Lord Burghley, was certainly no advocate of aggression.[2] Yet the commercial elements to whom such arguments were supposedly designed to appeal were probably less interested in northerly than in southerly projects. When London finally gave its backing to western planting it plumped for Virginia. Christopher Carleill's project, which did succeed in interesting both the Bristol merchants and the Muscovy Company, was for a colony 'in forty degrees . . . very apt to gather the commodities either of those parts which stand to the Southward of it, as also of those which are to the Northward'.[3] In so far

[1] D. B. Quinn, 'Some Spanish Reactions to Elizabethan Colonial Enterprises', *Trans. Royal Hist. Soc.*, 5th Ser., I (1951), 1–23.

[2] D. B. Quinn, 'Edward Hayes, Liverpool Colonial Pioneer', *Transactions of the Historic Society of Lancashire and Cheshire*, III (1959), 25–45.

[3] D. B. Quinn (ed.), *The Voyages and Colonising Enterprises of Sir Humphrey Gilbert* (Hakluyt Society, 2nd Ser., LXXXIII and LXXXIV), II, 356.

as the colonial movement did express commercial ambitions, these were mainly southerly ambitions. The writings of the elder Hakluyt, who had wide contacts among the merchants, indicate this trend of thought. His pamphlet, *Notes framed by a gentleman heretofore to be given to one that prepared for a discovery and went not*, was printed in 1582, but written in 1578, probably in connection with Sir Humphrey Gilbert's project of that year. Here he emphasises the desire to achieve commercial independence from Spain, France and Eastland, but the prominence of salt, wine, raisins, olives, cochineal, hides and southern fruits in the text suggests strongly that the writer had in mind a settlement in Mediterranean latitudes and that it was the Spanish trade he was most anxious to replace.[1] And this theme receives even more stress in his *Inducements to the liking of the voyage intended towards Virginia*, written in 1585.[2] These writings of the elder Hakluyt express no consciously aggressive purpose, but their economic nationalism has a southward bias. The London groups whose support mattered—and in particular the Iberian traders who might see America as an alternative to Spain—were presumably interested chiefly in the produce of lower latitudes—Mediterranean, sub-tropical and tropical. But these were precisely the latitudes that approached and encroached upon Spanish dominion in the western hemisphere. Thus even the most pacific aspect of the colonial movement acquired anti-Spanish implications.

In this early, projecting phase, however, the gentry played a larger and more active role than the merchants and characteristically they contributed a distinctly predatory and aggressive note to the movement. Grenville's plan for the discovery and colonisation of 'Terra Australis Incognita', put forward in 1574, had the support of William Hawkins and 'certain gentlemen of the West Country'. In spite of the pious plea of its author for permission to extend the Christian religion and England's overseas trade, neither de Guaras, the Spanish ambassador, nor the queen was to be convinced, and the patent for the voyage, though granted, was revoked, for fear of violence and the disruption of the precarious entente so recently achieved between the two countries.[3] It was left to Drake three years later to show what the presence of the English

---

[1] E. G. R. Taylor (ed.), *The Original Writings and Correspondence of the Two Richard Hakluyts* (Hakluyt Society, 2nd Ser., LXXVI and LXXVII), I, 116–22.
[2] *Ibid.*, II, 327–38.
[3] A. L. Rowse, *Sir Richard Grenville of the Revenge*, pp. 83–112.

in the Pacific really meant, which he did by returning with half a million in stolen treasure. And it was left to Sir Humphrey Gilbert to reveal how colonial schemes could be used as a cover for an assault on Spain's shipping and empire. His 'Discourse how her Majesty may annoy the King of Spain' (1577) advocates an expedition to Newfoundland for the capture of Spanish and Portuguese shipping 'either by open hostility, or by some colorable means, as by giving of licence under letters patents to discover and inhabit some strange place'. This proposal was accompanied by another, with a similar title, expounding the advantages of a surprise attack on Cuba and Hispaniola.[1] Such was the immediate background to Gilbert's first colonial venture in 1578. The exact nature of his objectives cannot now be defined with certainty, but it seems most likely that he did intend to plant a colony and that this was to be situated well to the south in eastern North America and used as a base of operations against the Spanish empire, though it is also likely that a part of the fleet was intended for an attack on the West Indies, or perhaps on the treasure fleet. In fact none of these plans materialised; Gilbert's chief associate, Henry Knollys, broke with Gilbert and left Plymouth with three ships which subsequently committed a number of piracies in European waters without attempting to cross the Atlantic; Gilbert himself left with seven vessels, but seems to have got no further than Ireland; Raleigh, in one of the seven, probably attempted a West Indies raid, but turned back on reaching the Cape Verde Islands. Gilbert's partners in this disorderly expedition were pirates and gentry of the Devon, Cornish and South Welsh coasts.[2]

In the complex of colonial enterprises projected in 1582–3 under Gilbert's patent, attention was focused on the Norumbega region rather than the more southerly coasts. The investors and participants were still for the most part gentlemen, but the acquisition of land appears to have replaced plunder as the main incentive and the idea of using a colony for anti-Spanish operations now took second place in Gilbert's schemes.[3] This deviation from the generally aggressive tendency of the gentlemen adventurers is interesting but explicable. The predatory activity of the gentry was essentially a reaction to the growing gap between rents and prices. Spanish bullion was only one possible answer to the problem.

---

[1] *The Voyages and Colonising Enterprises of Sir Humphrey Gilbert*, I, 170–80.
[2] *Ibid.*, I, 35–49, 169–238.   [3] *Ibid.*, I, 55–7.

Treasure might also be found in the vast tracts of North America farmed out by Sir Humphrey Gilbert. If not, a colonist might at least have a huge feudal estate at his disposal. Knowing only of the riches of Central and South America, the more imaginative and adventurous gentry understandably saw Norumbega as a magnificent new way to pay old debts.

But this proliferation of plans produced no concrete result save Gilbert's own tragic voyage to Newfoundland. War now loomed near, and in 1584 the focus of interest moved decisively southward. In this year the younger Hakluyt wrote his *Discourse of Western Planting*, which in its reconciliation of the economic and political cases for colonisation seems to epitomise the fusion of the commercial and the predatory elements in the movement. The younger Hakluyt had already demonstrated his anti-Spanish bias in his proposal for the seizure of Magellan's Strait in 1580. Now, however, in expounding the cause of Virginia, he was concerned to demonstrate to the Queen the national benefit, both political and economic, to be derived from a project that was already afoot, and his patron now was its prime mover, Walter Raleigh.

Western planting and privateering were thus two manifestations of the same dynamic; they came into full being at the same time, in 1585, with the onset of the Spanish war; they developed in embryonic forms alongside each other during the previous two decades, equally fostered by the expansionist drive of the English merchants and gentry and by the deterioration of the political situation in Europe. Inevitably the connections between the two activities were very close once the war began.

Raleigh's main purpose in his Virginia enterprise was to establish a base from which English ships could operate against the Spanish Indies and the treasure fleet.[1] In the early months of 1585 various English offensive measures in the Atlantic were planned; the extent and manner of co-ordination of these movements would depend upon events, but it is sufficiently clear that they were seen as complementary. Accordingly Grenville departed in April to plant the first English colony as a shore base within striking distance of the plate route. In June Bernard Drake, who had made ready a small force to follow Grenville, received orders to make

---

[1] The following account of the Elizabethan Virginia enterprise is based largely on *The Roanoke Voyages*, though in concentrating on the connection between privateering and colonisation I have possibly given this aspect more emphasis than Professor Quinn does.

for Newfoundland instead, there to round up Spanish and Portuguese shipping. Finally in September Sir Francis Drake sailed for the West Indies with the main object of capturing Cartagena and commanding the Isthmus. Meanwhile in May English shipping had been arrested in Spain, and the issue of letters of reprisal began in July. Grenville's expedition, therefore, was the first of a series of moves and counter-moves that mark the opening of the maritime war.

In these circumstances privateering was the natural and inevitable accompaniment of nearly every Virginia voyage. On his first voyage Grenville picked up prizes in the Mona Channel on his way out, and after leaving Ralph Lane in charge of the Roanoke colony, took a very valuable prize off Bermuda. Grenville himself put its value at £12,000 to £15,000 and estimated that this would 'answer the charges of each adventurer'. On the other hand the evidence of a Portuguese merchant on board the prize suggests very strongly that it was worth far more, and that the total return of the prizes amounted to some £50,000. The significance of this is far-reaching. Privateering could cover the expenses of colonisation, and in the circumstances it was the obvious, indeed the only way of maintaining such an enterprise. Since the state would not underwrite it, the Virginia experiment had to pay for itself. If it could in turn provide further facilities for privateering it might be reckoned worth while. Unfortunately the site initially chosen was quite unsuitable for a privateering base, since no deep-water harbour was found, and subsequent events frustrated the search for a better site. In consequence the promoters rapidly came to the conclusion that settlements ashore were merely a liability and a distraction from the more important and profitable business of plundering the Spanish Indies. Bernard Drake's highly successful venture in the *Golden Riall* underlined the lesson of Grenville's voyage, for Drake captured rich prizes of sugar and fish in addition to the Iberian fishing fleets.

In June 1586 Sir Francis Drake made contact with Lane's settlement. Drake, having just done his best to destroy the Spanish base at San Agustín, evidently still had positive hopes of the colony, and Lane accepted his offer of substantial help in shipping, supplies and men. The hurricane which scattered Drake's fleet led to a radical change of plan and Lane's decision to abandon the settlement and return home with Drake, and one important factor in this decision was that Drake was now unable to offer a ship suitable for use in the search for a good harbour. Thus the first faltering in the Virginia enterprise was due in part to Lane's disillusionment with Roanoke as a privateering base. Raleigh's supply-ship, which Lane had been expecting for Easter, arrived immediately after his departure, and Grenville with a small fleet a few weeks later. Raleigh's men did not wait for Grenville, and the latter himself did not stay long, leaving only a small holding party of fifteen or eighteen men. Grenville had taken prizes on the way out and was probably keen to pick up more on the return voyage, which may explain why he left so soon. In the event the prizes taken did probably pay for Raleigh's supply-ship and Grenville's expedition. By the end of 1586, in fact, the colonial project had made no material progress and seemed likely to offer nothing towards the prosecution of the war, whereas the high profitability and direct usefulness of prize-hunting had been clearly demonstrated.

In January 1587 a shift of emphasis in the colonial plans was marked by the appointment of John White as first governor of the City of Raleigh. The aim was to establish on Chesapeake Bay a colony of settlers instead of a paid garrison. The settlers would be granted land and would have a direct investment interest in the colony. This does not mean that the strategic possibilities of an English foothold in Virginia ceased to interest the projectors; it does suggest, however, a new concern with the creation of a stable, self-supporting community. Hence there now began to appear signs of conflict between the claims of the colony and the attractions of privateering. Already on the way to Virginia in 1587 the friction between White and his skipper, Simón Fernández, was evident, and so far did they succeed in thwarting each other that they obtained in the West Indies neither prizes nor supplies for the settlers.

Continuing interest in Virginia as a privateering base, however, is suggested by the activities of Grenville and Sir George Carey. Grenville appears to have planned a reprisal venture with three vessels in 1587, but he probably abandoned the project. Carey, who had probably been interested in the earlier Virginia ventures, set forth the *Commander*, the *Swallow* and the *Gabriel* in 1587 and came to some arrangement for co-operation with White. Carey was presumably interested mainly in settlement as an aid to privateering, and the visit made by William Irish with these three ships to the Virginia coast may have had no other

o   A.E.P.

object than to test the facilities which the settlement could offer to privateers. On the other hand it is quite likely that Irish carried settlers and stores. In any case, however, Irish failed to make contact with White or with any survivors of the previous colonies. As for White, he planted his settlers, but on Roanoke Island instead of Chesapeake Bay, a change of plan forced upon him by Fernández, who refused to take them any further because 'the summer was far spent' and presumably he wished to spend the rest of it in search of plunder.

Meanwhile in Europe the great crisis was approaching and the thoughts of men in the position of Raleigh and Grenville were dominated by the needs of home defence. Even still, when White reported progress at the end of 1587, Raleigh at once prepared to send a pinnace followed by a full-scale expedition under Grenville. By the end of March Grenville was ready to leave, but the Privy Council finally forbade him to go and ordered him to hand over his shipping to Drake. Two small vessels were spared, however, and with these—the *Brave* and the *Roe*—White sailed for Virginia in April 1588. He never arrived. His captain in the *Brave*, Arthur Facy, wasted time chasing prizes, and was finally pursued and savagely subdued by a Rocheller. The *Brave* managed to crawl back to Bideford, there to be joined by the *Roe*, which had likewise abandoned the voyage. In this year of the Armada very few ships escaped the general stay, but a squadron of four privateers did reach the West Indies. These were the *Drake*, the *Examiner*, the *Hope* and the *Chance*, which left London in March, were probably in the West Indies in July, and reached the Strait of Belle Isle, between Newfoundland and the Labrador coast, in August. There is no evidence that they called at Virginia, but it is possible that the *Chance* was Carey's ship and that this was, at least in part, Carey's venture. The owner of the *Drake* and the *Examiner* was John Watts. The chief pilot in this voyage, Roger Kingsnode, seems to have returned in time to join another expedition to the West Indies which may have left England before the end of the year. But again there is no evidence of any Virginia visit.[1] Nor did the whole of the year 1589 see, so far as is known, any expedition for the relief of White's colony, though a number of voyages to the western hemisphere were permitted.

The last of the Roanoke voyages took place in 1590. John Watts was setting forth three privateers—the *Hopewell*, the *Little John* and

[1] For these two privateering ventures see *E.P.V.*, pp. 40–58.

the *John Evangelist*—on a West Indies venture. Again there was a stay of shipping and as a result a bargain was arranged whereby Raleigh acquired for Watts the licence to depart while Watts promised to ship John White, with stores and additional planters, to Virginia. It was also arranged that the London merchant William Sanderson (since 1587 deeply interested in the colonial project) should send his ship the *Moonlight* with Watts' privateers. Independently (at least, so far as is known) Carey's ship the *Bark Young* also sailed for the Caribbean with the further intention of visiting the colony, and at some stage joined forces with the *Falcon's Flight*, which belonged to John Norris of Barnstaple, a merchant formerly associated with Grenville's expeditions. Finally, in consortship with the *Moonlight* sailed the pinnace *Conclude*, owned by Thomas Myddelton and partners. The operations of these vessels in the West Indies were fairly successful, though Watts and his men probably gained far more than the rest; the visit of the *Hopewell* and the *Moonlight* to Roanoke, however, yielded nothing except the unsolved mystery of the lost colony.

The next year saw further collaboration between Raleigh, Carey and Watts—in the West Indian expedition we have already examined. But despite one or two references to the prospect of 'wintering in the country' and one mention of a rendezvous evidently north of Cuba, there seems to have been no serious interest left in Virginia as a practical proposition. The quick dividends of privateering were obviously much more attractive than the dead loss of investment in Virginia; but it is at least as important that Virginia had never come near to playing its intended role as a base for maritime warfare, and in 1591 the likelihood of its doing so seemed far more remote than in 1585. Since then there had been so many accumulating difficulties, so many disheartening setbacks, that it would have required almost superhuman optimism and determination to make the fresh start that was probably necessary. Moreover, the Virginia project had been essentially a strategic concept of the 'men of war' and Elizabeth's refusal to make it completely her own is significant; inevitably Virginia was sacrificed to higher needs in 1587–8; but the fate of the colony after the defeat of the Armada was a matter of strategic choice; if the state wished to pursue the campaign for Atlantic power it must now take over from Raleigh; its failure to do so not only ensured the death of the colony but also signified the death of Atlantic strategy.

The close association of privateering with other colonial schemes during the war is equally marked. Raleigh's Guiana project was in his view one of 'those attempts that might either promise return of profit to ourselves, or at least be a let and impeachment to the quiet course and plentiful trades of the Spanish nation, who in my weak judgement by such a war were as easily endangered and brought from his powerfulness as any prince of Europe'.[1] Guiana would not serve as a base, but was seen as a source of treasure, the key to power. Raleigh had been one of the most active promoters of privateering since the onset of the war and it was a natural and logical sequel for a man of such ambition to employ his privateering resources in the search for gold. He also employed his wide privateering contacts. The Lord Admiral provided the *Lion's Whelp*, for example, and Raleigh secured the co-operation of Sir Robert Dudley as well as that of Captains Preston, Somers, Popham and Willis. Raleigh's Guiana ventures, indeed, from the 1593 voyage of Sir John Burgh to the 1597 voyage of the *Watte*, stemmed directly from the privateering war. Nor is there any clear break in this case between the war-time voyages and the first attempts at settlement. Already in 1597 Raleigh's men found a certain Captain Leigh with a bark called the *John* of London in the River Corentine. This cannot have been the Charles Leigh who explored the Wiapoco River in 1602 and settled the first English colony there in 1604, but it may perhaps have been the John Ley who went captain of Watts' *Alcedo* in Cumberland's expedition the following year, but 'went out of her into his own pinnace upon his own private voyage to the India where he sped well'.[2] Whoever he was, this captain was only one of many who frequented the Guiana coast from this time until and after the end of the war, bringing cloth, slaves and manufactures for pearls and tobacco, and combining the trade with West Indian plunder. And it was out of this situation that there developed the colonial experiments of Charles Leigh, Robert Harcourt and Sir Thomas Roe. Robbing the Spaniards, of course, remained a popular pursuit even after the war, and Leigh had considerable trouble with some of his men, who, led by the Bristol sailor Martin Pring, preferred the attractions of West Indies raiding to the arduous tasks

---

[1] *Principal Navigations*, x, 347–8.
[2] G. C. Williamson, *George, Third Earl of Cumberland*, p. 178. Charles Leigh sailed to Newfoundland in 1597.

facing them in Guiana. In the end Pring deserted the colony and joined a Dutch ship.[1]

The northward voyages of the nineties to Newfoundland and the region of the Gulf of St Lawrence, though less warlike in intent than the Guiana ventures, were by no means untouched by the temptations of plunder. Attacks upon Spanish and French vessels were frequent and the sailors, as usual, showed themselves much more eager for pillage than for exploring. Leigh, in his voyage of 1597, had a substantial foretaste of the annoyance and frustration he was to feel years later in Guiana, since on both occasions the predatory instincts of his men obliged him to change his plans. In the short run privateering could and often did distract attention from exploration and planting—examples of this are not difficult to find for Virginia, Guiana or the Gulf of St Lawrence. But it is worth remembering that Leigh himself sailed home in a prize in 1597 and sent his consort to the Azores 'to spend his victuals for a man of war'; could he have afforded the luxury of exploration without the bread and butter of prizes?[2] Even the pacific Brownists, when they petitioned in 1597 to be allowed to emigrate to Canada, suggested that they might 'in time also greatly annoy that bloody and persecuting Spaniard about the Bay of Mexico'.[3]

The colonial movement, though not completely stopped, undoubtedly suffered something of a depression during the nineties. When it revived in the early years of the new century it had much more solid financial backing than it had found in the eighties. The chief difference, indeed, between the schemes of the eighties and these of Jacobean times was that the gentlemen promoters were now joined by a considerable number of substantial merchants. Among these are to be found many of the leading privateering promoters—Watts, Myddelton, Farrar, Seckford, Goddard, Hopkins and Cletherow's son, for example, were among the founding members of the Virginia Company; Robert Auldworth backed Martin Pring's expedition in 1603; Thomas Auldworth, Richard Fishbourne and Sir John Dodderidge (son of the Barnstaple mer-

---

[1] J. A. Williamson, *English Colonies in Guiana and on the Amazon, 1604–1688*, p. 32. Hostility towards the Spaniards remained an important element in the Guiana colonies for some time.

[2] *Principal Navigations*, VIII, 166–80.

[3] S.P. Dom. Eliz., cclxvi, no. 56—an interesting anticipation of the Providence Island Company.

chant) were prominent in the Newfoundland project of 1610. Among the gentlemen, too, a leading part in colonisation was played by successful privateering promoters. Sir John Gilbert, Sir George Somers, William Parker and George Popham were among the pioneers of the Virginia scheme, and they were soon joined by Sir Amyas Preston, Sir Stephen Ridlesden and captains William King and Christopher Newport. The fluid capital which had been lacking in the eighties was now available, and it must have been drawn to a considerable extent from the profits of privateering.[1]

But the contribution of privateering to the eventual success of western planting was not merely financial; perhaps even more important was the substance of sea-power. For the last action of the Spaniards in connection with the English Virginia settlement was taken in 1588, when Vicente González reconnoitred the coast. After this, though much was planned, nothing was done, because the Spanish were too busy elsewhere. As Professor Quinn has shown, 'it is an interesting and ironical result that the sea war between England and Spain, which obstructed and finally ended the first series of English attempts to settle colonists on the North American mainland, also, in the end, prevented the establishment of Spanish forts and settlements there, which, in their turn, might have made the English Virginia settlement of 1607 impossible'.[2] In the early years of James the Spanish showed their dislike and suspicion of the Virginia promoters—and again they were not entirely wrong in attributing anti-Spanish sentiments to many of them—but they could do little to stop the settlement because now and henceforth they lacked the maritime strength to impose their will. The English had in fact the freedom of the Atlantic, and this was in no small measure due to the efforts of the privateers.

Practical sea-power, however, also implies a certain quantity and quality of shipping and seamanship, embracing knowledge of the ocean and its shores and mastery of the organisation and conduct of large, long-distance expeditions. The progress the English had made in all these respects is obvious from a comparison of the voyages of Sir Humphrey Gilbert with those made to North America from 1602 to 1607. Experience of the Atlantic, rare in 1580, was common in 1600. Bartholomew Gosnold had been

[1] Brown, *Genesis*, I, 32–63, 209–28, 390.
[2] D. B. Quinn, 'Some Spanish Reactions to Elizabethan Colonial Enterprises', *Trans. Royal Hist. Soc.*, 5th Ser., I (1951), 20.

captain of a privateer in 1599;[1] Martin Pring had been in the West Indies in the *Susan and Parnell* in 1602;[2] Sir George Somers had cruised the Caribbean in 1595; Christopher Newport probably knew American waters by the end of the war better than any Englishman had known them before it. And behind such captains stood organisers like Sir John Gilbert the younger, Sir Humphrey's son, whose practical contact with maritime matters was far wider and deeper than his father's had been. Not all the advance since 1585 was the result of privateering, of course, but the 'interruption' of the colonial movement by fourteen years of sea war (1588–1601) was perhaps a pause necessary for the gathering of sufficient strength to ensure the success of the post-war efforts.

[1] H.C.A. 24/67, no. 5/6.   [2] H.C.A. 13/104, 8 July 1602.

Chapter 10

THE PORTUGUESE TRADES

English penetration of the Portuguese commercial empire began, as we have seen, before the Spanish war and even before the Spanish occupation of Portugal. In Morocco the English were already well established by 1585, Portuguese pretensions in that country having been finally destroyed at the battle of Alcazar in 1578. The only important effect of the war here was to give the Barbary merchants the chance to supplement their trading profits with prizes. For sugar dealers like Ofield and Cordell the addition of West Indian or Brazilian prize sugar to Barbary sugar was especially attractive. After the war the trade continued, probably at about the same level. Further south, the Senegambia and Guinea trades were on a much more precarious footing. Physically the Portuguese were not strong enough to prevent English interloping in the fifties and sixties, but diplomacy eventually did win them some respite, since there appears to have been little or no English trade in this region in the seventies and early eighties. The war, however, brought a resumption of English enterprise, again in conjunction with privateering, though trade was probably more spasmodic on the Guinea coast than in the nearer and less hazardous area of Senegambia. After the war English commerce in West Africa seems to have developed slowly and haltingly, but by the middle of the seventeenth century it had become a regular and fairly important branch of trade.

In sum, there was nothing sensational about the progress of English trade in West Africa before, during or after the war, but progress there was, and in the long run these footholds were valuable. What makes them seem small—and to some extent actually kept them small—was the phenomenal success of the Dutch, who in shipbuilding, seamanship, capital resources and commercial technique far excelled their island rivals. In these trades the Portuguese did not lose many ships to English privateers, but to the extent that privateering did weaken the Portuguese, it merely served to open the way for the Hollanders, who were much more capable of exploiting Portuguese weakness than the English were themselves. The situation in the Brazil trade, though different in some respects from that in the West African, reveals this tendency more clearly, for here the English wrought much greater damage, but achieved less trade than in West Africa, while the Dutch reaped an enormous harvest. It is worth looking at the Brazil trade in some detail because it presents in an exaggerated, and therefore easily recognisable form the typical relationship of Portuguese, Dutch and English in the struggle for colonial trade.

To some English merchants Brazil seemed to offer practical prospects of colonial trade in 1580. There was reason to hope that here a direct and peaceful trade could be established without great difficulty. Brazil, as a plantation colony, needed manufactures, and these the English could surely supply; and Brazil afforded two main commodities—sugar and brazilwood—that were much coveted by the southward-trading merchants. Furthermore, this was not a region in which the Portuguese held their trade by virtue of naval and military force, as was the case in West Africa and the East Indies. Already in 1578 a certain John Whithall had written from Brazil to his old friend Richard Staper, offering sugar in return for cloths and other manufactures. The same man wrote again to John Bird and Robert Walkden, and the response from London came when Bird, Christopher Hodsdon, Anthony Garrard, Thomas Bramley and William Elkin sent out the *Minion* of London in 1580. All those mentioned except Elkin are known to have been prominent merchants in Spain, Portugal or Morocco, and in their letter to Whithall the five promoters of the venture laid great stress on their desire for peaceful trade. Nevertheless, the *Minion* had a troublesome voyage. The master, Stephen Hare, seems to have been unable to control the merchants' factors or the crew, but the main obstacle to trade was religion. At Santos the English were well received by the local people and officials, but the visit was cut short when the *ministrador* of Rio de Janeiro, hearing that the heretics had actually attended a funeral service in Santos, hurried to the city and demanded to see the English master. At this the *Minion* promptly sailed for Bahia, where relations between ship and shore were much less encouraging. The pilot, Edward Cliffe, decided to turn friar, and through him the Portuguese got wind of certain heretical books aboard. Hare refused to surrender these or to come ashore. Thereupon he was denounced as a heretic and some of the crew on shore were arrested. What happened next is obscure: although the men were released, there may have been an attempt to seize the ship; at any rate shots were exchanged and the *Minion* made off in haste. Very little trade was done at Bahia, but two of the factors remained there with a stock of goods for sale and it looked as though there was still a chance of peaceful trade.[1]

Meanwhile, however, the war party was not idle. Terceira in the Azores did not acknowledge Philip's sovereignty, and this seemed to the earl of Leicester, Walsingham and Drake, even to Elizabeth, an excellent opportunity for intervention on Dom Antonio's behalf. Preparations went ahead to garrison the island and base a fleet there to cut the flow of treasure to Spain. This tempting project fell through partly because the English, the French and Dom Antonio failed to work amicably together, and partly because the scheme was vehemently opposed by the merchants trading to Spain and Portugal. The French force which eventually attempted the operation in 1582 was crushingly defeated by the Spanish under Santa Cruz. But English privateers were already taking to the sea under the Portuguese pretender's flag. Among them were Thomas Walton's *Diamond*, the *Archangel* of London, the *Prosperity* under the pirate Clinton Atkinson, the *Greyhound* under Thomas Beavyn, John Young's *White Bear* under the pirate John Storye, and the *Antonio*, which sailed from Plymouth to join the pretender's forces at La Rochelle. In April 1582 one Henry Roberts brought a sugar prize into Bristol and in the summer Henry Oughtred's *Susan Fortune* raided the Portuguese fishing fleet off Newfoundland. Again Hawkins was one of the moving spirits. Four prizes brought into Plymouth by Dom Antonio's ships in March 1582 were said to have come into his hands, and he probably had an interest in the *Bark Talbot*, the earl of Shrewsbury's ship, which accompanied the *Bark Allyn* to the Azores that year. Sir Francis Drake also sent two ships to Terceira. Much of this activity was but thinly disguised piracy, and for men like

---

[1] Willan, *Studies*, pp. 5–9, recounts the facts of the case (which we have apparently discovered independently) in greater detail. See also above, p. 85, and in addition to Willan's references, H.C.A. 13/24, 28 Feb. 1581/2, 31 May 1582, 1 June 1582, 11 Dec. 1582. Another Brazil voyage of 1580 was said to have been made by a Guernsey ship set forth by Sir Thomas Leighton, but the report may be simply a pirate's explanation of his possession of Brazil goods (H.C.A. 1/43, 11 March 1583/4).

Atkinson Dom Antonio's licences served the same purpose as Huguenot or Dutch commissions had done in the seventies. But after 1580 the number of marauders increased and the anti-papist bias in English sea-robbery became more pronounced than ever, the chief victims being the Portuguese. Such was the background to the merchants' hopes of trade with Brazil.[1]

The biggest setback for the Brazil trade, however, was the result of what was ostensibly a trading venture—the voyage of Captain Edward Fenton in 1582–3.[2] Nothing illustrates better than this the confusion of English policy in the early eighties. After the failure of the Terceira project Leicester and Walsingham turned their attention to what had been an incidental item in their plans for that enterprise—a voyage for the Moluccas. Leicester himself was the main shareholder in the revised venture, the next largest shares being those of Henry Oughtred and Drake. A number of leading courtiers also subscribed. Thus far the investors were what might be expected for an ambitious voyage of plunder; but the list also included Lord Burghley, Customer Smythe and a contribution from the Muscovy Company which was worth more than all the other ventures put together. The Muscovy Company was keenly interested in developing peaceful trade with the East Indies, and the two Muscovy men most active in the management of this voyage—William Towerson and Alderman George Barnes—were also leading figures in the Spanish Company.[3] Of the other merchants mentioned by name in connection with the voyage a high proportion were Iberian traders, and later prominent in the privateering business—Thomas Cordell, Thomas Pullison, Thomas Starkey and Robert Sadler.[4] Towerson was of course the

---

[1] H.C.A. 1/40, 23 Feb. 1582/3; H.C.A. 1/42, 6, 9, 15 Aug. 1583, 30 March 1585, 24 July 1585; H.C.A. 13/24, 22 Oct. 1582, 31 Dec. 1582, 15 Jan. 1582/3, 21 March 1582/3, 25–27 April 1583; H.C.A. 13/25, 6–9 Sept. 1583, 16–17 Oct. 1583, 15 Aug. 1584, 31 July 1585, 20 Aug. 1585; A.P.C. XIII, 385, 391, 392; E. G. R. Taylor (ed.), *The Troublesome Voyage of Captain Edward Fenton, 1582–3*, (Hakluyt Society, 2nd Ser., CXIII), p. 29.

[2] The following account is based chiefly on E. G. R. Taylor's recent edition of materials relating to Fenton's voyage (*op. cit.*). These documents show that the conventional view of Fenton's role in the venture is mistaken.

[3] V. M. Shillington and A. B. W. Chapman, *The Commercial Relations of England and Portugal*, appendix. Barnes obtained letters of reprisal in 1585 (Lansdowne MS 143, f. 322) and a certain George Barnes went captain of the *Edward Bonaventure* in the 1587 Cadiz expedition [H.C.A. 25/2 (5), 13 March 1586/7].

[4] *Cal. S.P. Colonial, East Indies, 1513–1616*, pp. 73–4. On Cordell, Pullison and Starkey see above, ch. 5. Sadler was a member of the Levant Company in 1592; he

old pioneer of the Guinea trade and his namesake, who sailed with Fenton in this venture, was to become an active privateering promoter and commander after 1585.

For the present, however, the commercial interest was not set upon open aggression. They saw to it that the ships were freighted with suitable merchandise, they arranged passages for several factors and they gave strict instructions for a peaceful procedure by way of the Cape of Good Hope. Unfortunately they picked the wrong man for their 'general'. Captain Fenton, who replaced Frobisher in this capacity in the last stage of the preparations, was certainly no man of peace, as some historians have seemed to suggest. Vain, choleric and irresolute, he entertained during the course of the voyage almost every possible plan of action except the one outlined in his instructions. Sharply opposed to him were Drake's men, among whom young William Hawkins and John Drake were the leaders. Their one idea was to repeat the exploits of Drake's circumnavigation, though they had been forbidden to pass the Straits of Magellan except in case of absolute necessity. Only the factors and the chaplains stood by the original plan— and they were for the most part ignored. Fenton's first thought on reaching the West African coast was to seize St Helena and capture the Portuguese carracks. When this suggestion failed to evoke enthusiasm it was resolved, without consulting the factors, to make for the Magellan Straits. Thus the expedition found itself, as if inevitably, well down the Brazilian coast in about 28° S in November 1582. Here, however, they had intelligence of a powerful Spanish fleet on its way to guard the Straits.[1] Fenton and Drake's men, already angry and jealous of each other, now violently disagreed. John Drake went on south alone in the *Francis* to his own disaster. Fenton and the rest, who seem to have regarded the easterly route as impracticable at this stage, turned north to replenish their ships at S. Vicente, even more resentful of each other now that failure stared them in the face. The only substantial hope remaining was to sell their merchandise in Brazil and return with some small profit, but the Portuguese would not trade so long as a

was owner or part-owner of the *Adonia*, the *Globe*, and the *Marlian* of London and had a hand in the ventures of the *Bark Bond* of Weymouth, the *Grace of God* of Topsham and the *Lion's Whelp* [H.C.A. 25/3 (9), 31 March 1592; and below, appendix].

[1] Actually this fleet, under Don Diego Flores, had already turned north again; the English, had they made for the Straits then, might well have arrived first.

Spanish fleet was in the offing. While the English dallied three Spanish warships appeared and attacked. The English out-gunned them completely, sinking one of the enemy and killing numbers of their men with trifling loss to themselves. They then moved north to Espirito Santo and made another attempt at trade, but soon had to move off when news of the recent battle reached the town. Fenton, who had been toying with the idea of establishing a kingdom for himself in southern Brazil, now had a notion to commandeer Newfoundland. But his ship had not sufficient water for the voyage and there was nothing left but to come home and face the music.

The effect on Brazil trade was immediately felt. John Hawkins had refused to subscribe to Fenton's venture, pleading debts and liabilities arising from the Terceira project. In fact, however, the Hawkinses were hatching their own venture, having obtained authority from Dom Antonio to make a trading voyage to Portuguese Africa and America. In 1582 William Hawkins, now aged sixty-three, set forth with several ships to the Cape Verdes. Here the Portuguese showed unmistakable hostility; they launched a surprise attack and reduced Hawkins' force considerably. He had intended to go on to Brazil, but decided against this when he learned from a prize of the Spanish alert on the Brazil coast, following Fenton's visit. Instead he made his way to the Caribbean and brought home eventually a rich cargo of pearls, treasure, hides and sugar. But he also had to unload all the merchandise he had taken out to sell in Brazil.[1]

In 1583 Thomas Cordell, William Garraway and others sent out the *Merchant Royal* with a cargo of victuals for the relief of Brazil, which was suffering from famine. The English commander was Robert Flick. He had been a factor in Bruges at the age of twenty-one and three years later, in 1575, had transferred his activities to Portugal, where he continued to do business for other Englishmen and on his own behalf until 1586. He was in fact an expert in Portuguese trade and was obviously chosen for this reason. Having sold some of his cargo in Olinda, he departed, leaving three men to complete the sales. One of these may have died, but the others continued their business until the arrival of Don Diego Flores, admiral of the fleet that had frightened Fenton away from the Straits. The Spanish accused the two English factors of being Fenton's men, confiscated their goods and sent the

[1] J. A. Williamson, *Hawkins of Plymouth*, pp. 218–24.

unfortunate couple in irons to Seville, whence they were transferred to Lisbon. Only after four months of negotiation did Flick
secure their release and even then the concession was made only in
consideration of the food supplies the *Merchant Royal* had provided.[1] In the same year the Southampton merchant Edward
Cotton sent out a ship for Brazil, but this one never arrived—it
was wrecked on the coast of Guinea with most of the company
'through mere dissolute negligence'.[2] Still the merchants did not
give up. When the *St John the Baptist* of Vianna was captured in
1585 by Raymond and Drake, her cargo of sugar was claimed by
Richard King of London, Thomas King of Ipswich, Thomas
Cordell, Henry Beecher (another London wholesale sugar dealer)
and others. King's own factor, it was said, had been out to Brazil
to supervise the deal and the freight was to be delivered direct to
London.[3]

In 1584 Philip of Spain confirmed the privileges of the English
merchants in Portugal and it was not until 1589 that they were
finally expelled from Lisbon.[4] But the whole situation was
changed by the Spanish confiscations of 1585. English privateers
now regarded Portuguese shipping anywhere as fair game. The
Iberian merchants soon assumed the leadership of the anti-
Lusitanian campaign. Flick was still in Portugal in February
1586, but early in 1587 he was deputed to lead a fleet of London
merchantmen to seize the carracks on their way from Lisbon. He
sailed in the *Merchant Royal*—a sweet revenge—and with him in
the *Susan* went James Lancaster, another expert in the Iberian
trade. William Towerson, who had been with Fenton in 1582,
now commanded the *Margaret and John* and George Barnes went
captain of the *Edward Bonaventure*. Thomas Cordell's name heads
the list of the promoters, followed by those of Watts, Bayning,
Simon Boreman, Hugh Lee and Robert Flick. This was the
fleet of eleven Londoners that joined forces with Drake to singe
the king of Spain's beard.[5] As for English trade with Brazil, it

---

[1] H.C.A. 13/22, 21 Nov. 1576; H.C.A. 13/25, 3, 6 Sept. 1585; H.C.A. 13/29,
1 July 1591.
[2] *Principal Navigations*, VI, 408–12.
[3] H.C.A. 13/25, 6–8 Dec. 1585, 22 Jan. 1585, 26, 30 April 1588.
[4] Shillington and Chapman, *Commercial Relations*, pp. 147, 158.
[5] H.C.A. 13/26, 22 April 1586, 7, 9 March 1586/7; H.C.A. 14/28, no. 167;
H.C.A. 25/2 (5), 13 March 1586/7; Corbett, *Spanish War*, xix, 105. Flick again
commanded the *Merchant Royal* in the Armada campaign. In 1589 he adventured

came to an abrupt stop. When Cumberland's ships sailed into Bahia in 1587 there was no thought of amity on either side. The English were greeted with a volley of gunfire and replied by cutting out several prizes and planning an attempt on the town itself.[1]

The Portuguese Brazil trade suffered more heavily than any other from the depredations of English privateers. It required forty or fifty ships a year to carry away the sugar and brazilwood to Europe, and in the three years following the Armada English privateers captured no less than thirty-four such vessels.[2] By 1589 the losses were so great that the ships were instructed to sail north of Scotland to Hamburg, but the losses continued. In 1592 King Philip asked the supreme court of Portugal why the masters of Portuguese vessels allowed themselves to be taken by corsairs so easily, and in the same year he imposed a three-per-cent duty on colonial merchandise in order to establish a fleet for the protection of the Brazil trade. This measure does not appear to have diminished the losses to any appreciable extent.[3]

Thus the English merchants obtained the imports they had so long coveted, sending out powder and shot instead of cloth. The chief beneficiaries were those especially interested in sugar, like Thomas Cordell, Roger Ofield, Henry Topfield, Thomas Myddelton, Nicholas Farrar, Erasmus Harby, Henry Beecher and the Auldworths of Bristol. These and others were busy not only organising their own voyages of plunder, but buying the large quantities of sugar now pouring into the country. Prize sugar was coming mainly from Brazil, but also from the West Indies, the Canaries, the island of São Thomé and Morocco. From 1589 to 1591 sixty-nine prizes carried sugar as a main item of cargo, and the sugar captured in these three years by the privateers alone was worth at least £100,000.[4] Considering that sugar imports before the war, mainly from Morocco, totalled some £20,000 or £30,000

£1,000 in the Lisbon expedition, as well as 'setting forth himself and twenty men with muskets'. In 1591 he led the City of London's expedition to reinforce Howard at the Azores and in 1598 he represented the Londoners' interests in Cumberland's expedition (originally intended as a Brazil venture), commanding the *Ascension* as rear-admiral of the fleet.

[1] *Principal Navigations*, XI, 202–27.
[2] See above, Table 7, p. 130.
[3] S.P. Dom. Eliz., ccxxiv, 11; F. Mauro, *Le Portugal et l'Atlantique au XVIIe Siècle*, pp. 433–4, 447.
[4] See above, p. 133.

a year,[1] it is clear that an unprecedented sugar boom took place in England in the war years. Already in 1591 a Spanish spy reported 'that English booty in West India (i.e. American) produce is so great that sugar is cheaper in London than it is in Lisbon or the Indies themselves'.[2] The surveyor of the London custom house, Richard Carmarden, expressed the opinion in 1593 that 'although the Hollanders and Hamburgers have the only trade of other commodities that the Spanish trade can afford them, yet sugars they cannot have now in any quantity but from us, as the case standeth, by reason of the great quantities taken by reprisal from Spain and Portugal'.[3]

Carmarden's statement was made in a letter to Lord Burghley arguing against one Robert Zinzan's proposal to establish a monopoly of sugar refining. Suggestions of a similar nature were put forward in 1595, 1596 and 1597 by other would-be monopolists.[4] They were all rejected, but the fact that they were made is an indication of the growth of the industry in this period. In the middle forties there had been two refineries, which, according to John Stow, served the whole realm for twenty years. Later many others entered the business. Stow, writing in 1592, mentions nine by name and refers to others. He asserts that they made small profit by it, some becoming bankrupt, but it is not clear from the context whether he means to include the nine in this generalisation.[5] Certainly four of the nine—Bateman, Cordell, Ofield and Topfield—were successfully combining privateering with sugar-refining in the war years.[6] He does not mention Myddelton, Farrar and Harby, who were clearly making substantial profits in the nineties according to Myddelton's account book. Nor does he mention any of the foreigners who were said to be engaged in the

---

[1] L. Stone, 'Elizabethan Overseas Trade', *Economic History Review*, 2nd Ser., II (1949), 31–58; Willan, *Studies*, p. 314.

[2] *Cal. S.P. Venetian, 1581–91*, p. 527.

[3] Lansdowne MS 75, f. 105.

[4] Willan, *Studies*, pp. 318–22.

[5] John Stow, *A Survey of the Cities of London and Westminster* (ed. Strype, 1720), II, 244.

[6] Robert Bateman was doing business with Myddelton and Co. and took over the management of their sugar house in 1593: A. H. Dodd, 'Mr. Myddelton the Merchant of Tower Street', *Elizabethan Government and Society* (ed. Bindoff, Hurstfield and Williams), p. 269. Of the others, Nicholas Barnsley, grocer, became a member of the East India Company in 1599, and William Holman had a share in the venture of the *Bark Bond* in 1589.

business at this time. It may not have been true, as some believed, that London had replaced Antwerp as the main sugar-refining centre for the European market,[1] but it can hardly be doubted that the English industry had become a serious rival to the Dutch and German refineries. After the war English refining developed much more slowly—another indication, if any were needed, that the precocious expansion of the war years was almost entirely the result of privateering. Not for nothing did Robert Auldworth of Bristol call one of his privateers the *Sugar*.

With supplies of sugar thus rapidly mounting in the early nineties, the appetites of the merchants were still not satisfied. The returns of normal privateering were, after all, a matter of chance—a captain might as easily come in with a cargo of fish or wine. Hence presumably the decision to assault the main source of Brazilian sugar and gut the warehouses of Pernambuco. The promoters of this venture were all London merchants—John Watts, Paul Bayning, John More, Simon Boreman, William Shute, Roger Howe, Arthur and John Jackson and Roger Ofield. Ofield, the Barbary trader, was the chief sugar dealer here. Howe, who partnered Boreman in privateering on other occasions, was perhaps related to Robert Howe of the Barbary Company. The Jacksons had been active in reprisal ventures and carried on trade with Spain and the Levant at the same time. William Shute was trading to the Mediterranean in 1597 and owned two privateers—the *Prosperous* and the *Galleon Shute*. The rest we have met.[2]

As for the leader of the expedition, James Lancaster was born in Basingstoke, probably in 1554. He once observed that he had been brought up among the Portuguese and had served with them as a soldier and lived with them as a merchant. We know that in 1581

---

[1] De Castries, cited in Willan, *Studies*, p. 316.
[2] Howe and Boreman backed William King's West Indies venture in 1592 (*E.P.V.*, pp. 209–18) and obtained letters of reprisal for the *Salomon* and the *Roebuck* in 1593 [H.C.A. 25/3 (9), 23 Feb. 1592/3]. Howe later subscribed to the East India Company. Boreman had lived in Seville for some time and there had married Isabel de la Salde, returning to England with her and their infant son Simon in 1576. The younger Simon sailed with Lancaster in 1595 and was captured in the Caribbean in 1601 (see above, p. 177). The Jacksons had collaborated with Lancaster in the reprisal ventures of the *Mary* (or *Bark Smith*), 1589–91 [Lansdowne MS 142, f. 109, 30 July 1589, 11 June 1591; H.C.A. 13/29, 27 Jan. 1591/2, 16 June 1591; H.C.A. 25/3 (9), 11 June 1591; Harleian MS 598, f. 5]. For their trade and losses in Spain see H.C.A. 30/842; H.C.A. 13/26, 9 March 1586/7. For Shute, see pp. 119–20 above.

and again at the beginning of 1585 he was a factor in Seville. On this later occasion he was managing business for Alderman Thomas Starkey of the Skinners Company. Lancaster himself belonged to the Skinners. In all probability he had gone out to Portugal in the late sixties or early seventies as a lad, and had perhaps been apprenticed to Starkey. It was presumably in 1580 that he had taken up arms, to fight with Dom Antonio against Philip's invasion. In 1585 he was among those who lost property in Spain, and in 1587 he began his privateering career as captain of Bayning's *Susan* in the Cadiz expedition. He had charge of the *Edward Bonaventure*, Cordell's ship, against the Spanish Armada, and the following year he took the *Salomon* (belonging to Howe and Boreman) to Lisbon in the unfortunate Portugal expedition. So far Lancaster's career had been strikingly similar to Robert Flick's, and in 1590 he took to the seas with another of his old friends of the Iberian trade—Samuel Foxcroft. Together in the *Merchant Royal* and the *Edward Bonaventure* these two now took prize the *Hope* of Flushing with a cargo of sugar, woad and brazilwood consigned by a Dutchman at the Azores for Middleburg. The English were indicted for piracy on their return; in the subsequent investigation the Dutch sailors accused Foxcroft of having tortured them, and there is strong evidence that he did personally commit horrible brutalities upon them. Lancaster was not actively involved in this deplorable incident, but he was at least a consenting bystander who expected to benefit from the proceedings. The piracy charge was presumably dropped, however, and the two captains in the same ships departed next year with George Raymond for the East Indies. This was a disastrous venture, from which Lancaster did not return until 1594, but he soon managed to persuade his merchant friends to support him in a fresh endeavour—the Pernambuco raid. Only Cordell among his former privateering associates did not subscribe to the new venture, and this was possibly because he had other fish to fry.[1]

[1] Cordell helped to back the almost exactly contemporary venture of the *Rose Lion* (*E.P.V.*, pp. 338–76). For Lancaster's East India voyage of 1591–4 see below, pp. 214–15. For his career to 1591 see Foster, *Lancaster's Voyages*; H.C.A. 13/26, 3 June 1586, 7 July 1586; Lansdowne MSS 142, f. 109; 143, f. 322; H.C.A. 25/2 (5), 13 March 1586/7; Laughton, *Defeat*, II, 326; *Monson's Tracts*, I, 184; H.C.A. 13/28, 8 Oct. 1590, 15 Nov. 1590, 3 Dec. 1590, 28 Jan. 1590/1; H.C.A. 14/27, no. 50; Lansdowne MS 134. Foster, *op. cit.*, is the chief authority for the Pernambuco raid; see also Lansdowne MS 78, no. 59; S.P. Dom. Eliz., ccliii,

Lancaster left the Thames in October 1594 with the *Consent* (240 tons), the *Salomon* (170 tons) and the *Virgin* (60 tons). On his way out he recruited his force by taking several small prizes and by accepting the consortship of Edward Fenner[1] in the *Pilgrim* (or *Peregrine*) of Portsmouth and Martin Phillips in the *Welcome* of Plymouth, who also had a Biscayner prize and a pinnace with them. From one of the prizes Lancaster learned that a carrack returning from the East Indies had been cast away at Pernambuco and her goods brought ashore—news that no doubt strengthened his already formed determination to take the place. When he arrived there in April 1595 he found three large Dutch vessels in the mouth of the harbour. These had been sent out to convey the carrack goods to Europe, but they fortunately remained neutral while Lancaster proceeded to take possession of Recife, which was the port town of Pernambuco and contained all the valuable merchandise. There was no effective opposition to the attack itself, but in the ensuing thirty days of occupation, while Lancaster laded his own and the Dutch ships and a further five French privateers, the Portuguese repeatedly tried to retake the town or burn the English ships. Lancaster's careful management frustrated these efforts until just before the departure, when his subordinates' rashness led to the unnecessary loss of thirty-five men, including his two chief lieutenants and the French commander.

Indeed Lancaster's conduct of the whole venture was exemplary. He avoided all the snares into which so many captains fell: he wasted no time in diversions on the way out; he did not hesitate to attack when he arrived at the objective; he maintained good discipline and adequately covered his force against counter-attack; he dealt fairly and generously with both Dutch and French. One particular episode tells us a great deal about the attitude of such merchants to their former business acquaintances, now their enemies. A deputation of the Portuguese sought to parley with the English commander, who promptly went aboard one of the Dutch vessels and stayed there until his visitors had retired. Some of Lancaster's officers were puzzled by his action and he therefore

nos. 24, 32; H.C.A. 24/63, nos. 39, 41, 127–35, 162, 180; H.C.A. 13/31, 23 June 1595, 6 Aug. 1595; H.C.A. 13/102, 1 May 1596; Harleian MS 598, f. 34.

[1] The texts in Foster invariably refer to him as 'Captain Venner'. Foster calls him John, but there is no textual evidence for this, and the various other sources make it certain that this was Edward Fenner. They also show that Henry Roberts' report of Fenner's death (Foster, p. 69) was premature.

explained: 'Sirs, I have been brought up among this people. I have lived among them as a gentleman, served with them as a soldier and lived among them as a merchant, so that I should have some understanding of their demeanours and nature; and I know, when they cannot prevail with the sword by force, then they deal with their deceivable tongues, for faith and truth they have none, neither will use any, unless it be to their own advantage. And this I give you warning, that if you give them parle, they will betray us; and, for my part, of all nations in the world it would grieve me most to be overtaken by this nation and the Spaniards; and I am glad it was my fortune to pay them with one of their own fetches, for I warrant you they understand me better than you think they do.' And he went on to order that whoever came next from the enemy should be warned that he or any other approaching again would be hanged out of hand. The order was carried out and no hangings proved necessary.

At length the ships were ready. At eleven o'clock at night, one month after the taking of the town, fifteen vessels stocked tight with loot cleared the harbour. Only one—a Spanish prize—failed to arrive home safely. It was a magnificent haul of prize-goods, the greater part in value being made up of the carrack's cargo of pepper, cloves, cinnamon, mace, benjamin (benzoin), frankincense, gum-lac, indigo, aloes, calicoes, silks and 'blond stones'. The *Consent* and the *Salomon* brought in £31,000 worth of these eastern goods, and more came into Plymouth in Fenner's three ships. The *Virgin* and two of the three Dutchmen were laden with sugar and brazilwood to the value of £15,000, and more Brazil goods of unspecified value came home in Fenner's ships and the other Dutchman. As for the French, they seem to have taken brazilwood only. In all, the English must have harvested well over £50,000 worth of plunder.[1]

This was the climax of English depredations on the Brazil trade, but by no means the end of them. It was the intention of Cumberland and his merchant backers in 1598 to repeat Lancaster's exploit, and only the leakage of intelligence to Spain altered their plans. The influx of sugar continued after 1595, but probably ceased to rise from the level it had reached in the early nineties.

---

[1] The French had a generous share, considering that they arrived after the capture of the town; but their leader, Lenoir, had helped Lancaster in time of some need in 1593 and the Englishman now had a chance to show his gratitude. The Dutch ships did not share the booty, but were merely freighted by Lancaster.

The English merchants thus turned from trade to plunder. Clearly this was not a change they themselves desired, but one forced upon them by the trend of political circumstances and the aggressiveness of certain of their compatriots. Once plunder replaced trade, the merchants made the best of it, and the profits they made on captured sugar and brazilwood contributed to the mounting stock of fluid resources available for commercial expansion. But from the fast-growing Brazil trade itself they found themselves almost completely excluded by the Dutch. Already in 1578 a Dutch firm in Lisbon was sending brazilwood to Arnemuiden; by 1602 Amsterdam had a well-founded brazilwood industry. In 1587 Cumberland's men found a Dutch flyboat trading at Bahia —the *Unicorn* of Flushing, which they compelled to join them in their depredations. In the same year Robert Flick captured off the Portuguese coast two Dutchmen laden with Brazilian produce— the *Ruby* and the *Angel Gabriel*. Lancaster found three large Dutch merchantmen at Recife in 1595. Between 1587 and 1598 sixteen Dutch vessels are known to have traded in Brazil and fourteen others sailed with Brazil as their destination. During the truce of 1609–21 between half and two-thirds of the carrying trade between Brazil and Europe was in Dutch hands, and shortly after this the Dutch took direct control over a considerable part of the country. English participation in the Brazil trade in the first quarter of the seventeenth century was relatively unimportant and only increased when the Portuguese were faced with a Dutch invasion of their colony. The fact that the English could not compete successfully with the Dutch even after the Spanish war is sufficient indication of their technical inferiority. As a bulk-cargo carrier the *fluitschip* was far cheaper and more convenient than anything the English could build, and it was particularly suitable for the Brazil trade. But the Dutch had other advantages: they were well established in Lisbon before 1585 and remained there throughout the war, penetrating the colonial trade from within while the English weakened it from without. It is of course impossible to assess with any degree of accuracy the contribution of English privateering to Dutch supremacy in the Brazil trade, but it was undoubtedly a considerable factor.[1]

The story of the English attempts to penetrate the East India

[1] F. Mauro, *Le Portugal et l'Atlantique au XVIIe siècle*, p. 143; Engel Sluiter, 'Dutch Maritime Power and the Colonial Status Quo, 1585–1641', *Pacific Historical Review*, XI (1942), 29–41; C. R. Boxer, 'English Shipping in the Brazil

trade, culminating in the foundation of the East India Company, is better known, but it is not generally realised how large a part the privateering merchants played in this. English aspirations to the spice trade date far back in the century, but it is not our purpose here to trace them from their origins. The conquest of Portugal in 1580 gave renewed impetus to the quest, at the very moment when Drake returned triumphant with the news that he had established contact with the Sultan of Ternate. The next step was the abortive venture of Edward Fenton, which already indicated the eastern ambitions of the Iberian traders and future privateering promoters. At the same time Osborne and Staper of the Turkey Company were supporting the efforts of Newbery and Fitch to reach India and Cathay by way of Aleppo, Bagdad and Hormuz. Both did reach India and Fitch went further, but in 1591, after eight years of travel, he returned with a discouraging report of Portuguese hostility. In the same period attempts to find a route to the Pacific by the north-eastern and north-western passages were intensified, though of course with no success. The gentleman adventurers preferred the south-west route by way of the Magellan Straits, because they were interested mainly in plunder. Cavendish, however, was the only one who succeeded in repeating Drake's exploit; and he did very little to further the cause of East Indies trade.

Meanwhile the open rupture of Anglo-Portuguese relations led a group of London merchants in 1589 to propose an expedition by the Cape route. The ships to be used were the *Susan* of Paul Bayning's and the *Merchant Royal* and *Edward Bonaventure*, which belonged to Thomas Cordell. This petition, which urged the voyage 'as well for the annoying of the Spaniards and Portingalls (now our enemies) as also for the venting of our commodities', had no immediate result.[1] But in 1591 Cordell's two ships eventually set forth in the company of George Raymond's *Penelope*. Raymond was the 'general' and Samuel Foxcroft and James Lancaster commanded respectively the *Merchant Royal* and the *Edward*. This was not designed as a trading venture; a commission

Trade, 1640–65', *Mariner's Mirror*, XXXVII (1951), 197–230; V. Barbour, 'Dutch and English Merchant Shipping in the Seventeenth Century', *Economic History Review*, II (1929–30), 261–90; C. R. Boxer, *Salvador de Sa and the Struggle for Brazil and Angola*, p. 40; *Principal Navigations*, XI, 202–27; H.C.A. 13/27, Feb. and March 1587/8; H.C.A. 13/101, 29 March 1588, 25 Oct. 1588; H.C.A. 24/56, no. 54; Lansdowne MS 143, ff. 180, 197–230.
[1] *Cal. S.P. Colonial, East Indies, 1513–1616*, no. 239.

of reprisal was granted by letters patent and little cargo was carried. The purpose was to plunder Portuguese shipping and to explore the possibilities of trade. The talk of cloth sales was perhaps merely publicity to win the approval of the government. Cordell presumably had partners in this venture, but, whoever they were, the association of the names Cordell, Lancaster and Foxcroft (not to mention Bayning) is sufficient to point a connection between Iberian trade, privateering and East Indies trade.

The voyage of 1591 was an unmitigated failure. Scurvy took a heavy toll on the way out to the Cape, and consequently it was decided at Table Bay to send the sick home in the *Merchant Royal*. Then, soon after doubling the Cape, the *Penelope* went down with all hands in a storm. Foxcroft was already dead, and now the loss of Raymond in the *Penelope* left Lancaster in command. He succeeded in plundering a number of Portuguese vessels in the Indian Ocean, but lost many men from disease and was at one point himself very near to death. At length he agreed to lead his thirty-three starving and mutinous men home, and they struggled back round the Cape in March 1593. But their troubles were not yet over. The men insisted on taking the direct course for England and the result was six weeks of frustration in the Doldrums, which compelled them to make for the West Indies for provisions. Here after some difficulties they arrived at the island of Mona off Hispaniola and were able to recruit their health and spirits sufficiently to set sail again for Newfoundland. But they met storms which drove them off course and eventually forced them back to the Caribbean. The crew were now desperate. Five of them went ashore on some islands near Puerto Rico and refused to rejoin the ship. The remaining twenty-five made once again for Mona, and here, while the rest were ashore, five men and a boy cut the cable and sailed off, only to be wrecked in Ocoa Bay in Hispaniola. The five survivors surrendered to the Spanish, and though James Langton, then privateering on that coast, secured some of the *Edward*'s artillery, the bulk of it went to strengthen the fortifications of Santo Domingo. Meanwhile about Christmas 1593 Lancaster and eleven others were rescued from Mona by French ships. Of the seven left on the island, three were killed by Spaniards, two lost their lives seeking fowls on the cliffs and two at length were taken off by Frenchmen in March. Lancaster himself arrived home in May 1594.[1]

[1] Foster, *Lancaster's Voyages*; *E.P.V.*, pp. 284–97.

This experience was naturally discouraging to those interested in eastern voyaging, whether for plunder or for trade. Only one other attempt was made in the nineties—Sir Robert Dudley's venture under Benjamin Wood. Again, although two merchants accompanied the ships, this was primarily a privateering venture. Dudley was no trader and Wood was a notable privateering captain. He had sailed with Chidley in 1589 and was now intending to make another attempt to get through the Magellan Straits. This intention was evidently abandoned, however, and Wood made his way to the Indian Ocean via the Cape. There he plundered as Lancaster had done and suffered a similar decline of strength until his last ship, the *Bear*, was wrecked. The few survivors, save for a single Frenchman, seem to have perished in their attempt to struggle home.[1]

Prospects of eastern trade did not seem bright in the nineties. It was cheaper to spoil the enemy's shipping than to enter into risky and long-term projects of trade with the East, involving considerable outlay in merchandise, equipment, victuals and wages. Hence every eastern venture from 1585 to 1599 was primarily a plunder cruise, with trade-prospecting either neglected or completely ignored. And since even as privateering ventures these voyages invariably met disaster after Cavendish's return in 1588, they were abandoned in favour of Atlantic privateering. Lancaster turned immediately to western plunder after the catastrophic 1591–4 voyage, and the difference in the results was an object lesson to the London merchants, though they scarcely needed one, for Atlantic privateering had been booming since 1585. To men like Bayning, Cordell and Towerson, who had shown themselves willing to risk money in eastern projects, the conclusions were already obvious. There was, after all much more chance of capturing the coveted spices between the Azores and Lisbon than between the Moluccas and the Cape, and if one could not count on spices there were plenty of other desirable cargoes to be had for the taking without sending ships and men to their doom in the Indian Ocean. Consequently it was only when the Dutch had already completed two successful expeditions that the English merchants bestirred themselves. Even then progress was sluggish and the subscriptions promised in the first flush of enthusiasm were slow to come in. Privateering thus probably helped to delay the initiation of English trade with the East Indies, and might

[1] Foster, *England's Quest of Eastern Trade*, pp. 136–43.

have delayed it further had it not been evident at the end of the nineties that the war would soon end. With rumours of peace abroad, and with the certainty that the issue of eastern trade would be raised in any negotiations, it became imperative to establish a *de facto* claim.

Nevertheless the contribution of the privateering merchants to the foundation of far-eastern trade was of first-rate importance. It is not exaggerating to say that they provided the effective leadership. The majority of the 1599 and 1600 'committies' had privateering interests, but even more impressive is the composition of the working committee of seven set up on 10 October 1600 to organise the first voyage. Its members were Paul Bayning, the treasurer, at whose house the committee was to meet; Richard Staper, the great Levant Company leader, who had obtained letters of reprisal for the *Toby*, and had been interested in prizes taken by the *Salomon*, the *Susan Parnell* and the *John and Francis*, though he was no promoter of privateers as such; Thomas Cordell; James Lancaster, Thomas Allabaster, who was closely associated with the earl of Cumberland; Roger Howe, who had backed William King's West Indies expedition in 1592 and Lancaster's Pernambuco raid in 1595; and Richard Weych, brother-in-law of Thomas Myddelton. Finally John Watts himself, the prince of privateers, was called in to advise on the preparation of the voyage. In 1601 he replaced Sir Thomas Smythe as governor of the company, and he in turn was succeeded by Sir John Hart, who had taken the lead in financing Cumberland's Puerto Rico venture.[1]

The prominence of the privateering merchants was not merely due to their undoubted experience in the management of large and long-range expeditions. They also provided much of the economic 'drive'. They had for many years past been building up trade in luxury imports, originally by the Iberian trade and its extensions, and latterly by privateering. The activities of Oliver Stile, a member of the Barbary Company and the Levant Company, a privateering promoter and a committy of the East India Company, are typical. Stile was a warden of the Grocers' Company. Sir John Hart, Bayning and Edward Holmden (another committy) were also of the Grocers, as Thomas Myddelton was. But

---

[1] Stevens, *Dawn*, pp. 6, 12, 40, 57, 67. For Staper's interest in prizes see H.C.A. 25/3 (9), 15 Aug. 1592; H.C.A. 24/66, nos. 6, 15, 16. Allabaster was another Iberian trader (H.C.A. 13/26, 9 March 1586/7).

in practice men in other companies went in for wholesale grocery —Ofield the sugar-refiner was nominally a fishmonger and Cordell a mercer. Such men had been handling increasing quantities of pepper, cochineal, indigo, ginger, sugar, brazilwood and similar exotic products during the war years. Some of this was no doubt re-exported, but increasing home consumption of such commodities was a widely remarked feature of contemporary social life. The Levant trade was of course contributing in no small measure to this process, and the Levant traders themselves were much to the fore in the establishment of the East India Company. But many of the Levant traders in the new organisation, particularly its leaders, were also privateering promoters,[1] and many of them had been interested in Iberian trade before 1585. One reason for the foundation of the Levant Company had been the instability of political relations with Spain, and privateering had developed from the same root cause. Both formed, in their different ways, bridges between the pre-war Iberian trade and the post-war East Indies trade.

The most urgent requirement of the East India company in its early years, as its records show, was capital, and as we have seen privateering was one of the most important means of the accumulation of capital in the fifteen years before the company's first voyage. Over a quarter of the £30,000 initially subscribed or promised in 1599 came from men known to have invested in privateering. Again, the company could not have survived for long without large and powerful ships, and privateering, particularly of the kind combined with trade, had done more than anything else to stimulate the building of such vessels in the last decade of the century. In the first company voyage the *Dragon* had been Cumberland's man-of-war, built for privateering in 1595; the *Ascension* had been built for William Garraway in 1597, and had been used for privateering and trade; the *Susan* was possibly Bayning's ship, which had also been employed in both types of venture. As for the captains and masters in the early company voyages, many of them were experienced privateering com-

---

[1] Of the working committee of seven, Bayning, Staper, Cordell and Weych were Levant traders. The 1600 committee of twenty-five included thirteen identifiable Levant traders, five of whom were major privateering promoters, and two of whom had a minor interest in privateering. Ten of the twenty-five were major privateering promoters and four others had a minor interest. Only five members of this committee were not, as far as we know, interested in either Levant trade or privateering.

manders: James Lancaster, John Middleton, William Broadbent, Henry Napper and Roger Hankyn in the first voyage alone; and later David Middleton, Nicholas Downton, Anthony Hippon, Christopher Newport and William Parker, all well-known as reprisal men. In sum, the economic and maritime strength required to establish and maintain East Indies trade was to a large extent the direct result of fifteen years of continuous commerce-raiding. Again in these respects the contribution of the Levant trade can hardly be distinguished from that of privateering.

How far this activity weakened the Portuguese merchant marine and thus prepared the way for the Dutch and English interlopers it is difficult to say. It was reported in 1597 that 'the merchants of Seville and Portugal who used to venture to the Indies are broken by losses of goods and ships since the wars', but the mention of Seville makes this observation too vague to be of much value.[1] Nevertheless the English did capture three carracks, sink another and cause the loss of two more, which the Portuguese themselves destroyed by fire. These varied a great deal in value, from the enormously rich *Cinco Chagas* to the rather poorly laden *St Valentine*, taken by Monson in 1601.[2] Their loss was of course serious, but the damage done by the English seems to have been a small matter in comparison with the losses by shipwreck. One Portuguese writer puts the number of wrecks at thirty-five in the years 1580 to 1610. Another states that of the seventeen carracks which left Lisbon for Goa in 1590–2, only two returned in safety.[3] The contribution of the privateers was not negligible, but it merely assisted a process of commercial decline which was bound to result from losses on this scale.

Contemporaries could not but be aware of the intimate connections between privateering and the East India trade. Cumberland, for example, appreciated and even exaggerated the possible effect of his own depredations upon Portuguese commerce. His 1598 expedition had prevented the sailing of the carracks from Lisbon that year, and Cumberland wrote that 'if another year they

---

[1] *Cal. Salis. MSS.*, XIV, 30.

[2] The three captured were the *San Felipe* in 1587, the *Madre de Dios* in 1592 and the *St Valentine* in 1601. The *Cinco Chagas* was sunk by Cumberland's fleet in 1594. The *Santa Cruz* was destroyed by fire at Flores in 1592 and another carrack was similarly burned at St Michael's in the Azores in 1597.

[3] C. R. Boxer (ed.), *The Tragic History of the Sea* (Hakluyt Society, 2nd Ser., CXII), p. 24.

come not, then without fail it will be performed and the great and rich people (of the East Indies) be left greedily gaping for any nation to trade that will bring the like commodities, which I dare undertake the merchants of London shall do if her Majesty shall stay the carracks from going thither'.[1]

The English East India trade was thus in many ways the outcome of the privateering war, and it inevitably bore the marks of its origin. Trade, as the merchants explained to Lancaster, was now the main aim, but they had no objection to the plunder of enemy vessels provided it was done 'without prejudice or hazard of the said voyage'.[2] Lancaster saw fit to avail himself of the opportunity so offered and captured two Portuguese ships. Indeed, he deliberately and successfully schemed to catch Portuguese shipping in the Malacca Straits by surprise, and so make his voyage. When in consequence he took a very rich prize, 'he was very glad of this good hap, and very thankful to God for it. . . . For, saith he, He hath not only supplied my necessities to lade these ships I have, but hath given me as much as will lade as many more ships as I have, if I had them to lade'.[3] The trade itself was primarily concerned with imports from the East. As early as September 1599 it was decided to ask permission to send out coin, and to export merchandise free of custom for six years, 'for that many experiments are to be made before the country shall be fitted with merchandise vendible there'.[4] In its first twenty years the company exported £548,090 in bullion, and £292,286 in cloths, lead and tin. The Far East did not prove much of a market for English woollens. But goods bought in the East Indies in the same period for £365,288 were sold at home for £1,914,600.[5] The company thus carried to an extreme point the characteristics of the southward trades developed in the preceding half-century.

Here once again the Dutch did far better than the English. They not only reached the East Indies first, but within a short time beat the English out of the area. This triumph, however, had little to do with privateering. It is true that the slow English start was partly due to the counter-attractions of Atlantic plunder, but it is doubtful whether the English would have been able to compete at all without the maritime and commercial strength derived

[1] G. C. Williamson, *George, Third Earl of Cumberland*, p. 221.
[2] Stevens, *Dawn*, p. 118.   [3] Foster, *Lancaster's Voyages*, p. 108.
[4] Stevens, *Dawn*, p. 8.
[5] S. A. Khan, *The East India Trade in the Seventeenth Century*, pp. 16–17.

from privateering. For the Dutch owed their trading pre-eminence to sheer superiority in shipping, capital resources and commercial technique. They were already in advance of the English in these respects before 1585, and the events of that year enabled them to lengthen their lead. They continued their trade with the Iberian countries throughout the war, in spite of difficulties, whereas English trade with the enemy was negligible. Thus while the English had no alternative but to turn to privateering, the Dutch were in a much better position to exploit the decline of Iberian shipping. Naturally it was this side of the matter, rather than the real commercial superiority of the Dutch, that caused most comment in England. As John Chamberlain complained, 'we for their sake and defence entering into the war, and being barred from all commerce and intercourse of merchandise, they in the meantime thrust us out of all traffic to our utter undoing'.[1] The resentful jealousy of Anglo-Dutch relations in Stuart times was born and bred in the Spanish war.

[1] Quoted in *Monson's Tracts*, II, 91.

Chapter 11

THE CONSEQUENCES OF PRIVATEERING

Throughout much of the mediaeval and early modern periods privateering was no more than an incidental concomitant of war. When war occurred men with suitable ships simply took advantage of the opportunity to plunder enemy commerce, and merchants, as shipowners and import dealers, were naturally to the fore in this activity, particularly when their trade was interrupted and their shipping unemployed in consequence of war. For most of this time, indeed, privateering, though an interesting phenomenon, indicative of the temper and conditions of sea-faring, can hardly be considered a very significant one, since it had no permanent effect on the volume or distribution of trade nor on the sea-struggle between the nations; if it made a few fortunes and unmade others, this was but a personal and transitory matter of little relevance to the main lines of historical development. All this is true of the period before the domination of the oceans became a considerable issue in European wars—i.e. before 1585; and it is equally true of the period when oceanic power, now a great issue, was decided by the strength and effective use of state navies—i.e. from about 1650. It is not true, however, of the particular period in question, the period of the Spanish war, during which the significance of this issue actually emerged, but during which the initiative in sea warfare, at least on the English side, still fell largely to the private and voluntary effort of the seagoing and mercantile community. This is an exceptional period, when the maritime and commercial forces of the nation strove to achieve modern ends with mediaeval means, only half conscious of their purpose and of the inadequacy of their resources and technique. In these transitional conditions privateering played a special role and produced exceptionally important results.

The results were important most directly and obviously for England's own development, but their true significance, even for England, arises from the nature of the European setting. For the war with Spain was part of a European war, and this war was itself a phase—the decisive phase—in a longer struggle for supremacy. Spain reached the height of her power in the early eighties; in the following two decades her effort to dominate the northwest by securing the Netherlands was utterly and permanently defeated. Her failure implied at first merely the survival of England, France and the United Provinces, but ultimately the passing of European hegemony to these northwest countries. Her failure, moreover, was the failure not merely of her armies, but of her economy and of the complex commercial and financial network associated with it. The period which saw the political defeat of Spain also witnessed the establishment of northwestern economic hegemony over southern Europe. By 1609 French, Dutch and English traders were carrying all before them not only in the Mediterranean but in the Iberian peninsula itself. While Spain's bankers staggered from one crisis to the next, increasingly obsessed with the annual transfusion of blood from America, increasingly aware of the pernicious anaemia of their commercial system, the merchants of the north-west, with the backing of their governments, passed over to the offensive on and beyond the oceans. By the middle of the seventeenth century the military supremacy in Europe had passed from Spain to France, while the only economic rivalry that mattered was between England, France and the United Provinces. But it would be mistaken to imagine that the economic victory of the north-west was the result of military victory, or *vice versa*. Commerce and warfare were so intimately and variously connected as to make this struggle total, in the sense that every aspect affected every other.

The southward commercial drive of the north-west into the Iberian peninsula and the Mediterranean was already noticeable in the seventies, and as the excessive strain of war and inflation told upon Spain and her dependencies, so the offensive continued. There were two main attractions: markets for the growing cloth industries of France, Holland and England; and access to the produce of southern Europe as well as to that of the wider world to which the Iberian countries and the Levant were alike stepping stones. The colonial ambitions of the Dutch, English and French were not merely incidental to the Spanish war to which these countries were committed in Europe, but had their roots in the long-term economic shift within the continent, a shift that the war itself hastened.

Such was the international context of Elizabethan privateering.

What was its direct contribution to the defeat of Spain? In the first place it is clear that privateering was not an adequate substitute for the kind of blockade Hawkins dreamed of. The English never captured a treasure fleet and thus never succeeded in paralysing the Spanish war effort. The amounts of treasure they captured here and there were insignificant in proportion to the bullion reaching Spain, which increased throughout the war period—in fact precisely until England retired from the war. It was only when they occasionally caused the postponement of the Havana sailings that the corsairs achieved some direct impact upon the Spanish war machine. Yet the cumulative effect of continual shipping losses upon the Iberian economy was probably serious. Even allowing that the figures for the years 1589–91 may have been unusually high, and that they include some vessels that were returned to their non-Iberian owners, there still must have been something over a thousand Spanish and Portuguese ships captured by the English during the course of the war. The figures given by the Chaunus seem to indicate that losses by enemy action were quite small in the Atlantic trades to and from Seville, but this was only one branch of Iberian trade, and there is good reason to suspect that the figures are inaccurate.[1] It is probably true that the *flotas* themselves lost

[1] See Pierre et Huguette Chaunu, *Séville et l'Atlantique, 1504–1650.* The great value of this immense and formidable work is not in question here, but the remark of the authors themselves about the tables of losses should be noted: 'Ils risquent de paraître décevants, parce qu'on ne peut avoir l'absolue certitude qu'ils aient bien tout englobé . . .' (t. VIII₂, p. 698). For the war period Table 635 (t. VI₂, pp. 922–3) shows a total of thirty-six ships lost to corsairs or by enemy action in the Seville-Atlantic trade in both outward and return voyages. For the individual year 1591 Table 633 (t. VI₂, pp. 918–19) records the loss to corsairs of one ship only—the *San Juan.* As it happens we know that Watts' and Carey's men, who took this vessel, also captured eight others at that time—seven Santo Domingo ships and the richly laden *Trinity* of Seville—all of which were on their way to join the homeward-bound fleet at Havana. The same table gives a nil return for captures and losses by enemy action in 1590, whereas we know that this year's Virginia expedition took three Santo Domingo men on their way to Havana, including the valuable *Buen Jesus* of Seville, and sank two more, as well as two of the Mexican fleet (*Roanoke Voyages,* pp. 586–91). But in both these years there were other captures, some of which at least were of ships bound to or from Seville, which should therefore (but do not) appear in the tables. The Spanish sources in fact not only fail to provide a detailed guide to losses by capture, but actually give a false impression of the scale of such losses. It must be remembered, moreover, that the Chaunu tables take no account of ships not actually engaged in the Seville-Atlantic trade—e.g. ships engaged in local West Indian trade or operating illegally from ports outside the Andalusian monopoly, quite apart from the large numbers employed in non-

comparatively few vessels to corsairs, but the Chaunus have themselves detected a remarkable depression in the volume of shipping arriving at Seville from the Atlantic trades, a depression coinciding exactly with the years of the war with England.[1] Nor is this depression strange in view of the constant reports of enemy activities at sea. 'Presque toutes les lettres qui parviennent des Indes à cette époque nous signalent, en effet, la présence des corsaires anglais et font état de sérieux démêlés.'[2] No wonder that the Spanish were increasingly worried by what the Chaunus have called 'la crise de tonnage' and by what the Casa de Contratación described as 'la poca seguridad de la mar por los muchos enemigos'.[3] By 1599, when this complaint was made, the shortage of vessels for the transatlantic trade had become chronic. The average age of ships employed in the *Carrera de las Indias* declined from eight years in 1576–80 to 3·8 years in 1596–1600.[4] Writing in 1608, the shipbuilding expert Tomé Cano asserted that twenty-five years before there had been in Spain more than a thousand seagoing ships belonging to private owners, and in Portugal more than four hundred, together with fifteen hundred caravels; and of all of these, he maintained, there were hardly any left in either country.[5] Undoubtedly there were other causes of these fantastic losses— notably deficiencies in shipbuilding and seamanship—but it seems probable that privateering was at least as important as any other factor. The system of the *flotas* was of course maintained, but in the tremendous effort to preserve this one lifeline the Spanish government virtually abandoned the rest of Iberian shipping to the corsairs, just as it abandoned the local trade of the Caribbean in

Atlantic trades. This is no criticism of the tables themselves, since they are concerned specifically with the Seville-Atlantic trade; but the student should bear in mind Usher's opinion that 'the trade to the New World was less important in volume than the northern trade in wool, naval stores, dried fruits and metals' (A. P. Usher, 'Spanish Ships and Shipping in the Sixteenth and Seventeenth Centuries', in *Facts and Factors in Economic History—Articles by Former Students of E. F. Gay*, p. 210).

[1] T. VIII₂, pp. 862–3. The figures given are: 1581–5, 84,000 toneladas; 1586–90, 74,500; 1591–5, 65,000; 1596–1600, 78,000; 1601–5, 78,000; but in a footnote Chaunu confines the depression exactly to the years from 1583–4 to 1603–4; see also p. 879. At the same time the volume of outward-going shipping steadily rose.

[2] *Ibid.* t. IV, p. 71 (referring to 1598, but this might have been said of any year from 1585 to 1603).

[3] *Ibid.* t. IV, p. 83. [4] *Ibid.* t. VIII₂, p. 770.

[5] Quoted in Federico de Castro y Bravo, *Las Naos Españolas en la Carrera de las Indias. Armadas y Flotas en la Segunda Mitad del Siglo* XVI (Madrid, 1927).

favour of the treasure. What we know in detail of the prizes reveals clearly enough that it was the middling and lesser shipping that suffered most and that in this respect it was the same story on the Iberian coasts and among the Atlantic islands as in the Caribbean. It was reported in December 1597 that 'the merchants of Seville and Portugal who used to venture to the Indies are broken by losses of goods and ships since the wars'. In the following year Richard Hawkins wrote from Seville that 'Spain is utterly without shipping of regard' and added, significantly: 'that the war with Spain hath been profitable no man with reason can gainsay; and how many millions we have taken from the Spaniard is a thing notorious'.[1] The wholesale destruction of the enemy's merchant marine did not indeed win the war for England, but it helped in the long run to undermine the Iberian economy by making it dependent on foreign shipping. In the last decade of the sixteenth century the number of foreign vessels employed in the Atlantic trades mounted dramatically.[2] The northwestern countries were beginning already to reap their harvest; the largest share fell to the Dutch,[3] but the English did most of the sowing.

What, then, did the English themselves gain from privateering? Here again it is the long-term context that lends significance to the matter. Already before Elizabeth's accession England's overseas trade had entered a profound crisis which was to persist until the middle of the next century. Fundamentally this crisis arose from too great a dependence upon exports of woollen cloth to northern and central Europe. In the course of the century from 1550 to 1650 continuous efforts to find new markets resulted in only one major break-through—the penetration of the southern European and Levant markets. This success undoubtedly compensated to some extent for the stagnation of the older trades. The prosperity of the Iberian, Italian and Turkey trades in the first half of the seventeenth century was remarkable. But the significance of this new

---

[1] *Cal. Salis. MSS.*, XIV, 30; *Monson's Tracts*, II, 94.

[2] Chaunu, t. VIII₂, p. 772; Usher, 'Spanish Ships and Shipping in the Sixteenth and Seventeenth Centuries', in *Facts and Factors in Economic History, Articles by Former Students of E. F. Gay*, p. 210. Henri Lapeyre speaks of 'une très grave crise commerciale qui atteint l'Espagne dans les dernières années du regne de Philippe II, crise évidemment due à la guerre contre l'Angleterre'. In effect, 'l'Atlantique a cessé d'être une mer nourricière pour devenir un champ de bataille' (*Simon Ruiz et les Asientos de Philippe II*, pp. 72, 104).

[3] Engel Sluiter, 'Dutch Maritime Power and the Colonial Status Quo, 1585–1641', *Pacific Historical Review*, XI (1942), 29–41.

growth lay not only in the 'vent' it provided for English cloth, but also in the profitableness of the imports obtained. The Levant trade, indeed, had this in common with the Barbary and Russia trades, that each of these areas on the fringe of Europe offered terms of trade especially favourable to the industrially more advanced parts of Europe, so that the trade assumed a quasi-colonial character. Exports to these areas were not unimportant, but the main profit probably lay in the margin between the buying and selling prices of such goods as raw silk, currants and sugar. Further afield, in the West Indies, Brazil, West Africa and the Indian Ocean, the trade which now developed, albeit slowly, was essentially colonial, and the volume of exports mattered much less than the high rate of profit on the imports and the broadening and balancing effect of this trend upon the mercantile economy as a whole. Such evidence as we have for the first two decades of the seventeenth century shows a distinct relative increase in imports from southern Europe and extra-European areas.[1] These new trades were not yet dominant, but the main direction of the change that was taking place in English overseas interests is clear. The general pattern of the 'rich trades' was emerging and England had set foot on the road that was to lead her to the position of a world entrepôt, controlling a large share of extra-European commerce and harvesting immense wealth from the carrying trade and re-exports. The new trades had other features in common. They were for the most part relatively long-distance trades, requiring considerable capital to undertake; and most of them required powerful and therefore expensive ships. Only the great merchants —the Londoners and a few others—could finance such enterprise, and even they usually did so collectively.

In all these developments the Spanish war marks the vital turning-point and the contribution of privateering was far-reaching. The long-term significance of the Spanish war for English commercial development was inevitably concealed from the eyes of contemporaries because its immediate and obvious effect was a depression in the cloth trade. The loss of the Iberian

---

[1] See the figures in R. H. Tawney, *Business and Politics under James I*, p. 33. For the position in the later seventeenth century, see R. Davis, 'English Foreign Trade, 1660–1700', *Economic History Review*, 2nd Ser., VII (1954), 150. For the character of the Mediterranean trade, see R. Davis, 'England and the Mediterranean, 1570–1670', in *Essays in the Economic and Social History of Tudor and Stuart England in Honour of R. H. Tawney* (ed. F. J. Fisher), pp. 117–37.

trade was a heavy blow to the whole country, but particularly to those outports that depended largely upon Spanish markets— Bristol and Chester, for example. The mayor of Chester in 1598 ascribed the decay of the town to the 'restraint between her Highness' subjects and Spain, a place wherewith the merchants had all their intercourse'.[1] Moreover England's trade to Spain and Portugal had been closely connected with her northerly trades, and the loss of the one created difficulties for the other. There was at least a grain of truth in the report of a Spanish agent from London in 1586: 'The whole country is without trade and knows not how to recover it; the shipping and commerce here having mainly depended upon the communication with Spain and Portugal.'[2] The period of the war saw no satisfactory adjustment of the cloth trade to this unfortunate situation, and relations with the Dutch and the Hanse, as well as with Poland, Denmark and Sweden, were further strained by English seizures of contraband. The reckless behaviour of privateers was a continual source of embarrassment to legitimate traders who relied upon the goodwill of foreign governments, and towards the end of the war the ravages of Dunkirk raiders upon the shipping of the southwest and northeast ports threatened to bring the coastal trade of those regions to a standstill. The contrast between this state of affairs and the trade boom of the post-war years—a boom based largely indeed on the revival of the Iberian trade—is so striking that the less obvious but more permanent effects of the war have usually been overlooked.

For the depression itself had its positive aspect. The decay of the outports meant increasing concentration of trade and wealth in London; while small vessels were confined to port and small men went out of business, the joint stock companies and the great merchants throve. This may not have increased the prosperity of the country as a whole, but the accumulation of commercial power in the capital was essential for the great enterprises of the future—the successful launching of East India trade and the colonisation of North America. When, in the next reign, Sir Edwin Sandys alleged that the custom on London imports amounted to six or seven times the custom on imports for the rest of the country he was unwittingly attesting one of the chief commercial gains of the war.[3] His reference to imports, moreover, points attention to the distinctive feature of London's progress as a

---

[1] *Cal. Salis. MSS.*, VIII, 298.   [2] *Cal. S.P. Span., 1580–86*, p. 651.
[3] *Journals of the House of Commons*, I, 218.

commercial centre. For while cloth exports languished, the trades concerned chiefly with imports steadily advanced, in association with that special trade of wartime—privateering, itself the largest source of lucrative imports.

The relationship between trade and privateering was by no means simple. At one level privateering was merely a substitute for trade, employing the ships of Bristol, for example, that would normally have plied to the Iberian ports. As a substitute it failed, of course, to satisfy the needs of the country; it offered no outlet for the cloth industry, and the goods it returned were not necessarily those required. Large captures of pepper, cochineal, sugar and similar commodities would glut the market; outport men could not handle such goods in quantity and had to ship them to London. But as a substitute for the Iberian trade and the trade of the Iberian empires, privateering was in one respect successful: it was the means of acquiring in plenty and at little cost the coveted produce of those countries. Hence 'the cheapness that all Spanish commodities do now [1598] bear in England, having no trade with Spain, that they be for the most part of less price in England than in Spain or the Indias'.[1] To the Iberian and southward traders who had, for example, probed the Brazilian sugar trade before the war, a regular supply of prize Brazilmen was good enough, at least for the time being. In this sense war for them became a continuation of commerce by other means.

At another level privateering was an adjunct to trade, offering a super-profit to those who owned suitable ships and were engaged in the appropriate lines of trade—notably the Barbary and West African. Again it was not the health of the English economy that benefited, but the pockets of London shipowners and grocery dealers. This direct combination of trade and plunder was less common in the Levant trade, but the alternation of trade and plunder voyages by the powerful Levant merchantmen performed much the same function. How much the Barbary, West African and Levant trades owed to the bolstering effect of prize profits it is impossible to say, but the debt must have been considerable in each case.

Again—and this is far more important—privateering acted in various ways as a lever for the further development of trade. It is sufficiently clear that privateering organised by the great merchants and their professional allies was a highly profitable business. And

[1] *Cal. Salis. MSS.*, VIII, 212.

the mere incidence of profits on this scale of tens of thousands a year was important for the future of English commerce. The accumulation of liquid capital in Elizabethan England was a slow and painful process; the rate of interest was high and the great bulk of wealth lay in the land. In such circumstances windfalls assumed an unusual importance, and no other trade or business provided anything comparable to the showers of windfalls yielded by privateering. This capital came, moreover, directly or indirectly in substantial measure into the hands of those who could use it to the best advantage of commerce. Those merchants most active in privateering were in any case the southward traders who owned the powerful ships and had a strong interest in the products of the colonial and quasi-colonial areas. The capital accumulated by Watts, Bayning, Myddelton and their fellows from privateering played no small part in the launching of the East India Company and the financing of the Virginia plantation. Less directly it served to irrigate all trade, for the increased wealth of the London merchant community promoted all kinds of commercial enterprise in the new century and contributed largely to the post-war boom.

Perhaps even more valuable than these liquid assets were the gains in shipping, and in maritime experience. The precise measurement of the expansion of England's merchant marine during the war must await research specifically devoted to this subject, but it can hardly be doubted that a substantial growth did occur. In 1582, just before the war, a muster of ships and mariners gave a total of 223 ships of over eighty tons burden for the country except Northumberland, which accounted for 25 more. This may be compared with State Paper lists of later dates which show the number of newly built ships of over a hundred tons burden—those on which bounty was paid. For the period 1581 to September 1592 28 are mentioned; 18 more were built between October 1592 and July 1594, 30 between July 1594 and October 1595 and 57 between October 1595 and April 1597.[1] After this date, unfortunately, we have no further lists—only scattered docquets for the payment of bounty. The evidence as a whole, however, suggests a rapid advance in the rate of shipbuilding and an especially sharp rise in the number of large ships of over two hundred tons burden (72 out of the 133 built in the period 1581–

[1] *Monson's Tracts*, III, 188–92. S.P. Dom. Eliz., ccl, no. 33 ; ccliv, no. 33 ; cclxii, no. 126.

1597). Equally remarkable is the overwhelming share of London, for no less than 106 out of 133 were Londoners. Some of the new ships no doubt replaced old ones, and the war itself, by causing losses at sea, must have increased the demand for replacements. But even in the absence of statistics we may be sure that captures of enemy vessels outweighed such losses; and if this assumption is correct, the increase in English shipping during the war was greater than the shipbuilding data appear to indicate. Nor were these new vessels built for the old lines of the cloth trade. Some of them were intended primarily for privateering; others can be traced by name to the Levant, Barbary and Muscovy trades; many of them brought home prizes at one time or another during the war. In short, the war witnessed a shipping boom, a boom associated with the newer commercial trend and above all with privateering. These conclusions are graphically confirmed in every respect by the contemporary observer Sir Thomas Wilson, who, writing in 1600, estimated the merchant marine to be some twenty times the size of the queen's navy. 'This may well be conjectured,' he writes, 'by this, that when there was a fleet of 240 ships of war sent into Spain and 4 other fleet of merchants to the Levant, to Russe, Barbary and Bordeaux, all at one time abroad, yet should you never see the Thames betwixt London Bridge and Blackwall, 4 English miles in length, without 2 or 300 ships or vessels, besides the infinite number of men of war that then were and ever are roving abroad to the Indies and Spanish Dominions, to get purchase, as they call it, whereby a number grow rich.'[1] He no doubt exaggerates the numbers, but the general impression he gives of a flourishing maritime force, with some emphasis on the 'force', rings true.

And with the ships, of course, there grew up a race of skippers who knew the ocean as their forefathers had known the Channel, and could take a ship like Watts' 400-ton *Alcedo* to Alexandria, Senegal, Bantam or Chesapeake Bay according to their owners' instructions. These men—Newport, Parker, Somers and many more—were trained in the school of privateering. Their contribution to the new East India trade was indispensable, since men with the relevant practical experience of ocean voyages, men of proved judgement and responsibility, could hardly have been produced overnight. As for the Virginia plantation, it owed an immense

[1] F. J. Fisher (ed.), 'The State of England (1600). By Sir Thomas Wilson', *Camden Miscellany*, XVI (1936), 36–7.

debt to those who made themselves 'well practised for the western parts of America' during the war. Ships and seamen were rightly seen by Elizabethan statesmen as the key to mercantile power, and the contribution of these two decades of private warfare to England's maritime strength made possible her rise to commercial pre-eminence in the following century.

These gains in capital and maritime strength were important in the long run. It may well be considered, however, that the adverse effects of privateering upon trade during the war more than offset these long-term gains. Privateering, it is often suggested, distracted capital from normal trade, delaying, for example, the founding of the East India Company and the successful plantation of Virginia. In both cases there is some truth in the allegation, though it is arguable that neither project stood much chance of success until towards the end of the war because until then the necessary maritime knowledge, skill and experience were lacking. Moreover the revival of the Virginia project and the first East India voyage did take place before the war ended, when privateering was still very much alive. In fact neither Lancaster nor the North American pioneers of the late war period spurned prizes; it would have been unnatural in them to have done so, since they themselves had usually been engaged in privateering for years, as had their ships, their personnel and their backers. Thus such delay as privateering may have caused in the launching of these ventures only served to accumulate the impetus necessary for their success. In the case of the West Indies it has been shown in detail how the erosive effects of continuous depredations prepared the way for trade, which arose naturally out of and alongside privateering; and the same might be said of the tenuous connections with the Guiana coast. Here, as on the West African coasts, trade and plunder went hand in hand. Indirectly, too, privateering stimulated the demand for extra-European produce. In the short run it may have satisfied the market and reduced prices, but luxury consumption in England spread rapidly at this stage, giving the Elizabethan renaissance its characteristic lavishness. It was now that sugar and perfume, for example, became popular, and the increasing extravagance of fashion, especially in dress and jewellery, was the subject of much censorious comment. Goldsmiths like Shute and the Glanvilles, grocers like Myddelton and the Stiles, enriching themselves from these spoils of war, were understandably eager to forward schemes of Far Eastern and New World trade.

Nor is it true that privateering caused any serious interruptions of established trade. Fenton ruined the chances of Brazil trade, but his was ostensibly a trading venture, which in any case took place before the onset of the war and of privateering. The Levant Company was occasionally embarrassed by the activities of privateers in the Mediterranean, but its trade 'appears never to have been interrupted'.[1] Disputes arose over high-handed seizures in practically every branch of trade, but the only major repercussion was the banishing of the Merchants Adventurers from Germany in 1597, in response to an official act—the seizure of Hanseatic ships trading to Spain. Even in this case the company continued, after a short interval, to frequent the mart at Stade, and the chief result, far from diminishing the volume of trade, was to open Nuremberg and other parts of Germany to a swarm of English interlopers.[2] The important breach of trade in the war years was caused by the closing of the Iberian ports to English ships, but this was a fundamental fact of the war—the cause of privateering, not its result.

In sum, while the war itself brought evil days for England's traditional trades, privateering brought something other than compensation, inflating rapidly a younger side of the mercantile economy. This precocity is to be seen most clearly in the sugar industry, which underwent an extraordinary war boom and probably contracted considerably after 1603. As war dissolved into peace in the first few years of the new century the West Indies trade also withered, not to revive until Spain plunged once more into the struggle for supremacy. The war had acted as a forcing house of the newer type of trade, but what was viable in the new growth survived the cold and bracing blasts of peace.

The positive influence of privateering on England's commercial development is much easier to define than are its wider implications. For privateering was something especially characteristic of Elizabethan England, bearing in its own features the stamp of its national origin, but at the same time contributing to the change in the national structure and spirit that was to produce the Jacobean age. Privateering itself fused, as other pursuits were fusing, the energy and resources of the various social groups: court and country gentlemen, merchant magnates and local traders, captains and masters, those thrusting yeomen of the sea, and the mob of

[1] A. C. Wood, *History of the Levant Company*, p. 23.
[2] *Cal. Salis. MSS.*, VII, 543–4.

sailors, old hands or raw recruits, their part being no passive one. These all rubbed shoulders and spoke the same language equally, with that directness and immediacy of metaphor that no age since has known. There was an element of democracy in privateering, strongest at sea, where the mariners were inclined to take the bit between their teeth and gentlemen often had to haul and draw with the rest, but also present in the preparation of a venture and its winding up, since both were free for all. This was a popular war and privateering was the most popular aspect of it; it canalised the anti-Spanish sentiment present in all classes, though most prevalent in the mercantile part of the population; it gave his chance to any man who wished to wage war on his own account; it was the directest expression of the nation-in-arms. It thus embodied and developed that sense of confidence and pride in mere Englishness so well documented by Hakluyt and so well symbolised by the queen. At least until the civil war men would look back to the 'queen's time' as to an age of glory, not so much because they could point to great victories as because traditional memory filled them with nostalgia for the active unity and common participation of those days. The thousands of minor engagements were soon forgotten, but for them all as an archetype stood the defeat of the Armada, just as Drake came to stand for a great galaxy of privateering captains. The popular and democratic character of privateering is nowhere more obvious than in the writings of Henry Roberts, the sailor-poet. Himself a participant, a Devon man and a Londoner, he reproduces in all its naïvety the crude patriotism of the common man, patriotism mixed with godliness and greed and conscious pride in the deeds of citizens other than 'cavaliers'. This is the literature of the Elizabethan groundlings, and it is significant that its subject was privateering.[1]

But if privateering was a special vehicle of national feeling, this was due to the peculiar circumstances of the time: the dependence of the Elizabethan state upon the initiative of its subjects; its reluctance to bear the burden of full-scale sea war; its inability to impose maritime discipline; the readiness of great persons, even the queen herself, to draw a ticket in this lottery of fame and riches. Late Tudor government was in many respects based on popular consent—that was the strength of its weakness—but in this sphere of sea warfare it was almost the case that popular government was

[1] See L. B. Wright, *Middle Class Culture in Elizabethan England*, pp. 515–24; also above, pp. 150–5.

based on royal consent. The royal navy itself seemed, in the days of Drake and Hawkins, to be no more than a part of the national sea-force, a spearhead cast by the mercantile sea-gentry out of their own metal.

The peculiar aptitude of the Elizabethan English for privateering was not merely a political, but a social phenomenon—the product of the coexistence of ambitious traders and predatory gentry. Before 1585 these two wings of English maritime endeavour did not work in unison—Fenton's voyage illustrates their disharmony—but the war brought them into alignment and the great strength of the privateering movement was based on their collaboration. The ties between the business aristocracy and the naval captains and admiralty officials were now made strong. Henry Cletherow became 'he that doth buy all things for Hawkyns'.[1] Myddelton took financial charge of the great joint stock expeditions of 1591, 1592, 1595 and 1596. Watts and Raleigh joined forces in the Virginia expedition of 1590 and the West Indies cruise of the following year. Sir John Burgh accepted the aid of Newport's merchant syndicate. Ridlesden and Bragg, admiralty men, combined with John More and partners, City men. Meanwhile the gentlemen amateurs either went out of business, like the Sherley brothers, or out of existence, like Chidley, or became essentially the junior partners of merchant syndicates, as even Cumberland did in the end. At the same time, though for different reasons, the lesser kind of outport reprisal dwindled and the chief privateering bases came increasingly under the control of London interests. Thus there emerged a new social pattern of maritime force. From the ranks of the sea-gentry and the skilled mariners developed the nucleus of a 'managerial' element in shipping, consonant with the increasing size of the ships engaged. As for the ordinary seamen, though they held their own during the war by fair means or foul, the basis of their traditional independence was gradually being undermined by the evolution of the large, ocean-going merchantman. And over all stood the great merchants, backing the professional gentry, who depended on them for capital and for the realisation of their profit, employing the seamen, skilled or unskilled, owning the ships, commanding the market. These trends were no more than trends—there was no revolution in the maritime social structure—but they were of great significance for the future, constituting as

[1] Corbett, *Spanish War*, p. 222.

they did the social counterpart of the commercial advance we have noticed.

Recent work has focused attention upon certain marked features of early Stuart society and government: the great wealth and power of the metropolitan merchant oligarchy; the venality of the court and the bureaucracy; the dependence of the Crown upon London's money. The City, in fact, not only controlled most of England's foreign trade, much of her industry and a considerable part of real estate business, but oiled the wheels of a corrupt régime. Undoubtedly financial scandals, peculation and hectic competition for office did not begin with the accession of James I, though they may have multiplied remarkably from that time. As Sir John Neale long ago pointed out, their origins must be sought in the reign of Elizabeth, and particularly in its last decade.[1] But one of the fundamental facts of this last phase of Tudor rule was that England was at war—a war longer and more serious and expensive than any since Lancastrian times. The role of war in promoting the fortunes of the *haute bourgeoisie*, and with them the corruption of the state, is a familiar enough theme to French historians—why not to English? Perhaps because until recently we have been less interested in corruption and warfare and their intimate connections, so slowly have we awakened from the ideals of the nineteenth century to the realities of the twentieth. War was of course much less important for English development in 'Tawney's century' than for France in the same period, but this is no reason to leave it out of account as a formative influence. It is no accident that the admiralty was notoriously one of the most corrupt branches of the law and the administration. The sea war was waged for profit; the queen expected to make it pay, and her officers and her merchants made an investment of it. The Cadiz expedition, perhaps the biggest scandal of the nineties, grieved the queen because it failed to yield her a dividend, but it lined the pockets of many a soldier and sailor, among whom, we may reasonably suspect, the queen's own secretary-at-war, Sir Anthony

---

[1] *Essays in Elizabethan History*, pp. 59–84. Lawrence Stone's article, 'The Fruits of Office', in *Essays in the Economic and Social History of Tudor and Stuart England in Honour of R. H. Tawney* (ed. F. J. Fisher), pp. 89–116, dealing with the younger Cecil, would appear to support Neale's thesis. The politics of finance and the finance of politics in the Jacobean era are particularly well described in R. H. Tawney, *Business and Politics under James I* and in Robert Ashton, *The Crown and the Money Market, 1603–1640*.

Ashley, was to be counted. In such national enterprises, with all their opportunities for malversation, private and public interests were inextricably mingled. Of some 150 vessels engaged in the Cadiz voyage, only 15 or 18 belonged to the Crown; the rest, apart from 24 Dutch ships, were supplied by port towns and private owners. A high proportion of the privateering captains sailed, and they were led by Charles Howard, Essex and Raleigh —each in his own way a champion of pillage as a system of politics and a method of waging war.

Drake and Hawkins were dead and their places were soon to be taken by men of the calibre of Sir William Monson, Sir Robert Mansell and Sir Richard Leveson. The last owed his promotion to his marriage into the Howard family; the first was dishonest and vain; and of Mansell our greatest naval historian has written: 'It is the rise of this man that marks the commencement of a reign of selfishness and corruption that almost brought the navy to ruin in the next reign.'[1] By the end of the war the Howard régime in the admiralty had already undermined that sense of unity and devotion that had shone through in the hour of crisis; the pernicious influence of the Howards was a manifestation of the disease inherent in the system of patronage, a manifestation worse than most because the opportunities for private gain at the public expense were greater here than elsewhere and because the normal restraints of law and morality were more easily overborne where the proper business of all concerned was robbery with violence.

Ordinary corruption may easily arise when a government department has to deal with private interests; when those private interests actually dominate the department, corruption is liable to get out of hand; but when, as in the case of the Elizabethan admiralty, the department is itself a private interest, corruption becomes a wasting disease, and the health—even the life— of the state is endangered. At the top the Lord Admiral and the queen's principal secretary used the resources of the Exchequer to finance their private sea ventures, and while the high command thus exploited the state, lesser men were content to exploit the laxity of the Lord Admiral. Thus although the latter secured a considerable income by taxing prizes, he largely lost control over the business of reprisal. The sea war degenerated into an indecorous scramble for private profit, a scramble in which the queen's servants had peculiar advantages, but from which the Crown itself

[1] Corbett, *Successors of Drake*, p. 301.

could only lose. As we have observed in an earlier chapter, what was taking place was a disintegration of power, resulting from the conjunction of an antiquated system of government and the acquisitive drive of vigorous private interests in circumstances more than usually favourable to the latter. And among these private interests the great merchants gained most, not only by dominating the privateering world itself, but also by exercising influence in the official sphere. Their loans to the Crown became more and more frequent from 1585 and the part of men like Myddelton and Cletherow in the financial organisation of the sea war became more and more important. At the very end of the war, in February 1603, the government proposed a scheme for the formation of an auxiliary fleet of private ships to protect commerce in the Narrow Seas, tacitly admitting the inability of the royal navy to manage this duty. An independent committee, sponsored and assisted by the government, was to organise the new fleet, the main burden being borne by London; the treasurer was to be Paul Bayning. Prizes were to be free of customs and tenths, and the committee could discontinue the scheme if it proved unremunerative.[1] In the event the fleet was probably never formed, but the whole project bears eloquent testimony to the growing power of the City and of the privateering interest in particular, represented as it was here by Paul Bayning. Merchants' capital, like some parasitic growth, was gradually sapping away the power of the monarchy, thriving upon the rot it helped to spread.

[1] Corbett, *Successors of Drake*, pp. 397–9.

APPENDIX

APPENDIX

Note

The argument of this book is partly based on the information summarised below in two lists of privateers and prizes, one for 1589-91, the other for 1598. Each list is divided into sections according to the places of origin of the privateers: London, Southampton, Dorset, Devon and Cornwall, Bristol and Bridgewater, 'Other Ports' and 'Port Unknown'. The Southampton lists include ships of Chichester (signified by 'C'), Portsmouth ('P') and the Isle of Wight ('I.O.W.'). The Dorset ships are of Weymouth unless marked 'P' for Poole or 'L' for Lyme. In all places the sign 'U' indicates 'unknown'. Some of the prizes cannot be allotted to identifiable privateers; in cases where it appears that the privateer responsible is not mentioned elsewhere in the list, an unknown privateer has been added; otherwise the prize has been listed under 'Other Prizes' and no additional privateer is assumed.

It must not be imagined that the data assembled here represent simple, unassailable 'facts'. Each of the numerous statements concerning the privateers and the prizes is actually a conclusion based upon other statements of varying reliability.[1] Most of these original statements were made in connection with proceedings in the High Court of Admiralty, which was responsible for issuing letters of reprisal, adjudicating prizes and administering the law maritime. The records of this court are therefore rich in references to privateering. On the other hand this material has serious limitations. In the first place it is far from complete, partly because the records were not systematically kept and partly because a great deal of privateering activity escaped the notice of the court. Secondly, we cannot take on trust much of what was said by parties or witnesses in law suits. In using this material we have constantly to sift, judge and interpret.[2]

Next in importance is the list of the tenths of prizes allocated to the Lord Admiral in the period 1587-98.[3] It deals almost exclusively with prizes brought into Weymouth, Bristol and Southampton, and is incomplete even for these ports. Nevertheless this is an extremely useful source, since for most of the prizes mentioned it identifies the captor ship, its owners, captain and master, giving the nature of the prize-goods, a detailed inventory of the tenth

[1] The particular source references for each of the listed voyages are too voluminous to include here. They are given in full in my unpublished Ph.D. thesis in the University of London Library (1951).

[2] For a study of the court and its records see the introduction to *E.P.V.* and other works mentioned there.

[3] Harleian MS 598.

and some account of its sale and disposal. Several other lists, of considerably less value, occur in the Caesar Papers, which also contain many items of Caesar's correspondence and notes relating to Admiralty cases and other matters.[1] These are the main materials, but a great deal in the way of scraps has been garnered from miscellaneous sources.[2]

What follows, therefore, is not based upon any single body of material. Personal narratives are available for some voyages and not for others. Where we have a narrative and court material for the same voyage, we may find them supplementary or contradictory—usually both. In this fashion the materials do afford some check upon each other for many of the ventures, and such checks also demonstrate the dangers of dependence on one source alone for our knowledge of a voyage. For a single source may easily be misleading, especially in omitting mention of prizes taken, and in giving a false impression of the value of the prizes that are mentioned. What emerges from all this most clearly is that our lists of voyages are incomplete, and our lists of prizes even more so; the identifications of ships and personnel are fairly accurate, but the monetary valuations of prizes are often rather unreliable. As a general rule we have preferred the risks of under-estimation to the hazards of inflation. The tonnage figures for ships are given in tons burden, as was usual at this time, and are, like most sixteenth-century tonnages, merely approximate.

[1] The Caesar Papers are in the British Museum collections of Lansdowne MSS and Additional MSS.

[2] See 'Sources', above, pp. ix–xv.

LIST OF PRIVATEERS AND PRIZES

1589–91. LONDON SHIPS

ship	tons	promoters	date	captain	prize-cargo	value £	remarks
Adonia	u	Robert Sadler, Nicholas Clevinger, William Leckland, John Giles	1589				with *Grace of God* of Topsham
Amity	100	Henry Colthurst and Company	1589	Thomas White	wines, oil, raisins ⎫ wines, oil, raisins ⎬ Portuguese	u u	with *Dolphin* of London
		"	1590	Walter Crunnelowe	Leaguer with fish / Frenchman with Dunkirkers' goods	u	with *Eagle, Lark and Passport*
		"	1591	Thomas White	wines, oil, linen / u / u	u u u	
Balinus	40	George Bassett	1591	John White	wines—Portuguese	u	
Black Dog	60	William Michelson and Henry Cletherow	1588–9	William Michelson	wrought iron and manufactures	1800	West Indies. Other small prizes
Black Falcon	u	Edward Glenham	1591	Thomas Foscue			See *Edward Constance*
Bark Burr	130	Sir George Carey	1591	William Irish			See *Swallow* of Southampton
Centaur	120	John Watts and others	1591	William Lane			See *Harry and John*
Centurion	200	City of London	1591	Christopher Furth			See *Susan* of London
Cherubim	250	City of London	1591	Broothers	sugar, hides, ginger, sarsaparilla, brazilwood, treasure and other goods	2000	,,
Costly	200	City of London	1591	George Deane	woollen and other cloth figs, raisins, oil, wines—Portuguese	u	,,
Crocodile	u	Edward Fenner	1591			u	
Delight	40	John Barbor and Thomas Matthew	1590	John Thomas	hides, oil, raisins, olives	450	
			1591	John Ridlesden			

243

ship	tons	promoters	date	captain	prize-cargo	value £	remarks
Delight	u	Thomas Bramley and Roger Ofield	1590	Thomas Beste		u	See *Samaritan*
Discharge	50	Henry Seckford	1589	Robert Hutton	oil, secks, ginger	u	
		„	1590	Thomas West	Portuguese oil, cloth, pots, etc.	450	Spanish goods in French ship
		Thomas Fenner and John Bird	1591		Frenchman with Canary wines, sugar, etc.	u	Ship and one third of wines restored due to sail with *Golden Noble* of London, *Falcon* of Portsmouth, and *Elizabeth* of Plymouth
Dolphin	90	Henry Colthurst and Company	1589	John Maynard			See *Amity* of London
Dolphin	50	John Watts	1589				See *May Morning* of London
Eagle	u	Henry Colthurst and Company and Edward Holmeden	1589	Henry White	corn / sugar, cotton wool, and 'beveradge'	u / 1180	After deduction of freight and costs for the French owners
Edward Bonaventure	250	Thomas Cordell	1590 / 1590	James Lancaster	pitch, iron and grinding stones	u	See *Amity* with *Merchant Royal*. Shared *Amity's* fish prize. Spoil of *Hope* of Flushing
		„	1591	„			with *Merchant Royal* and *Penelope*. East Indies venture
Edward Constance	u	Edward Glenham	1591	Edward Glenham	figs and raisins—Portuguese oil	u / u	with *Black Falcon*. Attempted St. George's Island. Venetian argosy (mainly sugar) taken in Mediterranean

ship	tons	promoters	date	captain	prize-cargo	value £	remarks
Elizabeth	120	William Hall, John Howell, William Russell	1591	John Matthews	silks and other cloths—Italian	u	part of cargo declared good prize
Elizabeth and Mary	u	Thomas Myddelton	1589	William Myddelton	sugar and cotton wool—Brazilman	2000	
Examiner	u	John Watts and Thomas Sewell	1590	Anthony Barlowe	hides, money, jewels, gold	u	
Fancy (or Black Jolly)	60	Andrews Fones, Edmund Ansell, Philip Darrell	1590	Nicholas Webb	corn—a Lübecker	u	with Grace of God of Dover
"		"	1591	"	deal boards and corn	700	took two prizes, but these were wrecked with the Fancy
Fortunatus	40		1590	George Martin			
Globe	120	Edward Leckland and Robert Sadler	1591	Nicholas Nelson	fish—a Leaguer	110	See Bark Bond of Weymouth
Golden Dragon (or Red Rose)	150		1591	Roger Roidon			
Golden Noble (or Golden Phoenix)	200	John Bird and John Newton	1591	Edward Partridge			See Discharge, but also Allagarta. The Golden Noble eventually sailed with Cumberland's 1591 expedition
Grace of God	35	William Grafton	1591	William Grafton			
Greyhound	u		1591	Christopher Colthurst	sugar, wool, dyewood—Brazilman	2460	
Bark Hall	60	William Hall	1591	John Langford			
Handmaid	u	City of London	1591				See Susan
Hare	u	Thomas Myddelton and Erasmus Harby	1591	Geede			See Riall of Weymouth
Harry & John (or Hopewell)	150	John Watts, John Stokes, Henry Cletherow and others	1590	Abraham Cocke	hides, sugar, ginger, cochineal, pepper, sarsaparilla	6000	with John (or Little John) and John Evangelist. Consorted with Moonlight and Conclude. West Indies and Virginia
					hides, sugar, ginger, cochineal, sarsaparilla and silks salvaged from 2 other prizes	300	
					hides and wood	500	

1589-91. LONDON SHIPS (continued)

ship	tons	promoters	date	captain	prize-cargo	value £	remarks
		John Watts and others	1591	William Craston	hides, ginger and sugar	2000	with Centaur, John (or Little John), Pegasus and Fifth Part. Consorted with Bark Burr, Content, Swallow, Prudence and Lion (of Southampton). To the West Indies. (Two more prizes are counted for Swallow of Southampton.)
					hides, ginger and sugar	2000	
					hides, cochineal, silver and money	2000	
					hides, sugar and ginger	2000	
					hides, sugar and ginger	2000	
					bullion, cochineal, money, hides	18,000	
Harte	40	Thomas Myddelton	1591	Thomas Myddelton	bullion, plate, money, pearls	3000	captain a kinsman of the London merchant
John (or Little John)	100	John Watts and John Stokes	1589	John Mussett	São Thomé sugar	3435	consorted with *Minion* of Bridgewater
		,,			Canary wines	100	Spanish wine taken and the French ship released
John Evangelist	u	John Watts	1590	Christopher Newport			See *Harry and John*
		,,	1591	Michael Geare			See *Harry and John*
Lark	40	Henry Colthurst and Company	1590	William Lane			See *Harry and John*
			1590				See *Amity*
Magdalen	50	City of London	1591				See *Susan*
Margaret	60	Robert Cobb, John More, Robert Southwick	1589	Robert Hallett	oil	250	shared with *Supply*
		,,	1591	Christopher Newport	wines, almonds, copperas	u	with *Prudence* in the West Indies
Margaret & John	180	John Watts	1591	John Rickman	hides and sugar	500	See *Susan*
Mary (or Bark Smith)	60	John and Arthur Jackson, Edmund Aronsell and James Lancaster	1590	Edmund Barker	rice, oil, olives, wool, cochineal and other goods	230	shared in *Delight* of Southampton's sugar prize
			1591	Allan Coates	pots, salt, wines and oil—Portuguese	u	

ship	tons	promoters	date	captain	prize-cargo	value £	remarks
Mary	u	Arthur Stercke	1590	Matthew Stercke	resin and olives—Leaguer	u	See *Susan*
Mayflower	300	John Watts	1591				with *Dolphin*. To the River Plate
May Morning	50		1589	Abraham Cocke			See *Edward Bonaventure*
Merchant Royal	300	Thomas Cordell	1590	Samuel Foxcroft			See *Edward Bonaventure*
Mermaid (or Merman)	100	William Bond	1591	"			
			1591	Thomas Huckley	wines, raisins, oil, figs and olives—Leaguer	1140	
Moonlight	80	William Sanderson	1590	Edward Spicer	fish	230	See *Harry and John*
Moonshine	50	John Newton and John Bird	1590	John Myddelton	wines, walnuts, grapes, olives, etc.	100	Biscayan prize
		"	1591	"	cochineal, hides, sarsaparilla and treasure	5000	A French prize of oil and fish restored to owners
Passport	80	Henry Colthurst and Company	1589	Christopher Colthurst	sugar and brazilwood—Brazilman	2000	
		"	1590	Oliver Maister	fish and oil—Leaguer	200	See *Amity*
Pegasus	80	John Watts	1591	Thomas Rise			See *Harry and John*
			1591	Stephen Michell			
Penelope	u	George Raymond	1590	George Raymond	sugar, brazilwood and hides—Brazilman	2790	shared with *Pilgrim*
					iron	1248	
Post	30	Robert Cobb, Thomas Pullison and Thomas Starkey	1591	"			See *Edward Bonaventure* with *Amity*
			1590				
Pretence	60	Samuel Thomas	1591	John Thomas			See *Margaret* and *Harry and John*
Prudence	70	Robert Cobb, John More, William Jones and John Newton	1591	John Brough			
Return	u	Henry Seckford	1589	Thomas Philips	linen cloth		See *Discharge*
		"	1590	"		u	

1589–91. LONDON SHIPS (continued)

ship	tons	promoters	date	captain	prize-cargo	value £	remarks
Robert	u	Earl of Cumberland	1590	Nicholas Downton		2580	with Cavendish in his last voyage
Roebuck	240	Thomas Cavendish	1590	John Cocke	sugar, ginger and hides wines—Portuguese	550	
		,,	1591	,,			
Salamander	90	William Holliday	1589	Thomas Ellys	sugar and brazilwood—Brazilman wines	5000	
Samaritan	160	,,	1590	Anthony Potts	wines	800	Leaguer wines in a Scots ship
		Thomas Bramley and Roger Ofield	1590	William Jones	u	u	A French man-of-war
Seadragon	50	William Holliday	1589	Robert Naylor	Spanish wines / wheat—Portuguese / pots and salt—Portuguese / sugar and brazilwood—Brazilman	u / u / u / 2680	spoiled a French ship of some Canary wines
Squirrel	40	,,	1590	Anthony Ingram	hides—Portuguese	u	See *Susan*
Stephen	180	,,	1591	John Legatt			spoiled some Dutch vessels. In company of *Minion* of Bristol and *Tiger* consorted with *Gift of God* of Barnstaple with *Margaret*
		Andrew Fursland and John Cherry	1590	Thomas Horwell			
		,,	1591				
Supply (or *Black Pinnace*)	u	Henry Seckford	1589	Peter Lee	fish—Leaguer	u	
Susan	300	City of London	1591	Robert Flick	hides, cochineal and raw silk / hides, cochineal and raw silk / hides, sarsaparilla and indigo—Portuguese	6000 / 6000 / 6000	Flick led the City of London squadron sent to reinforce Lord Thomas Howard at the Azores in 1591. The City only took £6000 of the returns because Howard and his consorts claimed shares

ship	tons	promoters	date	captain	prize-cargo	value £	remarks
Swallow	70	John Rainbridge and Thomas Stepney	1590	George Raymond			shared a prize with *Dainty* of Plymouth
		,,	1591	John Johnson	hides, sugar, ginger, cochineal, dyewood, silver and rialls of plate	1500	shared this prize and another with *Globe* of London and *Bark Bond* of Weymouth with *Julian* and *Delight* of Lyme and *Unicorn* of Barnstaple
Swiftsure	80	George Raymond	1589	James Beare			spoiled some Dutch vessels. In company with *Minion* of Bristol and *Stephen*
Tiger	170	William Holliday, John Watkinson, Andrew Fursland and Ralph Bowes	1590	John Markham			
		William Holliday, Ralph Bowes, Martin van Bank and George Barnestrawe	1591	George Barnestrawe	spices	u	in company with *White Lion* of Weymouth. The spices were what was left of 2 valuable prizes which escaped
White Lion	340	John Chidley and others	1589	Thomas Polwhele			these ships, together with *Robin* of Bristol, formed John Chidley's South Sea fleet—see above, pp. 67–8
Wildman	300	John Chidley and others	1589	John Chidley			
Wildman's Club	25	John Chidley and others	1589	Richard Glover			

1589–91. SOUTHAMPTON SHIPS

ship	tons	promoters	date	captain	prize-cargo	value £	remarks
Bevis	60	Edward Hayes	1589	Edward Hayes	wines and figs	200	Dutch merchants secured return of about half of cargo
		,, Thomas Heaton	1590	,,	wines	u	also spoiled an Irish vessel
			1591		olives, oil and hides	455	With *William Bonaventure*
					olives, oil and hides	455	
					wheat and rye	455	

1589–91. SOUTHAMPTON SHIPS (continued)

ship	tons	promoters	date	captain	prize-cargo	value £	remarks
Blessing (P)	70	Thomas Heaton, George Raymond and William Bassett	1589	Davie Targett	sugar and cotton—Brazilman	3808	
Brave (I.O.W.)	35	John Jefferies	1591	Thomas Ardinge	u	u	a French bark
Chance (I.O.W.)	u	Oliver Knott, Henry Joliffe	1590	David Perrin	hides	1100	with Carey's *Swallow* and *Bark Burr* in the West Indies
Commander (I.O.W.)	200	Sir George Carey	1591	Thomas Page			
Content (I.O.W.)	u	Sir George Carey	1590	Nicholas Lisle			
Delight	u	Earl of Cumberland	1590	Thomas Covert	sugar—Brazilman	u	
					salt	60	
Eleanour	100	Thomas Heaton, Henry Cletherow and Lawrence Prowse	1590	Francis Brooke	brazilwood, sugar and wax —Brazilman	470	took a Dutch prize of salt, which was restored
					sugar and brazilwood— Brazilman	4030	
		,,	1591	Lawrence Prowse	sugar, ginger and hides	2000	
					sugar and cotton wool— Brazilman	2000	
Falcon (P)	u	John Bird and Thomas Fenner	1591	Edward Fenner	linen	u	
Galleon Fenner (P)	120	William Bassett	1591	John Dunn	butter	u	
Grace (P)	50	Dennis Rowse and Thomas Exton	1591	Henry Napper	salt	u	
Hare	30		1590		salt	u	
John Young (C)	60	John Young	1589	Benedict Haines			
		John Young and John Jefferies	1590	John Leye	São Thomé sugar	1320	with *Prudence* of Barnstaple and *Unicorn* of Dartmouth
			1591	William Hambourne	corn, sugar, linseed, etc.	u	

ship	tons	promoters	date	captain	prize-cargo	value £	remarks
Lion	80		1591	John Oker			in the West Indies. Shared in capture of Carey's *Swallow*'s prize of hides
Minion	60	William Dudson and Lawrence Prowse	1589	Thomas Prowse	iron	u	
			1590	John Legatt	salt and secks	u	a St Malo ship
			1591		wines, sugar, flax, cotton, sumac, molasses and wax	200	with Lord Thomas Howard's fleet
Phoenix (P)	60	Earl of Hertford	1590	Edward Grant	sugar and molasses—Brazilman	1355	
		"	1591				with Lord Thomas Howard's fleet
Prudence (C)	120	Thomas Heaton	1591	Thomas Bestige	wines, oils, figs, canvas, candles and paper	600	joined Cumberland's fleet in the Azores
Saucy Jack	u	Thomas Heaton	1589				
Swallow	70	Sir George Carey	1591	Ralph Lee	hides	1500	in the West Indies with *Bark Burr* and *Content*. Consorted with Watts' fleet
					sugar and pearls	2000	
William Bonaventure	u	Thomas Heaton	1589	William Heaton	wheat and rye—a Hamburger	180	ship restored to owners
		"	1590	John Elsey			took part in spoil of two Easterlings
Bark Young	u	John Young and John Crooke	1591	Brooke			in company of *Bevis*
			1590	William Irish	women's doublets, coarse thread, shirts, linen cloth and ivory	70	a prize of sugar and hides taken in West Indies and lost to Leaguers
u (I.O.W.)	u		1589	Henry Joliffe	fish—Leaguer	280	
					wools, resin, salt, etc.	u	
"	u		1590	Peter Edwards	salt	33	a French ship
"	u	Thomas Heaton and Lawrence Prowse	1590	John Austin	pitch and linen	u	a French ship
"			1591		fish	u	

1589-91. DORSET SHIPS

ship	tons	promoters	date	captain	prize-cargo	value £	remarks
Advantage (L)	u	John Davis, John Hazard	1590		sugar and cotton wool—Brazilman	700	
Aid (L)	u	Henry Pitt and Anthony Moone	1590	Richard Moone	wheat	u	
Alice Bonaventure (P)	60	Richard Goddard	1591	Paul Bush			
Amity	60	Nicholas Jones	1591	Nicholas Wright			
Anne Huddy	u	William Huddy and John Reynolds	1589	Hugh Preston	wax, fustians and hollands	50	
		"	1590	Henry Thin	sugar, brazilwood and hides —Brazilman	1000	
					fish	40	
Bark Bond	56	John Bond, William Pitt, Richard Pitt, William Holman	1589	David Geyer	sugar, brazilwood and cotton wool—Brazilman	4670	
		"	1590	Edward Bond	molasses, sugar, Málaga raisins, etc.—a Leaguer	660	
		"	1591	Roger Geyer	hides, sugar, ginger, ivory and other goods	1500	shared this and another prize with *Swallow* and *Globe* of London
Bark Brave	u		1589	Oliver Hillyard	a Brazilman	u	shared in Brazilman taken by a Plymouth ship
Bark Brooke	u	John Brooke, Thomas Bagg, William Hodder and John Willis	1590	Thomas Bagg	sugar and ginger—Brazilman	1715	
			1591	"	salt—Portuguese	u	
Carouse	30	Roger Page	1589	Oliver Knott	wheat	120	a small Brazilman
					u	u	
Catherine (or Little Catherine)	35	Robert White	1590	Robert White	sugar, cotton wool, brazilwood and hides— Brazilman	1465	
					sugar and brazilwood— Brazilman	2000	
			1591		sugar and cotton wool— Brazilman	2850	

252

ship	tons	promoters	date	captain	prize-cargo	value £	remarks
Delight (L)	u	Amyas Preston and George Somers	1589	John Newall			with *Julian* of Lyme
Endeavour (L)	u	Henry Rogers	1591	Ephraim Reynolds	cloth	u	a French ship
Foresight (L)	u	Robert Hazard and Richard Norris	1589				
Golden Hind (or *White Lion*)	120	Edward Lewes	1591	Edward Lewes	pepper and other goods	u	in company with *Tiger* of London. The pepper was taken from one of two prizes which escaped
Hopewell (L)	u	John Vinie	1591		wines		
Jane Bonaventure	20	Roger Geyer	1590	Roger Geyer	u	47	claimed a share of *Prudence* of Barnstaple's prize
Julian (L)	u	Amyas Preston and George Somers	1591	,,	hides, cochineal	5000	in company with *delight* of Lyme, *Swiftsure* of London and *Unicorn* of Barnstaple
			1589	George Somers	silver, gold, jewels, money, cochineal, silks, hides and campeche wood	25,000	
Little John (or *Gift of God*)	20	John Peters	1591	Richard Skinner	timber, wines, olives, figs, oil and salt—French ship	36	with *Revenge* of Lyme
Lyme (L)	u	Robert Davies	1591	Robert Davies	iron coulters, spikes, etc.	373	
Minion Rose (L)	u	George Somers	1591	Robert Brooke	pepper, cloves, mace, sugar, ivory, brazilwood, etc.	10,000	the cargoes were worth more than this, but some goods were probably recovered by the Italians who claimed them. *Riall* of Weymouth, *Discharge* of London, a ship of William Walton's and *Samaritan* shared the capture of the prizes
Bark Randall	60	John Randall, Sir George Carey, Sir Walter Raleigh and others	1590	Thomas Lother	pepper, etc. (as above) and precious stones	13,000	
					sugar	u	
					millet	u	
Revenge (L)	40	Richard Bedford	1591	Richard Skinner			with *Little John* of Weymouth

1589-91. DORSET SHIPS (continued)

ship	tons	promoters	date	captain	prize-cargo	value £	remark
Riall	160	Thomas Myddelton and Erasmus Harby	1590	William Myddelton		u	with *Bark Randall* of Weymouth
		"	1591	"	oil—a French ship	u	with *Hare* of London
Son (L)	u	"	1591	Thomas Myddelton	corn in a Hamburg ship	u	
				Robert Davie	sugar, molasses and wool—Portuguese	1000	
Sunday	u	Richard Norris	1589	Henry Duffield	fish	u	a French ship
Bark Way (or Bark Sutton)	70	Brooke	1589	Mark Bury	sugar	u	took a French ship, which was restored
u	u		1589		sugar	u	the privateer was a canter of Weymouth, a converted prize

1589-91. SHIPS OF DEVON AND CORNWALL

ship	tons	promoters	date	captain	prize-cargo	value £	remarks
Amity (Barnstaple)	30		1591				with *Prudence* of Barnstaple
Arthur (Plymouth)	u		1591	Arthur Pepott	iron horseshoes, spikes, bolts, hoops, calivers, etc.	300	
Bark Burton (Plymouth)	u	Sir Walter Raleigh	1589	Mark Bury	cochineal, hides and other goods	10,000	consorted with *Drake* of Plymouth and met Cumberland's fleet at Azores
Bark Bury (Plymouth)	u		1590	Thomas Bury			involved in the spoil of two Easterlings

ship	tons	promoters	date	captain	prize-cargo	value £	remarks
Chance (Plymouth)	50	John Weekes, Robert Crosse	1589	William Hobbes			with Sparke of Plymouth. Brought in some valuable prize-goods
Conclude (Plymouth)	35	Thomas Myddelton, James Bagg, Nicholas Glanville and William Finch	1591	John Crosse, Arthur Pepwell	sugar—Brazilman	u	consorted with Moonlight of London and joined Watts' fleet in West Indies
			1590	Joseph Harris	a Portuguese prize	u	
Dainty (Plymouth)	200	Sir John Hawkins	1591	Stephen Acham			with Unity and Fancy of Plymouth
			1590		u	u	sailed with Hawkins' 1590 fleet. The prize was the Holy Ghost, which carried a valuable cargo
Diamond (Dartmouth)	40	Gilbert Stapleyhill	1591	William Holland	walnuts and wood—Portuguese	u	undertook a special voyage to Lord Thomas Howard's fleet
Dolphin (Plymouth)	50	,,	1591	John Lidstone, Thomas Fleming	u	30	joined Cumberland's fleet in the Azores
Drake (Plymouth)	60		1589	John Davis			
Drift (Plymouth)	u	Humphrey Fones	1589				
Elizabeth (Plymouth)	60	John Bird and Thomas Fenner	1591	George Webb	a Portuguese prize	55	sent to Lord Thomas Howard's fleet
Elizabeth Bonaventure (Northam)	80	William Pallett	1591	Richard Adams			
Elizabeth Fishbourne (Plymouth)	70	Richard Fishbourne	1589	Richard Fishbourne	sugar and brazilwood—Brazilman	2720	the prize was lost to a Rochelle man-of-war and then re-taken by three English merchantmen
		,,	1590				involved in the spoil of two Easterlings
		,,	1591		a prize of Gascon wines	u	

ship	tons	promoters	date	captain	prize-cargo	value £	remarks
Elizabeth Glanville (Tavistock)	u	Nicholas Glanville	1590				set forth with Conclude and Nicholas of Plymouth shared Bark Young's prize
Falcon's Flight (Barnstaple)	u	John Norris	1590				
Fancy (Plymouth)	u		1591	William Finch	hides and other goods	u	with Unity of Plymouth took two prizes, both brought home by Conclude
Fly (Plymouth)	16	Richard Hawkins	1590	John Sled			
Flying Hart (Topsham)	u		1591	Richard Savidge	fish, resin, turpentine, combs, etc.	u	Biscayan
Fortmouth (Barnstaple)	u		1591		wines		
Fortune (Plymouth)	u		1590	Bodley		u	St Malo vessel spoiled. Goods to be restored
Francis (Barnstaple)	u	William Morcomb	1590	Richard Hill	u	1500	
Gift (Topsham)	25		1590	Norbrook	money	u	
Gift of God (Barnstaple)	80	Andrew Fursland and John Cherry	1591				with Stephen of London
Grace of God (Topsham)	80	Robert Sadler	1589				with Adonia of London
Greyhound (Plymouth)	u		1589		hides	560	
Bark Halse (Plymouth)	50		1589	Grenville Halse	u	140	
Hare (Plymouth)	u		1589	Turner	wheat	50	
			1590		woad	u	
Hazard (Plymouth)	u		1591	Henry Austen	a Leaguer prize	u	one of two Biscayan prizes taken jointly by this and other privateers
Michael Roscarrock (Padstow)	u		1590	Grenville Halse	iron	u	
Nicholas (Topsham)	u	Nicholas Turner	1590	Richard Woodcock	woad	1600	

ship	tons	promoters	date	captain	prize-cargo	value £	remarks
Nicholas (Plymouth)	40	Nicholas Glanville	1590				was to go with *Conclude* of Plymouth
Pagan (Falmouth)	u	Thomas Payne	1591	William Lestocke			spoiled a French ship of fish share claimed by *Jane Bonaventure* of Weymouth
Prudence (Barnstaple)	110	Richard Dodderidge	1590	William Batten	gold, pepper and ivory— Portuguese	16,000	
		„	1591		cloth, horseshoes and hides	u	with *Amity* of Barnstaple spoiled *Jonas* of Amsterdam; restitution ordered but some of cargo embezzled
Prudence (Dartmouth)	u		1590	George Drake	u	u	the three prizes were taken by *Prudence*, John Young of Chichester and *Unicorn* of Barnstaple, but appear to have been appropriated by Drake
					u	u	
					u	u	
Rainbow (Exmouth)	60	John Strong	1589			u	
Richard (Plymouth)	u	„ Richard Hutchins	1591	William Parker	salt, wines, iron, oil, etc.— Portuguese	u	
			1591		seed cotton—Portuguese hides	u	
					u	u	
Samarian (Dartmouth)	250		1590			u	with *Chance* of Plymouth
Sparke (Plymouth)	140	William Sparke	1589	William Sparke	hides, ginger and sugar	1375	involved in spoil of two Hamburg ships and a French vessel
			1590		u	u	
Trinity (Plymouth)	u	Grenville Halse	1591	Richard Smith	nuts and iron	u	

1589-91. SHIPS OF DEVON AND CORNWALL (continued)

ship	tons	promoters	date	captain	prize-cargo	value £	remarks
Unicorn (Barnstaple)	60	William Morcomb	1589	Charles Buckley			shared in the capture of Julian of Lyme
		,,	1590	William Collibeare	iron and sumac	u	also took part in the capture of Prudence of Dartmouth's prize
Unicorn (Dartmouth)	60	,,	1591	William Stockaber	iron and sumac	u	
			1589	Ralph Hawes			
Unity (Plymouth)	u		1591	William Hobbes	salt, Brazil sugar and other goods	u	with Fancy of Plymouth took two prizes, both brought home by Conclude
					hides and other goods	u	
White Hart (Barnstaple)	u		1591	Edward Jones	ivory	u	
u (a pink of Falmouth)	u	James Erisey	1589			u	spoiled a ship of Spanish wines bound for London

1589-91. BRISTOL AND BRIDGEWATER SHIPS

ship	tons	promoters	date	captain	prize-cargo	value £	remarks
Amity	u	Thomas Hopkins	1591	William Goslett	fish and train oil—a Leaguer	170	
Anne Fortune	80	Humphrey Clovell, Derrick Derrickson, Thomas Howell and Richard Cooke	1591	Thomas Howell	u	u	
Diamond (Bridgewater)	60	Robert, John and William Puddy, Thomas Holcomb and others	1589	George Watkins	pots and salt	75	
			1590		wines, kettles, etc.	u	
Diana	50	John Oliver and John Jolie	1591	William Morgan	wines, iron and pitch	140	
			1591	Nicholas Lilbart	fish and train oil—a Leaguer	180	

ship	tons	promoters	date	captain	prize-cargo	value £	remarks
Elizabeth Bonaventure	80	John Hopkins	1591	William Cole	fish—Portuguese; Málaga raisins—a Leaguer wines, oil, meal, earthen dishes, etc.—Portuguese; millet	u; 850; 670; 100	
Green Dragon	60	William Trenchard; "; "	1589; 1590; 1591	William Trenchard; "; Daniel White	hides; wines; fish; olives, oil and woollen cloth; salt, rye and timber; woollen cloth, oil, glasses, etc., church ornaments and plate; a small French ship	u; 105; u; 708; u	shared with *Jonas* of Bristol in capture of *Fortune* of Lübeck
Hopewell	u	Thomas Holcomb, Richard Barker and others	1590	John Higgins	gold, pepper and ivory—Portuguese	u; 12,000	
Jeromie	u	Roger Bowyer	1591	Robert Johnson	dry fish	480	restitution sought, probably unsuccessfully, by French owners
Jonas (Bridgewater)	15	Henry, William and Alexander Jones	1591	Thomas Stourbridge			
Jonas (or John)	60	Walter Denny, Hugh Griffen, Richard Powle, Richard Auldworth	1591	John Batten	fish and train oil; a Lübecker	270; u	prize was *Fortune* of Lübeck, which was used as a warship to convoy Spanish merchantmen
John	u	John Hopkins	1589	John Hopkins	sugar and brazilwood—Brazilman	4000	
John	u	Barnes	1590		salt—Portuguese	60	
Looking-Glass (or Little John)	100	William, John and Richard Walton	1591	John Winn	sugar and brazilwood—Brazilman	3060	

1589–91. BRISTOL AND BRIDGEWATER SHIPS (continued)

ship	tons	promoters	date	captain	prize-cargo	value £	remarks
Martin	30	John Sachfield	1589	Adams	sumac and other goods wines	270	spoiled a Scots vessel
		William Standlack and Robert Stone	1591	John Jeane	salt—Portuguese	70	
Mayflower (Bridgewater)	60	John Pike	1591	John Pike	hides, dyewood and pearls	u	valuation does not include the pearls
Merman	60	William Samford	1590	William Samford	sugar and brazilwood— Brazilman	2000	
Minion (Bridgewater)	50	Alexander, Henry and William Jones	1589			2985	in consortship with *John* of London in the Azores
Minion	190	,,	1591	George Watkins			in company with *Tiger* and *Stephen* of London with *Salamander* of Bristol
			1591	John Stratford			
Phoenix	60	William Walton	1590	John Giles	woad		
Pilgrim	80	William Standlack	1590	Andrew Batten	wheat	530	
Pleasure	150	Thomas James and Thomas Jennings	1590		salt, sugar and brazilwood— Brazilman	720	
Robin (or Delight)	120	John Chidley	1591	Thomas Jennings	hides, fish, train oil and other goods	790	a Leaguer
Salamander	120	William Walton	1589	Andrew Merrick	wheat—Leaguer	120	sailed with Chidley's South Sea expedition. Was wrecked on Normandy coast
Seabright	u	Christopher Pittes	1589 1590	Thomas Howell	sumac	230	
Toby	30	William Trenchard	1589 1591	William Higgins	olives, oil, wines and hides— Portuguese	450	to sail with *Phoenix* of Bristol
		Richard Powle, Walter Denning and William Higgins	1591	Walter Denning	a French ship	u	

ship	tons	promoters	date	captain	prize-cargo	value £	remarks
White Lion	60	Thomas Holcomb and Thomas Hopkins	1589	John Higgins	knives, linen, woollen cloths, pots, etc.	110	
			1590	William Harvey		5	
William	u	William Walton	1591	George Popham	salt		took part in spoil of a French vessel
u (a caravel of Bridgewater)	u	Sir John Popham	1589				
u (a ship of Bristol)	u	Certain Bristol merchants and Sir Walter Raleigh	1591	John Flegon	a French prize of fish	u	

1589–91. SHIPS OF OTHER PORTS

ship	tons	promoters	date	captain	prize-cargo	value £	remarks
Black Bishop (Yarmouth)	50		1591	Richard Bishop			with Flying Hart of Lynn
Blessing of God (Rye)	80	Town of Rye	1591				
Desire (Lynn)	40	William Parkins	1591	William Parkins	gold and pepper— Portuguese	4070	
Flying Hart (Lynn)	90	William Parkins	1591				
Grace of God (Rye)	40	Town of Rye	1591	Henry Bedford			spoiled a Swedish vessel
Harry Bonaventure (Chester)	90	Henry Bedford	1591	William Gilbert			spoiled a Lübecker laden with corn
Little Grace of God (Dover)	u		1589	„	raisins oranges }	770	
Primrose (Barry)			1590	William Morgan			took a cargo of green woad and São Thomé sugar, but was ordered to restore it to owners
Wheel of Fortune (Carmarthen)	u		1589	Richard Nashe	wines, calicoes, pepper and other goods	u	French ship laden with Spanish goods
u (a pinnace of Yarmouth)	u		1591				sailed with Black Bishop

1589-91. SHIPS OF PORT UNKNOWN

ship	tons	promoters	date	captain	prize-cargo	value £	remarks
Allagarta	80	Earl of Cumberland	1591	Baylie	four Hamburg ships laden with copper, lead, corn, ash, deal boards, pipe staves and other war materials	u	Cumberland's 1591 expedition. The Hamburg cargoes were declared contraband of war. Two sugar prizes and a great quantity of spices taken from Dutch ships were lost at sea
u (a bark)	u	Adrian Gilbert	1591	Randolph Cotton	sugar—Brazilman	u	one of Cavendish's fleet
Black Pinnace	u	Sir Thomas Cavendish	1591				one of Cavendish's fleet
u (a caravel)	40	Earl of Cumberland	1589	Pigeon	fish—Leaguer	u	various other prizes were taken, but lost at sea, including one very valuable cargo of hides, silver and cochineal, wrecked in Mount's Bay. Further booty was taken from the town of Fayal
					fish—Leaguer	u	
					fish—Leaguer	u	
					pepper and cinnamon	u	
					wines and oil	u	
					wines and oil	u	
					sugar, wines and sweetmeats	u	
					woad	u	
					u	u	
					u	u	
					fish—Leaguer	3000	
					sugar—Brazilman	3000	
					sugar—Brazilman	3000	
					sugar—Brazilman		
Charles	80	Lord Charles Howard	1591	Matthew Bradgate			with Lord Thomas Howard's fleet
Delight	70	Lord Charles Howard	1591				with Lord Thomas Howard's fleet
Desire	u	Sir Thomas Cavendish	1591	John Davis			one of Cavendish's fleet
Discovery	12	Earl of Cumberland	1591	Nicholas Lynche			Cumberland's 1591 expedition. See Allagarta

ship	tons	promoters	date	captain	prize-cargo	value £	remarks
Disdain	70	Lord Charles Howard	1589	George Fenner	sugar and brazilwood—Brazilman	1000	
		"	1590	Adam Seager	salt	u	with Lord Thomas Howard's fleet
		"	1591				
Discontent	u	Sir Walter Leveson	1590	William Edgerton	pipe boards, casks, ironwork linen and woollen cloth—Portuguese	260	
Galleon Dudley	250	Sir Thomas Cavendish	1590	John Clark	woollen cloth, oil, wines and other goods	u	spoiled a Flemish hulk of an English merchant's goods
					victuals	u	
		"		Stephen Seaver	hides	u	
					sugar, cotton wool and brazilwood—Brazilman	1340	
Renamed Galleon Raleigh		Carew Raleigh	1591	Henry Thynne	a French ship	u	restitution eventually ordered but some of the cargo was already sold and the rest sunk
					fish and oil—a French ship	u	
Frances	30	Earl of Hertford	1590		hides and sugar	u	
					a French prize	u	in company with Lord Thomas Howard's fleet
		"	1591	Philip Smith	a French prize	u	one of Cavendish's fleet
					hides	u	
Galleon Heart's Ease	u	Sir Thomas Cavendish	1591	Nicholas White	wines, iron, etc.—a Leaguer	u	
Lion's Whelp	90	Lord Charles Howard and Robert Sadler	1590	Thomas Roche	wrought and unwrought iron	u	with Delight of Southampton
Margaret	60	Earl of Cumberland	1589	Edward Wright			Cumberland's 1589 expedition. See caravel (port unknown)

ship	tons	promoters	date	captain	prize-cargo	value £	remarks
Meg	60	Earl of Cumberland	1589	William Monson			Cumberland's 1589 expedition. See caravel (port unknown)
Pilgrim	u	Sir Walter Raleigh	1590	Jacob Whiddon	sumac, raisins and almonds	500	shared in the capture of *Penelope* of London's prize with Lord Thomas Howard's fleet
			1591				
Bark Raleigh	u		1591	John Norton	fish	u	
Samson	260	Earl of Cumberland	1591			u	Cumberland's 1591 expedition. See *Allagarta*
u	u		1589/90	Miller	wines	u	
u	u		1590	Crauthorne	sugar	u	
u	u		1589	Sandy	sugar and brazilwood—Brazilman	1940	
u	u		1589/90	Grimes	wines	u	
u	u		1589/90	Jones	hides	1460	
u	u		1589/90	More	figs and other goods	u	
u	u		1589	May	corn	u	
u	u		1590	Walter Edney	sugar and other goods—Portuguese	u	
u	u		1590	Wye	woollen cloth and other goods in a French ship	20	
u	u		1589	Melchior Strangeways	wines	200	
u	u				sugar	u	

date	prize-cargo	value £	remarks
1589/90	wines	u	Norris' prize, brought to Dartmouth
1589/90	wines	u	Hill's prize, brought to Plymouth
1589/90	sugar	u	Batten's prize, brought to Topsham
1589/90	salt	u	White's prize
1589/90	wines	u	White's prize
1589/90	hides, cochineal, anil and bullion	u	Pitt's prize, brought to Padstow
1590	velvets, silks, linen cloth, etc.	u	Johnson's prize, brought to Dartmouth
1589/90	sugar and ginger	u	Drake's prize, brought to Topsham
1589/90	sugar	u	brought to Coombe
1589	u	790	Davies' prize, brought to Ilfracombe
1591	sugar	800	Davies' prize, brought to St Ives
1591	oil, cotton wool, soap and wines	u	brought to Portsmouth—a French prize
1591	figs	60	brought to Purbeck
1589	corn	u	brought to Weymouth
1589	corn	u	brought to Weymouth
1589/90	fish—French	u	brought to Plymouth
1589/90	fish—French	u	brought to Plymouth
1589/90	fish—French	u	brought to Plymouth
1589/90	u	u	brought to Plymouth
1589	wheat	25	White's prize
1590	u	u	William Walton's prize, brought to Padstow
1590	u	u	William Walton's prize, brought to Padstow
1590	wines	120	brought in by a ship belonging to John Bird and John Newton
1590	woad	360	prize brought in by George and Edward Fenner
1589/90	corn	440	prize brought in for Sir Walter Raleigh
1589/90	fish	u	prize brought in for Sir Walter Raleigh

1598. LONDON SHIPS

ship	tons	promoters	captain	prize-cargo	value £	remarks
Affection	120	Earl of Cumberland and others. John Watts owner	Thomas Fleming	a Brandenburg corn ship, bound for Spain	u	Cumberland's Puerto Rico venture
				sugar, ginger and other goods, including some brass ordinance, being made up of 9 prizes and the booty from the island	16,000	to count as 10 prizes at £1600 each
Alcedo	400	Cumberland and others. John Watts owner	John Ley. Thomas Catch on return			See *Affection*
Amity	200	Oliver Stile, Thomas White, Margaret Hawkins	Benjamin Gonson			with *Concord*. Took an Italian ship, which sank. A Barbary voyage
Ascension	400	Cumberland and others. William Garraway owner	Robert Flick			See *Affection*
Balzar	u					
Centurion	300	Cumberland and others. Thomas Cordell owner	Henry Palmer	wines and figs	212	
Concord	u	Oliver Stile, Thomas White, Margaret Hawkins	Olaf Maisters			took a Lübecker, laden with wool, flax, madder, copper kettles, fish, etc., bound for Italy
Consent	350	Cumberland and others. John Watts owner	Francis Slingsby			See *Affection*
Galleon Constance	u	Cumberland and others. John Watts owner	Hercules Foljambe			See *Affection*
Diamond	u		Edmund Brasey	u salt	u	
Experience	u		John Izad		u	took aboard at Lisbon a cargo of sugar and other goods freighted for Venice and brought them home as prize. Restitution ordered
Ferret	u	John Davies	John Johnson			claimed share of *Darling* of Portsmouth's prize

ship	tons	promoters	captain	prize-cargo	value £	remarks
Flying Dragon	290	Thompson	Hugh Robinson	sugar and hides	u	shared Merchant Bonaventure's prizes
Fortune	u	Thomas White	Cuthbert Grype	gold and brass guns	u	on a trading voyage to Barbary
Golden Dragon	220	Sir Thomas Sherley	Sir Thomas Sherley	pipes staves and hoops victuals	u	these goods were all that proved good prize out of the cargoes of four Lübeckers and three other neutral vessels
Golden Phoenix	u			goatskins, hides and sugar	400	
John	u	Henry White		millet and salt	u	
John (or Joshua or Jason)	u	John Davies	Nathaniel Harrison	salt and cider	118	Irish vessel bound for Spain. Also took a Bayonne ship bound for Spain. Restitution ordered
				tallow, iron and stagskins	u	
				sugar and brazilwood—Brazilman	u	
John & Francis	u	John More, Thomas Cordell, Richard Staper and others	John Wells	corn and barley—a Ragusan	u	with Solomon, Susan Parnell, Peregrine, Phoenix and one other London merchantman
				corn and barley—a Spanish ship	u	
Lion's Whelp	90	Earl of Nottingham	George Watson	u	u	also spoiled two French vessels
Lizard	30	Edmund Doggett and Dudley Hawkes	Edmund Doggett	u	u	
				sugar, wines, ginger and cotton wool	2555	
Maiden's Hope	u	Thompson				with Flying Dragon of London
Margaret & John	200	John Davies		brass pans, skins, pewter, wax, ivory, etc.—Portuguese	750	
				Danish ship with pipe-staves, arms and victuals	u	bound for Lisbon
				a Lübecker	u	bound for Lisbon
Margaret & John	200	Cumberland and others, John Watts owner				See Affection
Merchant Bonaventure	240		Nicholas Diggins	Brazilman with sugar	1300	
Merchant Royal	350	Cumberland and others. Thomas Cordell and William Garraway owners	Sir John Berkeley	salt—Scots ship	u	See Affection

1598. LONDON SHIPS (continued)

ship	tons	promoters	captain	prize-cargo	value £	remarks
Mermaid	220	Christopher Newport and Edward and Francis Glanville	Christopher Newport	hides, pepper and ginger	2700	See Report
Neptune	u			logwood, hides and tobacco	u	West Indies voyage
Pegasus	80	Cumberland and others. John Watts owner				See Affection
Peregrine	200	More, Cordell, Staper, etc.	Matthew Bond Peter Oliver			See John and Francis
Phoenix	180		John King			with Report 1597–8 and later in 1598 with John and Francis, etc.
Phoenix	250	More, Cordell, Staper, etc.	Bernard Drake	wheat	70	a Spanish man-of-war
Primrose	246	Richard Drake	Godfrey Markham	salt	u	See Affection
Prosperous	400	Cumberland and others. William Shute owner	James Langton. John Watts on return			
Red Lion (or Rose Lion)	170	Thomas Myddelton, Thomas Wygges, Nicholas Farrar Christopher Baker	William Saxey	Norwegian ship laden with Spanish salt	u	a Dutch ship bound for Vianna
Report	u	William Shute and Henry Anderson		deal, lead, oars, clapboard and wines	30	taken by Report, Mermaid and Phoenix on a Mediterranean trading voyage
Royal Defence	190	Cumberland and others. William Garraway and Mr. Cockayne owners	Henry Bramley	almonds, perfumes, beans, rice, etc. cloths	20	
Scorpion	u	Richard Thurston, John Stanton, Robert Mead				See Affection
Seamew	u	Mark Scoles	Mark Scoles	Brazilman with sugar and brazilwood	900	in consortship with Amity and Concord. Disputed John of London's Brazilman prize
Solomon	180	More, Cordell, Staper, etc.	Bartholomew Hoggett			See John and Francis
Sonne	250	John Watts and Bartholomew Matthewson	Lawrence Clayston	corn, victuals, arms, etc.	u	
Susan & Parnell	250	More, Cordell, Staper, etc.	Rowland Cortmore			See John and Francis
Thomas	200		Thomas Whitbrook	u	u	See John and Francis a valuable prize

1598. SOUTHAMPTON SHIPS

ship	tons	promoters	captain	prize-cargo	value £	remarks
Angel	80	Sir Oliver Lambert, Richard Goddard, Lawrence Prowse	N. Smithe	u	87	
u (a bark)	60	John Randall				
Darling	u	Sir Walter Raleigh, Sir Robert Cecil, Richard Burley, Francis Burley	William Palmer	salt	37	
Darling (or Diana) (P)	45	Matthew Watkins	John Sadler	sugar—a Madeira caravel	2180	
Elizabeth	30	Henry Carpenter	Henry Carpenter	wines and oil	194	
Mayflower	u	John Cornish	John Cornish	salt	30	
Phoenix Bonaventure	u	R. Hall		u	820	
Speedwell	40	Sir Oliver Lambert	Nicholas Lynche	u	1000	a West Indian prize
Welcome	u	Lawrence Prowse	Richard Scott	Spanish money	120	a West Indian prize
				iron	u	

1598. DORSET SHIPS

ship	tons	promoters	captain	prize-cargo	value £	remarks
Aid	u	John Mitchell	John Mitchell	pitch	30	
Catherine White (or Great Catherine)	u	Robert White	Giles Baynard	hides and other goods—a Guinea prize	110	
				hides, sarsaparilla, santomart wood, negroes, a gold whistle and £69 in coin	1000	a West Indian prize
Francis	u	Henry Drake	Henry Drake	sugar, brazilwood and preserves	2640	a Spanish ship
Grace	u	John Randall	Edward Baynard	u	u	
Maundlyn (L)	u	Richard Norris	Edward Giles	wines, salt and ginger	u	a French ship, but adjudged good prize

ship	tons	promoters	captain	prize-cargo	value £	remarks
Pearl	u	William Walton	William Hall	sugar, cotton wool, ivory, gold, negroes and succades	2200	a São Thomé man
Return (L)	u	Thomas Fisher, Richard Barnes	Richard Barnes	sugar, ginger and hides—Brazilman	2820	
Revenge (L)	40			salt, cloths, etc.	u	
Swift (L)	u			wheat	54	
Tobacco Pipe	u	John Reynolds	Ephraim Reynolds	salt	80	with *Revenge* of Lyme

1598. SHIPS OF DEVON AND CORNWALL

ship	tons	promoters	captain	prize-cargo	value £	remarks
Dolphin (Plymouth)	u		Gilbert Blackoller			shared in spoil of Amsterdam vessel
Fortune (Plymouth)	u	John Thomason and William Edwards	William Edwards			French ship with salt taken, but not good prize
Frances (Plymouth)	u	Emmanuel Silvester	Emmanuel Silvester	linen cloth, wines, and oil—Portuguese		committed several spoils
Gift of God (Barnstaple)	80	William Morcomb	Thomas Chichester	gold, silver and money		
Grace (Plymouth)	u		John Thomason		u	with *Plow* of Plymouth
Bark Pearse (Plymouth)	u		John Hills	iron, oars, linen, fustians and pitch	u	a French ship, taken in the Azores
Plow (Plymouth)	u		John Ridlesden	a Portuguese prize	u	spoiled a French ship of corn
Pretty Jack (Penzance)	u	Nicholas Halse	Francis Carey	wines and sumac—Portuguese	u	a French ship
Speedwell (Barnstaple)	u		Robert Hunny	u	u	
Spy (Plymouth)	u	John Waddon and Strange Browne		wines and other goods—Portuguese	u	
Tiger (Dartmouth)	u	William Blackall				returned from West Indies venture with a dubious prize

1598. BRISTOL AND BRIDGEWATER SHIPS

ship	tons	promoters	captain	prize-cargo	value £	remarks
Flying Dragon	150	William Walton	Jasper Norris	goatskins, hides and cloth	210	committed several acts of spoil
Mary Fortune	150	John Hopkins	Daniel White	almonds and dry fish	120	
Shiver	u		Reginald Williams	figs	24	

1598. SHIPS OF OTHER PORTS

ship	tons	promoters	captain	prize-cargo	value £	remarks
Panther (Arundel)	u	Sir Thomas Palmer, James Booth, Thomas, Richard and Anthony Earsfield	Richard Earsfield			spoiled two Irish ships

1598. SHIPS OF PORT UNKNOWN

ship	tons	promoters	captain	prize-cargo	value £	remarks
Anthony	120	Cumberland and others	Robert Careless. Andrew Andrewes on return			See *Affection* of London
Berkeley Boy	u	Cumberland and others	John Ley			See *Affection*
Discovery Frigate	u	Cumberland and others	William Harper			See *Affection*
Guiana	210	Cumberland and others. Sir Walter Raleigh owner	Christopher Colthurst. Gerard Middleton on return			See *Affection*
Malice Scourge	500	Cumberland and others	John Watts. James Langton on return			See *Affection*

1598. SHIPS OF PORT UNKNOWN (*continued*)

ship	tons	promoters	captain	prize-cargo	value £	remarks
Samson	300	Cumberland and others	Henry Clifford. Christopher Colthurst on return			See *Affection*
Scorn	u	Sir Thomas Gerrard	Thomas Broughton	Portuguese prize of salt French prize of fish	u u	
Swallow	u	Earl of Nottingham and Sir Robert Cecil	Alexander Vaughan Roger Hankyn			spoiled an Irish ship shared in the spoil of an Amsterdam ship
Truelove	u					

prize-cargo	value £	remarks
sugar	u	Captain William Gresham's prize, brought to Southampton
Madeira wines, sugar and conserves	u	
spices	u	brought in by Captain Peers Lemon

INDEX

u

ships named (*cont.*)
Seadragon (London), 37, 113, 136, 248
Seadragon (Weymouth), 142
Seamew, 268
Seraphim (London), 112
Seraphim (Weymouth), 143
Shiver, 271
Solomon, 268
Son, 254
Sonne, 107, 268
Sparke, 257
Speedwell (Barnstaple), 270
Speedwell (London), 94
Speedwell (Southampton), 269
Spy, 270
Squirrel, 248
Stephen, 248
Sugar, 146, 209
Sunday, 254
Supply (see Black Pinnace)
Susan 94, 110, 206, 210, 214, 218, 248
see also Wildman
Susan and Parnell alias Susan Parnell, 199, 217, 268
Susan Fortune, 202
Susan's Handmaid (see Wildman's Club)
Swallow (Isle of Wight), 42, 97, 165, 166, 193, 251
Swallow (London), 93, 143, 249
Swallow (Vaughan's), 272
Swan, alias Double Flyboat, 63, 145
Swift, 270
Swiftsure (Chichester and London), 93, 249
Thomas (London), 268
Thomas (Plymouth), 90
Thomas Bonaventure, 94
Tiger (Dartmouth), 270
Tiger (London), 37, 42, 113, 249
Tiger (St Malo), 75
Tobacco-Pipe (see Amity)
Toby (Bristol), 260
Toby (London), 217
Trial, 178
Trinity (Plymouth), 257
Trinity (Seville), 166, 224

Triton, 177
Truelove, 37, 89, 272
Unicorn (Barnstaple), 93, 258
Unicorn (Bristol), 152
Unicorn (Dartmouth), 258
Unicorn (Flushing), 213
Unity, 258
Victory, 72
Vineyard, 117–18, 184–5
Violet, 76, 143
Virgin (London), 211–12
Virgin (Sherley's), 54, 58
Watte, 196
Welcome (Plymouth), 211
Welcome (Southampton), 139, 269
Wheel of Fortune, 37, 261
White Bear, 92, 202
White Hart, 258
White Lion (Bristol), 261
White Lion (London), 38, 48, 67, 68, 249
White Lion (Weymouth), see Golden Hind
White Lion (Howard's), 89
Why not I?, 37
Wildman, 37, 67, 68, 110, 249
see also Susan
Wildman's Club, alias Susan's Handmaid, 67, 68, 110, 249
William, 144, 261
William Bonaventure, 145, 251
Wolf (see Black Wolf)
Shrewsbury, earl of (see Talbot)
Shute, William, 77, 119–20, 121, 184 209, 232, 268
Silvester, Emmanuel, 270
Simpson, John, 111
Skinner, Richard, 253
Skinners' Company, 111, 210
Sled, John, 256
Slingsby, Sir Francis, 76, 266
Sly, John, 140
Smith, Philip, 263
Smith, Richard, 257
Smithe, N., 269
Smythe, Sir Thomas (customer), 96, 203
Smythe, Sir Thomas (governor East India Co., etc.), 108, 217